Minority citizens in disasters

Minority citizens in disasters

RONALD W. PERRY

ALVIN H. MUSHKATEL

THE UNIVERSITY OF GEORGIA PRESS   Athens and London

Paperback edition, 2008
© 1986 by the University of Georgia Press
Athens, Georgia 30602
www.ugapress.org

Designed by Madelaine Cooke
Set in Times Roman with Helvetica display
Printed digitally in the United States of America

The Library of Congress has cataloged the hardcover edition of
this book as follows:
Library of Congress Cataloging-in-Publication Data

Perry, Ronald W.
Minority citizens in disasters / Ronald W. Perry, Alvin H.
Mushkatel.
xii, 205 p. ; 24 cm.
    Bibliography: p. 183-200.
    Includes index.
ISBN 0-8203-0830-7
    1. Disasters—United States—Psychological aspects. 2.
Minorities—United States—Psychology. 3. Minorities—United
States—Attitudes. 4. Disaster relief—Government policy—United
States. 5. Disaster relief—United States—Citizen participation.
I. Mushkatel, Alvin H. II. Title.
HV555.U6 P473   1986
363'.3'4'089 19   85-20820

Paperback ISBN-13: 978-0-8203-3141-6
ISBN-10: 0-8203-3141-4

British Library Cataloging-in-Publication Data available

To Our Children: Elizabeth, Jessica, Zachary

Contents

LIST OF TABLES   ix

PREFACE AND ACKNOWLEDGMENTS   xi

1   Minority citizens in disasters   *1*

2   Disaster warning processes   *23*

3   Social processes following warning   *59*

4   Citizen involvement in threat management   *88*

5   Emergency management policy and the local community   *125*

6   Retrospect: ethnic differentials in disaster behavior   *155*

BIBLIOGRAPHY   183

INDEX   201

List of tables

1.1 Survey completion summary   *18*
2.1 First warning source by ethnicity   *26*
2.2 Proportion of respondents ranking source as highly reliable by ethnicity   *32*
2.3 Warning message content by first warning source and ethnicity   *37*
2.4 Initial warning belief by message content and ethnicity   *41*
2.5 Initial perceived personal risk by message content and ethnicity   *43*
2.6 Initial warning belief by past experience and ethnicity   *46*
2.7 Initial personal risk assessment by past experience and ethnicity   *49*
2.8 Initial warning response by first warning belief and ethnicity   *53*
2.9 Initial warning response by first risk assessment and ethnicity   *56*
3.1 First source contacted for confirmation by ethnicity   *61*
3.2 Number of additional sources contacted by first confirmation source and ethnicity   *65*
3.3 All sources used for warning confirmation by ethnicity   *68*
3.4 Warning response by warning belief and ethnicity   *71*
3.5 Warning response by risk perception and ethnicity   *74*
3.6 Probability of warning compliance (evacuation) by warning belief, perceived risk, and ethnicity   *77*
3.7 Shelter destination by ethnicity and warning setting   *79*

3.8 Knowledge of shelter availability by ethnicity and warning setting   *81*

3.9 Mode of transportation by ethnicity and warning setting   *85*

4.1 Most important reason for evacuating by ethnicity   *90*

4.2 Protective actions undertaken by ethnicity   *96*

4.3 Total number of protective actions undertaken by ethnicity   *98*

4.4 Reasons for undertaking protective actions by ethnicity   *100*

4.5 Primary source of community emergency response information by ethnicity   *105*

4.6 Sources of past information on environmental hazards by ethnicity   *110*

4.7 Best way to communicate environmental hazard information by ethnicity   *116*

4.8 Preferred volunteer activity related to emergency services by ethnicity   *122*

Preface and acknowledgments

This book is based upon a series of studies sponsored by the National Science Foundation (grant numbers PFR-8019297, CEE-8120426, and CEE-8311868). All of the conclusions drawn are those of the authors and do not reflect official National Science Foundation policy.

We wish first to acknowledge our considerable debt to William A. Anderson. As the project technical monitor on all three grants, Bill consistently created a positive administrative atmosphere for our continuing research. As an experienced sociologist and field researcher, Bill provided many theoretical and technical insights that all eventually found their way into our work. He combined knowledge and encouragement over several years in a way that made our jobs as researchers both more enjoyable and easier to execute.

We have also amassed a considerable debt to Thomas E. Drabek for his careful and critical reading of our manuscript. We believe that Tom's professional suggestions and intricate knowledge of empirical studies of disaster behavior served to substantially enhance the intellectual depth of our work. Our debt to Gary A. Kreps is also great. Gary served above and beyond collegial duty by sorting through the original manuscript, identifying both gaps in the work and tactics for focusing the manuscript on key issues.

We are also grateful to Russell R. Dynes, José O. Marrero, and J. Rick Ponting, who provided initial suggestions for research design and much needed encouragement throughout the different projects. Marjorie R. Greene, both as a co-worker and later from her post in Yugoslavia, provided valuable intellectual criticism, colleagueship, and much technical guidance. Charles E. Fritz has also earned our respect and gratitude in two ways. It was his research on disasters, under University of Chicago–NORC auspices in the 1950s, that first raised the ethnicity question in a systematic fashion. Our work explores a small part of the path that he and his colleagues began to blaze nearly thirty years ago. Aside from his pioneering role in the field, we are grateful to Charlie for many years of patient tutorage and thoughtful encouragement. Finally, Enrico Quarantelli has provided much sage advice on conceptual issues and has lent us the benefit of his enormous field experience on several occasions. We are most appreciative of all the scholarly guidance offered us and have done our best to employ it effectively.

We are aware that this book represents only a very small step toward acquiring a better social scientific understanding of the role of ethnicity in disaster preparedness and response. Indeed, the analyses of our data from Denver, Mount Vernon, and Abilene raise more questions than they answer. For the present, this is a healthy outcome. The questions answered give us a small platform on which to stand while integrating ethnicity into existing sociological theories of disaster behavior. The questions raised constitute suggestions for future research agendas.

1 Minority citizens in disasters

The social scientific study of human behavior during natural and man-made disasters is a fairly recent phenomenon. Indeed, almost all of the empirical research now available has been conducted since 1950 (Quarantelli and Dynes, 1977). It is not surprising then that certain aspects of citizen response to disasters remain largely unstudied. This book focuses upon one such little-studied area: the response of ethnic minority groups to disasters. The need for knowledge about ethnic differentials in disaster behavior may be understood both from the perspective of social scientific theory and the viewpoint of applied emergency management.

From the standpoint of social science, the development of a body of knowledge that is idiosyncratic to any single racial or ethnic group presents serious limitations. Because disaster studies have been historically ethnically homogeneous, scholars interested in theoretical development are faced with the problem of an empirical gap regarding differences in disaster response between minority and majority group citizens. We do know that behavioral and attitudinal differences have been documented in connection with research on American ethnic groups (cf. Rose, 1973). Minority groups differ among themselves and from majority citizens in terms of world view, socioeconomic status, family organization and structure, and participation in religious and other voluntary associations and in terms of political efficacy and trust in

social and political institutions. And this short inventory is by no means complete. To the extent that these variables are important in understanding disaster
behavior, one would expect to find response variations between minority and
majority group citizens. Thus, the theorist intuitively knows that ethnicity is a
relevant variable but lacks the empirical building blocks to begin the theory
construction process.

Although they are quite sparse, the data that do exist on minority citizens
in disaster reinforce the idea that racial and ethnic differentials must be systematically identified and addressed. Much of these data may be seen as "outcome information" generated in the process of accounting for citizens after
disasters. In general, such information reveals that minority citizens experience different consequences from disasters than nonminority citizens. We
find, for example, differentials among ethnic groups in death and injury rates.
Red Cross fatality counts show that disaster-connected deaths are dispropor-
tionately high among minority citizens (Trainer and Hutton, 1972:5). Similarly, the Waco, Texas, tornado of 1953 left 4 percent of affected white families reporting at least one member seriously injured, while 12 percent of the
black families involved reported seriously injured members (Moore,
1958a:147).

The presence of ethnic differentials in death and injury rates suggests that
similar differentials could exist in regard to other variables as well. Death and
injury statistics focus on the outcomes of the disaster experience. While compelling in themselves, they inevitably raise the question of what concrete perceptions and behaviors lead to these outcomes. Do minority citizens suffer
more physical harm because they live in more vulnerable locations or less
hazard-resistant dwellings? Or do minorities perceive danger and understand
warning messages in fundamentally different ways and thereby behave in a
fashion more likely to result in injury? Ultimately, it is likely that *both* social
structural and social psychological variables contribute to outcome differences. From a theoretical point of view, it is therefore important to initiate a
process of tracing backward from outcome variables to identify antecedent
variables presumably responsible for ethnic differences.

The identification and explanation of ethnic and racial differentials in
disaster behavior are also important from an applied perspective. A primary
goal of professional emergency management is the safety of all citizens—
minority and majority. Thus, minority citizens become a special consideration
to the extent that they behave differently from majority citizens. For example,
one study reports that Mexican-Americans were less likely to believe flood

evacuation warning messages than whites, no matter how specific the wording of the message (Perry, Lindell, and Greene, 1981:97). Since it is known that citizens hesitate to comply with a message they do not find believable, this suggests that to successfully evacuate an area, emergency managers need to give concerted attention to devising and presenting warning messages that inspire belief in both minority and majority citizens.

One can extend this line of reasoning to citizen compliance with other emergency management measures that depend upon accurate communications from authorities to citizens. Consequently, one would anticipate ethnic differentials in citizen adoption of protective or mitigative measures such as flood or earthquake proofing of homes, purchase of hazard insurance, or development of family emergency plans. This concern logically extends to recovery measures as well, where one would anticipate differentials in understanding the availability and ultimately seeking of institutional aid. The accomplishment then of a wide variety of emergency management tasks may depend to some degree upon the ethnic composition of any given community of interest.

Consequently, reasoning from both theoretical and applied perspectives, it is clear that disaster researchers must begin to examine the role of ethnicity in disaster response and management. At a minimum, this task demands the specification of ethnic differentials in the way citizens prepare for, respond to, and recover from disasters. The existing data base from which one might begin to make such specifications is very slim. Among American field studies, race was first included in the National Opinion Research Corporation (NORC) disaster studies (Fritz and Marks, 1954) and then in a handful of subsequent studies (cf. Moore, 1958a; Mileti et al., 1981; Perry, Lindell, and Greene, 1981; Burton, 1972; Johnson and Burdge, 1973; Ives and Furuseth, 1980; Bates et al., 1963; Sims and Bauman, 1972). The National Science Foundation has sponsored one exploratory study aimed largely at documenting the presence or absence of ethnic variations in warning response (Perry, Greene, and Mushkatel, 1983). Apart from these efforts, however, only scattered empirical references to race or ethnicity exist in the literature on citizen response to disasters.

Minority groups and emergency management

This book examines the behavior of two minority groups—blacks and Mexican-Americans—relative to whites in three disaster events: a propane car railroad derailment, a nitric acid spill, and a flood. Considering the sparseness of the empirical record regarding ethnic differentials, it is important to establish parameters for interpreting the data presented here. This can be accomplished by undertaking two tasks: providing an overview of the activities that constitute emergency management, and examining the implications of ethnic differentials within the context of emergency management.

Comprehensive emergency management

The National Governors' Association (1979:11), through the conceptual work of Hillary Whittaker, has advocated an approach to community disasters that requires comprehensive emergency management (CEM). CEM refers to the challenge of developing a capability for handling all phases of disaster management activity—mitigation, preparedness, response, and recovery—in all types of disasters by integrating and coordinating the efforts and resources of many different agencies and levels of government. Thus, there are two particularly distinctive features of CEM. First, the focus is upon all phases of community disaster management by dictating a concern with (1) *preventing* (mitigating) disasters by eliminating or reducing their probability of occurrence where possible; (2) *preparing* protective measures for threats that cannot be controlled; (3) *responding* to disaster events when they do occur; and (4) *restoring* a social system after disaster impact. Second, CEM is characterized by a concern with managing all types of emergencies, including nuclear attack, natural disasters, technological disasters, civil disorders, and terrorism. This acknowledges that, although different types of disaster impose sometimes distinct demands, there are some generic functions that are common across different types and the same general system can be used for managing all emergencies. We will consider the process of devising and implementing emergency management policy more thoroughly in chapter 5.

The present study deals with citizen behavior in the preparedness and response phases of emergency management. Preparedness measures are undertaken to protect human lives and property in conjunction with threats that cannot be manipulated via mitigation measures or from which only partial protection can be achieved. Preparedness activities can be divided into two general categories: actions related to providing an alert that an impact is imminent, and actions designed to enhance the effectiveness of emergency operations. Preparedness measures related to providing an alert include the development and improvement of detection and prediction technologies that inform authorities of impending threats. Such technologies include, for example, riverine flood detection systems and radar detection and tracking of severe storms. In addition, warning systems that convey information from authorities to the public about threats such as tornadoes, tsunamis, and hurricanes also fall into this category. Preparedness measures aimed at enhancing emergency operations also entail a variety of activities. These activities include developing routing plans for evacuations, stockpiling materials for shelters, assembling lists of resources and their locations for possible use in responding to a given emergency, and training cadres and conducting drills or rehearsals of emergency plans.

Therefore, preparedness measures are conducted or undertaken *in advance* of any particular disaster event. They represent ways of protecting life and property when disasters do strike. Historically, research has shown that preparedness activities have received comparatively few governmental resources when compared with response and recovery programs. In general, both citizens and authorities show a great deal of interest in preparedness issues immediately following a major disaster, but this declines significantly as time passes. Because considerable time is often required to translate concern with a hazard into budget allocations and implementable programs, the development of preparedness measures frequently suffers.

Emergency response activities are conducted during and just after the period of impact, and they focus upon assisting the affected public as well as minimizing further damage from secondary or repeated impacts. Some of the more visible response activities include search and rescue, provision of emergency medical care, and the sheltering of evacuees and other victims. Operations also may be mounted to counter secondary threats, such as fighting urban fires in earthquakes, identifying contaminated water supplies and other public health threats during typhoons, identifying contaminated wildlife or fish in connection with a toxic chemical spill, or preparing for floods and mudflows in connection with a volcanic eruption.

Implications of minority differentials

It is within the structure provided by the concept of comprehensive emergency management that one can begin to answer the question of what social scientists and emergency managers should know about the behavior of minority citizens in disasters. Hence, it is clear that, at a minimum, there should be an understanding of the ways minority citizens comprehend and participate in the four primary emergency management activities. Furthermore, empirical documentation should be obtained for ethnic differentials in citizen participation and response patterns in connection with different hazard agents. It is necessary, of course, to understand the behavior of all citizens (whether minority or majority) relative to emergency measures for many types of disasters. In the overall scheme of emergency management, minority citizens form an issue only to the extent that they behave or are affected differently from majority citizens and thereby pose the necessity for modified management techniques to achieve the objectives of effective mitigation, preparedness, response, and recovery.

Approached from this perspective, it is clear that understanding the role of ethnic group membership in emergency management is not a simple task. It is certainly not an objective that can be achieved within the context of a single study. Indeed, as is the case in all social science, the production of knowledge regarding the behavior of minority groups in disasters is best seen as an ongoing process. Over time, and as a function of many studies, information can be progressively amassed that allows social scientists to document areas in which minority and majority citizens differ and to identify situations in which participation and response do not seem to differ.

The research upon which this book is based represents a first attempt to begin that larger process of knowledge accumulation. Given that this research is an initial step, an effort has been made to achieve a fairly broad coverage of the issues that constitute integrated emergency management. Thus, the data reported here focus upon two phases of emergency management—preparedness and response—and upon two types of disaster agents—a riverine flood and two hazardous material incidents. Studies of three communities' responses to threats from the environment make up the data upon which our analyses of minority versus majority group behavior are based. The specific research issues addressed in each community are, first, minority differentials in the warning process itself and, second, differentials related to citizen participation in the emergency preparedness process. Of special concern here too is the idea of making comparisons of citizen response to evacuation warnings in the different types of disasters.

As we have demonstrated above, there are numerous reasons for studying the response of minority citizens in disasters associated with filling gaps in social scientific knowledge. Yet it is also important to understand that from the perspective of managing communities disasters, great practical and operational benefit is derived from knowledge of potential response differentials among different minority groups. For example, consider the problem of issuing an evacuation warning message to an endangered population containing large segments of one or more minority groups. Ideally, the emergency manager formulates a message, delivers it via some mode (perhaps door-to-door contacts by police officers), and then oversees the citizens' departure from the threatened area. This simple description implies that a variety of assumptions made by the emergency manager will not be affected by the minority group composition of the community. A few of these assumptions are cataloged below.

- It is assumed that all citizens will be able to understand the message itself. If a warning is issued only in English, however, is it safe to assume that all minorities whose first language is not English will be bilingual or be able to get the message translated promptly?

- It is assumed that the emergency personnel who issue the message are seen by citizens as a credible source of threat-relevant information whose primary interest is public safety. Is it appropriate to believe that minority citizens, some of whom may have experienced discrimination or at least less than positive treatment from various community agencies and officials, will see those officials as having their best interests in mind and therefore as being credible sources of threat information?

- It is assumed that all citizens' views of the disaster threat will at least be somewhat consistent with that of the community authorities and that they will act upon the officially recommended protective actions. Is it safe to assume that the world view of minority citizens sufficiently overlaps that of majority group authorities to insure a consistent definition of the situation as dangerous and that minority citizens will embrace the suggested protective action as appropriate?

These questions constitute issues with which an emergency manager must grapple and regarding which there is little concrete research evidence.

Emergency services personnel are charged with protecting citizens and property from the dangers posed by natural and man-made hazards. Success in accomplishing this objective depends to a certain degree upon the smoothness and speed of emergency response operations. Without, among other things, accurate communications with citizens and a shared understanding of the nature of the environmental threat and appropriate strategies for dealing with it, there is little hope that response operations will run smoothly. For these reasons it is necessary to know if, and in what ways, minority citizens' responses to disaster differ both among themselves and from the majority group.

Disaster warnings in three communities

Disasters are usually thought of as catastrophic events, frequently associated with the forces of nature: earthquakes, tornadoes, hurricanes, or floods. Yet other events, such as explosions, chemical spills, or industrial accidents, are also described as disasters. In establishing parameters for the social scientific study of disasters, Charles Fritz has advanced a definition that concentrates on important distinguishing features of disaster events. He suggests that a disaster is any event "concentrated in time and space, in which a society or a relatively self-sufficient subdivision of society, undergoes severe danger and incurs such losses to its members and physical appurtenances that the social structure is disrupted and the fulfillment of all or some of the essential functions of the society is prevented" (1961a:655).

This classic definition stresses that disasters occur at a definite time and place and that they disrupt social intercourse for some period of time. Allen Barton embraces this approach, arguing that disasters exist "when many members of a social system fail to receive expected conditions of life from the system" (1970:38). Thus, both Fritz and Barton agree that any event that results in a significant change in inputs or outputs for a given social system is accurately characterized as a disaster. The important point to be derived from inspecting these definitions is that volcanoes, hurricanes, floods, chemical spills, explosions, or nuclear power plant accidents all fit equally well into either definition. Hence, at this level of abstraction, both natural and man-made disasters may be treated under the same conceptual rubric.

In comparing citizen response to different disaster threats, however, one must specify important characteristics of the threat agent. In so doing, the researcher is compelled to identify aspects of the disaster impact that could affect either the warning process or the nature of warning recipient performance. The most widely used scheme for describing disaster agents was devised by Barton (1970) and subsequently refined by Dynes (1970) and Kreps (1979). In his attempt to characterize the nature of social system stresses, Barton (1970:40–47) emphasized four basic dimensions: scope of impact, speed of onset, duration of impact, and social preparedness. Scope of impact is a geographic reference categorizing impact as involving either a small area or only a few people (narrow impact) or as encompassing a large area or many people (widespread impact). Speed of onset refers to the suddenness of impact or to the time period between detection of a threat and its impact on the social system. This dimension is usually classified as either sudden or gradual. Duration of the impact itself refers to the time that lapses between initial onset and the point at which the impact subsides. This can be a few minutes (short), as in the case of a tornado, or several hours (long), in the case of some riverine floods. Finally, social preparedness is used to characterize the extent to which a community has devoted resources and personnel to the preparedness phase of emergency management. Thus, social preparedness is conceptualized here as a continuum ranging from high (representing a community with an effective, in-place response plan and appropriate resources) to low (a community without a plan or with minimal resources).

By describing each of our three disaster events in terms of Barton's four defining dimensions, two general objectives can be accomplished. First, an overview of the circumstances of each incident is provided for the reader. Second, any incident-specific distinctive features can be identified and treated as factors to be incorporated into analyses of comparative warning response. Thus, in the absence of any more general barriers to comparative analysis, the incident-specific descriptions convey information that will make interpretations of between-event comparisons more meaningful. Finally, it should be pointed out that the analyses of disaster response behavior that follow in chapters 2 and 3 actually focus upon citizen actions when told to evacuate as protection from a potentially dangerous situation. Thus, in all three study sites citizens were responding to authorities' warnings of potential disaster. In Abilene, Texas, the potential threat actually materialized as a flood. In Mount Vernon, Washington, the threat posed by a derailed tank car carrying potentially dangerous propane did not turn into disaster because authorities were able to right the car, thereby defusing the danger. In Denver, Colorado, the threat posed by a large nitric acid spill was ultimately defused when atmospheric conditions allowed the gas plume to dissipate. Consequently, while disaster agent impact conditions varied across the three sites, our research focus remains the same: how did citizens respond to the warning of an impending environmental threat?

High water in Abilene

Abilene is a west-central Texas city of more than 100,000 citizens located approximately 200 miles west of the Dallas–Fort Worth metropolitan area. The town was founded in the early 1880s at about the same time the Texas and Pacific Railway was completed. Because of its favorable location near the railway, Abilene has evolved into a major center for retail trade, serving a twenty-two-county area hinterland. Aside from retail trade, its economy depends upon manufacturing, the petroleum industry, medical care, and farming and ranching. A major military installation located nearby also buttresses the local economy. It is a growing community with a young population—nearly 75 percent of its inhabitants are under the age of fifty.

The dry flatlands that characterize much of West Texas have a long history of flooding. Abilene is traversed by several creeks, sources of beauty but also flood vulnerability. Among the largest are the Lytle, Elm, and Cedar. These creeks are fed by nearby reservoirs and have a long history of flooding. During late October of 1981, the West Texas region experienced heavy thunderstorms that eventually deposited sufficient rain to cause the flood event studied here. Initially, rain fell steadily over a period of several days, allowing the normally dry land to become rain soaked and producing minor local flooding due principally to runoff. Then, in a period of three days, Abilene and its environs were pelted with 8.34 inches of rain, more than one-third of its average annual rainfall of 23.59 inches. With this impetus and the overflow of one lake, the creeks—particularly Lytle and Cedar—overflowed their banks, invading nearby homes. Two areas of localized urban flooding were selected for study here: the Carver-Woodlow district, a relatively low income area populated primarily by minority citizens (blacks and Mexican-Americans), and the Wyndrock district, a neighboring working-class neighborhood populated principally by whites.

Abilene is best characterized as having a high level of emergency preparedness. Within the town governmental structure there is an active office of civil defense, the director of which provides primary coordination for emergency management. Substantial community resources are devoted to planning for and responding to emergencies. The civil defense coordinator supervises the dissemination of general hazard information as well as overseeing all official communications to citizens during emergencies. The coordinator functions as the hub of communications; he receives, evaluates, and passes on communications from citizens to relevant local officials; serves as the primary contact with extracommunity organizations such as the National Weather Service, the State Department of Emergency Services, and the Federal Emergency Management Agency; and facilitates communications between community organizations involved in emergency response. While the performance of these functions is probably role incumbent-specific, it nevertheless promotes effective emergency response by forming a de facto command and communications center.

Thus, local authorities had approximately six hours' advance notice from the National Weather Service that flooding should be expected. With the very short communications delay in Abilene, authorities were able to begin monitoring both the reservoirs and creek levels promptly. The process of issuing warnings in areas to be evacuated therefore was based upon both Weather Service data and local observation. The lead time permitted effective deployment of personnel (police and fire fighters) to issue warnings, since they were dispatched on the basis of progressive threats from the gradually rising creeks. It is difficult to estimate the total number of families evacuated before flood impact or as part of search and rescue operations, but the area selected for study contained just over six hundred dwelling units.

Evacuees were initially advised of several evacuation centers established in different parts of town. Eventually these were combined into two primary shelters, one located at the civic center and the other in the gymnasium of a local university. Most resources for first aid, sleeping, and cooking as well as the emergency command post were housed in the civic center shelter. Operations at the smaller university shelter were geared to two primary activities: reuniting separated family members and helping evacuees relocate to temporary shelter in the homes of friends and family. In addition to managing these shelters, local Red Cross personnel provided fixed feeding stations in the main shelter and community churches for families without cooking facilities. Red

Cross volunteers continued an intensive family assistance program, including family counseling services provided by social workers from local universities, for approximately a week beyond the initial food impact. For families with extensive losses, services were extended until traditional community social service agencies were able to assume the cases.

There were no deaths and few injuries as a result of the flooding in Abilene. Property damage, however, was extensive. More than 113 private homes were classified as totally destroyed or sustaining major structural damage after initial damage surveys. Damage to public property, including streets, bridges, dams, and boats and city buses used in evacuations, was estimated at $2.7 million.

To summarize, Abilene represents a community characterized by a high level of emergency preparedness. This was particularly true for floods, which are seasonal and have frequently affected the city in past years. This particular flood can be characterized as having gradual onset in that officials were warned several hours in advance and were able to pass that warning on to most citizens before flood impact. The scope of impact was localized in two parts of the community and the duration of impact was short.

An emergency in Mount Vernon

Mount Vernon is a community of approximately 13,000 residents located near Puget Sound in northwestern Washington. The town was established in the 1870s in connection with the growth of the logging industry and its position of prominence as a regional trade center was cemented in the 1890s with the establishment of the Great Northern Railway, giving it links to the marketplace both by sea and by rail. Over the years, as the logging industry followed the forests eastward, Mount Vernon's economy came to be dominated by agricultural interests. At present agriculture remains the town's primary economic strength, but it is supplemented by food processing, a timber products industry, oil refining, fishing, and tourism. To appreciate the importance of Mount Vernon regionally, one must understand that it is one of only a few communities in the area that, as well as being a seaport, is situated such that the primary north-south highways and railbeds pass through it.

The hazard environment of Mount Vernon is characterized by a diverse collection of threats. Natural hazards to which the community is subject include riverine floods and earthquakes. The town is also situated near Mount Baker, an active volcano. The presence of oil refineries and related product storage facilities in and near Mount Vernon constitutes the primary man-made hazards. Finally, there is also a threat due to potential hazardous materials transportation incidents on the nearby highway and rail systems.

On one spring evening in 1981, local railroad employees were engaged in the routine movement of a train within Mount Vernon's city limits. At approximately 5:45 P.M., a tank car carrying 25,000 gallons of propane derailed on a spur near downtown. The tank car remained upright and appeared to be undamaged. It was subsequently determined that the accident was caused by mechanical problems with the wheels operating in concert with weak rail ties and the curvature of the track (Cantwell, 1981). Although conflicting reports exist, local railroad employees apparently made some attempts to get the tank car back on the tracks but were frustrated in their efforts. At this point, the train crew did not define the situation as posing any danger. Thus, with the work shift coming to an end, the crew determined that there was no leakage of hazardous materials and simply closed off the spur for the night. Railroad personnel did not notify local authorities of the derailment and presumably planned to right the car as part of the following day's work.

In retrospect, a local railroad spokesman pointed out that "the biggest mistake occurred when local railroad officials didn't notify the proper authorities" (Boardman and Burkhart, 1981). At approximately 7:45 A.M. on the following morning, an employee of a business located near the derailed tank car noticed the car (which was marked "liquified petroleum gas") and reported it to county authorities. Four local emergency organizations played key roles in responding to the incident: the local police and fire departments, the county emergency services office, and the county sheriff's office. After a site inspection, the emergency responders determined that hazardous materials were not being released into the environment and contacted railroad authorities regarding the derailment.

While there was apparently no formal written agreement at the time regarding notification of local authorities in the event of accidents, a railroad spokesperson indicated that routine instructions given to crews included notifying local authorities if hazardous materials were involved in a derailment (Boardman and Burkhart, 1981). Failure to notify local authorities immediately following the derailment resulted in a strained relationship between Mount Vernon emergency managers and railroad emergency responders. Also, town and county emergency managers, as a function of having the derailment first reported to them by a citizen, felt the necessity to conduct an independent assessment of the threat posed by the derailed tank car. Ultimately the town and county officials agreed with railroad representatives that as long as the tank car sat unmolested in its resting position, it did not pose a major threat to the community (Burkhart, 1981).

Substantial disagreement again arose, however, in connection with railroad plans to replace the propane-filled tank car on the track. Railroad officials continued to argue that the operation would pose no threat to the community. The local emergency managers felt that their charge to protect the public safety demanded that a very conservative position be taken regarding environmental threats. Thus, fire department officials reasoned that lifting the tank car back onto the tracks could produce sufficient strain on the tank itself to cause any preexisting weak spots to fracture, producing a release of propane into the environment. In the event of such a release, it was reasoned that any spark could either ignite the propane or produce an explosion that could in turn threaten nearby storage tanks that also contained liquified petroleum products (Burkhart, 1981). It should be noted that while there was no particular reason to suspect that the tank car contained weak spots, there was also no immediate means of confirming that such weak spots did not exist. Based upon this assessment of the risks associated with the derailment, Mount Vernon officials decided to evacuate the population in the surrounding area during the time the tank car was replaced on the rails.

At approximately 10:00 A.M., officials began the process of door-to-door, in-person notification of surrounding residences and businesses that evacuation was advised. The evacuation effort included an elementary school and a nearby nursing home. Citizens were advised that public shelter could be sought at designated schools and parks outside the evacuated area. County sheriff's deputies blocked off primary streets near the derailment site at 11:00 A.M. By 12:30 P.M., approximately 2,500 citizens had been evacuated from the endangered area. The tank car was returned to the tracks without incident, and beginning about 1:00 P.M. citizens were again allowed access to the evacuated area. The citizens involved in the evacuation represented two ethnic groups. The majority were working-class whites living in an older neighborhood adjacent to the derailment site. A number of Mexican-American citizens were also evacuated, some from a nearby working-class neighborhood but most from an area near the railroad and freeway. This latter area is heavily populated by agricultural laborers.

The tank car derailment in Mount Vernon is best described as an emergency that precipitated an evacuation rather than a disaster. Except for railroad equipment, there was no property damage, and no hazardous materials were released into the environment. Technically speaking, the concepts of scope and duration of impact do not apply to this emergency. For comparative purposes, however, it may be said that the *potential* scope of impact was narrow and the *potential* duration was short. In Mount Vernon, the onset of the threat was sudden, but local authorities and railroad employees retained enough control over the threat that sufficient lead time was available to warn citizens before the tank car was moved (and the threat became acute). Mount Vernon is characterized by a high level of emergency preparedness. Just prior to the emergency described here, the cognizant county emergency services office had been restructured and assigned a trained full-time director. Also, county and town emergency personnel had successfully conducted two evacuations in the county area in the six months preceding the derailment.

The Denver nitric acid spill

Denver is a large regional center of commerce and industry for an eight-state area. It has a well-developed and broadly based economy, including serving as the administrative office base for many national corporations and having a high technology (electronics, military production, energy development) industrial base that rivals California's Silicon Valley. Denver is a developed city that has experienced a very high growth rate over the past thirty years. Most recent growth has been in the suburbs; the city limits were essentially filled by the close of the 1960s. The structure of Denver is similar to many other major industrial cities in the United States. Denver is plagued by air pollution problems, urban sprawl, and a continuing battle to revitalize the downtown. Denver remains a cosmopolitan city, with a relatively young and still fast growing population. It is also an ethnically diverse city: the 1980 census reported that 18.7 percent of the residents were Mexican-American, 12.0 percent were black, and there were smaller concentrations of American Indians and Orientals, including recent immigrants from Southeast Asia.

On April 3, 1983, a rail car coupling pierced a tank car in the Denver and Rio Grande Western Railroad yard located near the central business district at the intersection of two interstate highways. The tanker ultimately spilled 18,000 gallons of nitric acid, used in the production of explosives, drugs, and fertilizer. Initially the spill ignited a minor fire and a yellow cloud of nitric acid gas caused explosions in some nearby electrical transformers, resulting in power outages in the area surrounding the railroad yard. No serious injuries were reported in connection with the accident itself.

As time passed, a large nitric acid gas plume formed over the rail yard. This gas cloud potentially threatened the nearby residential areas. The Denver Office of Emergency Preparedness, coordinating with the fire department, decided to evacuate an approximately five hundred–square–block area adjacent to the rail yard. Although part of the evacuated area consisted of factories and warehouses, there was also a number of low-income, inner-city residences. The area is populated principally by Mexican-Americans, blacks, and whites, with a very small number of Cambodian immigrants.

The warning process was begun at 5:30 P.M. with the sounding of emergency sirens. Warnings were also broadcast over local television and radio stations and an alert was issued over the National Oceanic and Atmospheric Administration (NOAA) weather radio. In addition, emergency services personnel warned citizens door to door in some areas and via mobile loudspeakers in other areas.

Approximately 2,300 persons registered at public shelters; officials estimate that more than 4,000 people were evacuated from their homes. Most of the evacuees were away from home less than twenty-four hours. By the afternoon of April 4, the fire department had neutralized most of the acid with soda ash and the gas plume had dissipated. Numerous citizens received medical treatment for minor eye irritations and respiratory difficulties, but none of those evacuated sustained serious injury.

Unlike the hazardous materials incident in Mount Vernon, the containment vessel was breached in Denver and emergency officials had to contend with an atmospheric release of nitric acid. The scope of impact was highly localized. The acid spill itself posed little threat to nearby homes. The danger to citizens came from the gas plume that formed above the spill and was subject to movement with the wind. The speed of onset was rapid; once emergency managers confirmed the existence of the plume and plotted trajectories to identify the threatened area, there was an immediate need for evacuation.

The duration of impact was short. Social preparedness in Denver, which maintains a city Office of Emergency Preparedness, is best described as high.

Data collection procedures

The same data collection procedures were used in each of the three study communities. The general design of the household surveys involved a "preletter-follow-up" strategy, which is fairly commonly used in surveys that employ trained interviewers to administer questionnaires (Perry, Lindell, and Greene, 1981:165–180). That is, the data-gathering procedure involved a series of contacts or attempted contacts with each potential respondent. First, a preletter describing the purpose of the study and explaining respondent selection procedures was mailed to each sampled household approximately six weeks before initial interviewer contacts were to be made. Following this initial communication, a trained project staff interviewer made three successive attempts over a period of one week to contact the potential respondent. As a function of this first attempt to make contact, all respondents were classified as (1) refused to be interviewed, (2) not in residence during relevant disaster and thus not interviewed, (3) partial or full interview completed, (4) unlocatable, or (5) moved and needed to be traced. Approximately one month later, project staff interviewers attempted again to locate and interview either in person or using a short form telephone questionnaire all potential respondents previously classified as either unlocatable or moved. After three such follow-up attempts by project staff members, respondents were either reclassified as having been located and refused participation, located and interviewed, or left in their original classification. The purpose of the elaborate call-back scheduling was to maximize the chance of reaching all potential study participants.

The return or completion rates generated via the above described field procedure were high enough to allow statistically meaningful analyses of the data and are comparable with the results yielded by similar study designs (Perry, Lindell, and Greene, 1981; Perry and Greene, 1982a). Table 1.1 summarizes survey completion information for both study sites. Line 10 shows that 79.9 percent of the Abilene respondents were interviewed, as were 73.3 percent of the Mount Vernon respondents and 85.5 percent of the Denver respondents.

Table 1.1
Survey completion summary

Description	Abilene	Mount Vernon	Denver
1. Total households drawn	239	206	159
2. Refused interview	11	8	6
3. Moved; could not trace	9	24	5
4. Could not contact	6	9	4
5. No dwelling standing or empty house	7	6	2
6. Not in town during disaster event	5	8	6
7. Total contacts made	207	167	148
8. Total interviews (partial or complete)	191	151	136
9. Percent total contacts interviewed	92.3	90.4	91.8
10. Percent total households drawn interviewed	79.9	73.3	85.5

We can now turn our attention to examining the nature of the sampling procedure used to select citizens to be interviewed. In all three communities, the target population was composed of those people who had heard an evacuation warning from any source. The procedure used to translate this target population into operational terms is one commonly used in studying warning response (cf. Mileti, 1974:70–87; Perry, Lindell, and Greene, 1981; Perry and Greene, 1982a). For each community sampled, a large map showing dwelling units was obtained. For each map an overlay was developed that delineated the areas of the community that were believed to have been warned by authorities. To increase the chance that the warned areas would be accurately delineated, a minimum of three informants was questioned about which areas were warned.

After the warning areas were identified on the map, the dwelling units within them at the time of disaster impact were enumerated. In each community, this list was constructed from the current *Polk's City Directory*. Completion of this exercise left us with a sample frame—a listing of the target population—for each community. From this sample frame a systematic or interval sample from a random start was drawn for all sites (Mueller, Schuessler, and Costner, 1977:378–380). The total number of dwelling units in the sample frame was estimated and a sample fraction chosen such that approximately 200 dwelling units were drawn from each site. The actual number of dwelling units drawn in Abilene was 239 (due to an incorrectly inflated sample fraction). There were 206 in Mount Vernon and 159 in Denver. This procedure yields *probability samples* of dwelling units within the areas believed to have received evacuation warnings. It should be emphasized here that probability samples were used to avoid any systematic bias in our pattern of selecting households to be interviewed; there is no interest in using these random samples to make population projections (for example, like political pollsters).

Finally, the sites selected for study were pre-screened as part of a disaster monitoring process to insure that selected communities contained enough minority group citizens who were affected by the evacuation warnings. Research project staff monitored news reports of natural and man-made disasters that involved evacuation of threatened populations. The first step was to assemble summaries of newspaper, radio, and television reports of disasters. After screening these sites for accurate reporting, basic population composition information was gathered from census documents, state fiscal planning offices, and town or regional chambers of commerce. Direct contacts were also made with town political and emergency management officials to estimate the approximate ethnic minority makeup of the evacuated people who had heard (from any source) an evacuation warning. The procedure chosen to translate the target universe into operational terms is one that is commonly used in the study areas. Final site selections were made on the basis of several criteria: (1) a preference for communities where more than one ethnic minority group was involved in the evacuation, (2) a preference for recent disasters, (3) a concern that authorities had sufficient forewarning to issue warning messages before impact, and (4) a selection of both natural and man-made disasters for study.

A note on external validity

As mentioned above, our utilization of probability methods in drawing samples was designed to minimize bias in the selection of cases for interview. The estimation of population parameters from sample statistics is not a primary goal of this research. Instead, our research thrust is exploratory. We are concerned with identifying and describing relationships among variables, particularly with regard to differences and similarities among ethnic groups.

Keeping our exploratory objective in mind, as is the case with all research, our sample sizes were determined by the available funding resources.

Given our desire to explore a wide range of variables, the sample sizes are numerically small. Consequently, we face a problem that has confronted many researchers before us: as matrices were constructed for tabular analyses, low frequency or zero cells began to appear. This is not a problem tied to tabular analysis. Other analysis techniques such as multiple regression simply handle missing data differently (for example, by supplying arithmetic averages). We believe that some sophisticated analyses risk obscuring or masking missing data problems rather than overtly addressing them. We chose cross tabulations because this technique involves displaying our data in a way that allows critical readers greatest latitude in interpreting the results—even to the point of reassembling and restructuring our scaling decisions. We have also made concerted efforts to alert readers to our conclusions and interpretations that may be artifacts of small cell sizes.

Independent of these analysis tactics, there still remains the question of the external validity of our results. To what populations or peoples do our results generalize? This question is particularly important because there is so little data currently available on minority citizen disaster behavior. To those scientists and practitioners who are anxious for a "quick fix" of the gap in empirical knowledge, our answer will no doubt be disappointing. In essence, this research is no different from any other exploratory study. It marks a beginning of the systematic assessment of ethnic differentials, not a conclusion.

In brief, one can have confidence in the external validity or generalizability of any research results drawn from any type of study design to the extent that those results are *replicated* over time and across different populations or study sites. This logic has been used for decades by scientists working in the areas of chemistry, physics, biology, and psychology. Confidence in a particular finding drawn from a particular data set is defined in two ways. To the extent that the result is replicated by other researchers at different times, one has confidence that a true effect has been isolated. To the extent that the result is replicated on different subjects (that is, in different settings), one can have confidence that the effect is prevalent in a variety of populations.

This view of knowledge accumulation in social science does indeed place strenuous demands upon the research community. The most formidable of these is that researchers must know the empirical record well and carefully coach interpretations of their data in the larger context of previous disaster studies. It is through this mechanism that we construct an empirical record in terms of which we can effectively assess the external validity of all disaster studies. In this sense, the size of the sample is a consideration in data analysis, but whether the sample size is large or small the generalizability of the conclusions must be examined in terms of their relationship to other studies.

Now, to the extent that conclusions drawn in this book represent consistencies across our three study sites, our confidence in the findings is enhanced. The more important test, however, still lies with the future. It is only as we develop a backlog of studies of ethnicity in disaster that we can evaluate, replicate, elaborate, or negate findings reported here. Perhaps the most functional way of viewing the results presented here is in terms of problem identification. Certainly, these results stand as firmly as the results of any single study. However, we can constructively view these findings as signposts identifying issues that merit further or more thorough study. While this tack is a useful approach in any research area, the paucity of data on ethnic groups in disasters makes it particularly appropriate here.

In closing, we wish to echo the sentiments of Professor Rodney William Stark. In 1972 Stark published the first study of collective violence in law enforcement titled *Police Riots*. In the preface, the author recounts his efforts to obtain additional resources (funding) to obtain a larger sample and conduct a major survey. When funds were not forthcoming, Stark assessed the situation: "my option was to say nothing or do the best I could with what I could get. Obviously, I felt silence was more irresponsible than risking error" (1972:iii). By risking error, Stark simply meant that he may document behaviors that were peculiar to his sample, behaviors that did not generalize well to other subjects or populations. Our view is that empirical science must start somewhere, and like Stark we feel that saying nothing is simply professionally unacceptable. Indeed, science is not a zero-sum game. Knowing that a trait is peculiar to a particular population under particular circumstances is just as important as discovering a trait that universally applies. In the philosophy of science, a finding is valuable in itself and in the context of other findings. While individual scientists may feel reinforced by findings that are consistent with theoretical edifices, a finding of "no statistically significant relationship" is also a valid research outcome.

Plan of the book

The research reported herein focuses upon disaster response and disaster preparedness issues. Chapters 2 and 3 describe citizen warning response behavior. Chapter 2 is concerned with the way people respond to the first warning messages they receive. Here we are particularly interested in examining the social processes and channels through which people are warned and the effects of warning source, mode, message content, number of warnings heard, and past disaster experience upon first reactions to the environmental threat. Chapter 3 reviews post-warning phenomena, including warning confirmation patterns, warning compliance behavior, and shelter utilization.

Chapter 4 deals with the participation of minority citizens in the planning and response process. Of prime importance in this chapter is the examination of a variety of potential operational problems that might be associated with minority citizens, including testing to determine if observed behavioral differences should be attributed to race or socioeconomic status, looking at minority patterns for gathering information about environmental threats, examining the feasibility of different types of outreach programs for disseminating hazard information to minority and majority group citizens, and examining the impact of language on understanding the content of warning messages.

In chapter 5 we change units of analysis from the individual to the community. An attempt is made here to examine the broader context in which citizen disaster response and planning take place. The emphasis is upon understanding the formation and implementation of emergency management policy in the context of emergency services delivery in the local community. Our approach involves surveying the nature and growth of emergency services policy and then examining the implications of citizen participation for the administration of emergency management.

The closing chapter of the book provides a detailed summary of our major findings. Careful attention is given to elaborating the implications of our results for applied emergency management, including suggestions for amending emergency services practices.

2 Disaster warning processes

From a technical standpoint, a disaster warning is a message indicating the existence of and describing some danger in the environment. The message itself is the product of a complex social process involving individuals (acting as organizational representatives) and technology. Whether the danger stems from natural forces or is man-made, the process that culminates in the issuance of a warning message can be described as including five primary activities: (1) scanning the environment to detect threats, (2) compiling descriptive information once a threat is detected, (3) evaluating threat characteristics and likely consequences for citizens, (4) deciding to issue a warning message when it is determined that danger will reach an unacceptable level, and (5) deciding upon content of message, mode of delivery, and timing of issuance. The first two steps usually involve technology, such as the use of weather radar in the case of hurricanes or radiation detection devices in the case of nuclear powered electricity generators. All subsequent steps describe decisions made by local authorities, usually a collection of organizations acting in concert. The issuance of a warning message also begins another fairly complex social process, namely, that of inducing threatened citizens to undertake behaviors that will ultimately reduce the negative consequences of disaster impact.

The purpose of this chapter is to examine citizen behavior when first confronted with a disaster warning message. Before issuing the warning message, local authorities must collectively define the environmental threat as likely to inflict serious harm upon citizens. In order to comply with protective measures suggested by authorities, citizens must come to share their definition of the situation as potentially dangerous. Much research has documented that people's very first reaction to a warning is disbelief; a feeling (or perhaps more accurately, a hope) that the danger described in the message will not materialize (Drabek, 1969; Moore, 1958a; Mileti, 1974). Following this, it is known that citizens typically begin an evaluative process of scrutinizing the disaster warning in an effort to either verify that the threat is real or eliminate concerns by determining that no danger exists (cf. Perry, 1982). This process involves three different but interdependent activities: evaluating the warning source, interpreting the message, and initiating actions related to the environmental threat.

These initial assessments are important processes that have received comparatively little research attention. From the standpoint of disaster response operations, the time consumed by such citizen evaluations affects the overall warning response time and consequently the extent to which life and property are potentially endangered. Also, in terms of theories of human disaster behavior, the outcome of citizen warning assessments determines the extent to which protective actions suggested in the warning message will be complied with or ignored. Our primary interest, then, lies in understanding factors that control or influence how a citizen responds to the *first* warning message received. A considerable backlog of research indicates that citizens' first response to a disaster warning is a function of their initial assessment of personal risk and the extent to which they believe that the warning message is accurate or describes a real environmental threat (cf. Perry, 1985). In turn, three variables are thought to be related to risk assessment and the development of a warning belief: warning source, warning content, and past experience with disasters. The following sections address each of these factors and their relationship to perceived risk and warning belief, followed by an examination of the relationship of risk and warning belief to initial warning response. In all cases, particular emphasis will be placed upon identifying differences among ethnic groups and between disaster events.

Warning source

Research on warning response has shown that the source from which an individual receives the first warning about an environmental threat influences the way in which the warning is evaluated (Perry and Mushkatel, 1984; Mileti, 1975:75; McLuckie, 1970:38; Drabek and Stephenson, 1971:192). At the outset, we acknowledge that it is sometimes difficult to separate warning source from communication channel (cf. Moore et al., 1963). The concept of warning source concentrates upon the person or agency that presumably constructs and delivers the warning message. Communication channel or warning mode refers to the mechanism through which a message is delivered. Emergency management authorities, police, fire fighters, friends, neighbors, relatives, and political authorities are all clearly warning *sources*. The warning message developed by these sources may be delivered via a variety of warning *modes*, including face-to-face verbal contact, a mobile loudspeaker, telephone, radio, or television. The distinction between source and mode is clear, analytically speaking, but very unclear in practice. Indeed, certain modes are commonly used, or even exclusively used, by certain sources. A warning from a friend, relative, or neighbor is likely to come face to face or via telephone. Emergency authorities may transmit warning messages via mobile loudspeakers, radio, television, or face to face. In the context of warning source, mass media may be conceived as either mode or source.

At one level the mass media, represented by radio, television, and newspapers, are *channels* through which information passes. In the context of environmental threats, an emergency manager might formulate a warning message and then choose to send it to the public by asking radio, television, or newspapers to reproduce the message. More direct dissemination may be achieved by activating the Emergency Broadcast System, whereby an emergency manager can read a message that is transmitted via cooperating media. In both the preceding examples the media are channels rather than sources.

Mass media can be warning sources as well as channels, however. This is particularly true in the case of multiple impact disasters or environmental threats where the period of forewarning is long. In such cases, the mass media fulfill their normal news function regarding the environmental threat. A quantity of information from multiple sources is gathered by reporters and then assembled, interpreted, and disseminated to the public. Such information may include specific information attributed to emergency managers, but it is also likely to include descriptive information about the current threat derived from different sources as well as coverage of past and/or related threats. In this situation, the medium becomes a source: it gathers information about the threat and interprets the information for the public. In our analyses we are concerned with the mass media as sources, not channels. In all three disaster events, the mass media—represented by local radio and television stations— did relay warning messages to the public. Although the lag time available for such warnings was lowest in Mount Vernon and Denver and highest in Abilene, respondents in each community could meaningfully designate radio or television bulletins as their first warning of danger.

Table 2.1 shows ethnic group membership by first warning source for each community studied. The classification of warning sources follows the scheme developed by Drabek (1969), where "authority" refers to personnel from emergency services organizations (including police, fire, and sheriff's personnel) and "mass media" includes radio and television broadcast stations. In connection with the Abilene flood, the three ethnic groups show different

Table 2.1

First warning source by ethnicity

First warning source	Blacks		Whites		Mexican-Americans	
	N	%	N	%	N	%
Abilene						
Authority	44	68.8	7	8.5	4	10.5
Mass media	18	28.1	52	63.4	18	47.4
Relatives/friends	2	3.1	23	28.0	16	42.1
Mount Vernon[1]						
Authority	0	0.0	37	42.0	9	25.0
Mass media	0	0.0	12	13.6	11	30.6
Relatives/friends	0	0.0	39	44.3	16	44.4
Denver						
Authority	14	32.6	10	25.6	7	14.3
Mass media	9	20.9	8	20.5	7	14.3
Relatives/friends	20	46.5	21	53.8	35	71.4

[1]There were no blacks in the Mount Vernon sample.

patterns of first warning source. Most blacks (68.8 percent) were first warned by an authority; 28.1 percent cited mass media and only two respondents (3.1 percent) reported relatives or friends as the source of their initial warning. On the other hand, the majority of whites (63.4 percent) received initial warning through the mass media. Among these respondents, relatives or friends were the second most frequently cited source (28 percent), and only 8.5 percent were first warned by an authority. Finally, the majority of Mexican-Americans were about evenly split on first warning source between the mass media (47.4 percent) and relatives or friends (42.1 percent); only four respondents (10.5 percent) cited an authority as first warning source.

Because of the progressive nature of the warning process in Abilene (the areas with the highest proportions of minority citizens were threatened first and thus warned first by the authorities), minority citizens had a slightly greater opportunity to be warned by authorities than did whites. Indeed, as stated above, only 8.5 percent of the whites first heard a warning message from authorities. The authorities used door-to-door contacts in issuing warnings and progressed through the danger areas, thereby creating a sequential lag wherein heavily minority areas were warned early in the process and heavily white areas were warned later. However, at the same time authorities began issuing warnings, mass media began broadcasting warning bulletins, so all citizens tuned to the media had an approximately equal chance of hearing an initial warning message via this source. Dependence upon the media for first warning was highest among whites and Mexican-Americans, where approximately half the respondents in each ethnic group were first warned by radio or television.

To receive a first warning message from relatives or friends requires a two-step process. First, the relative or friend must receive a warning or some information about the environmental threat. Then, that warning recipient must contact another person to relay the message. Consequently, in our samples the proportion of persons warned by relatives or friends serves as an index of the level of social network activity among warning recipients. In Abilene, this social networking behavior was highest among Mexican-Americans, suggesting that kinship and friendship contacts serve as important channels for information exchange. Considerably fewer whites—who had an equal opportunity for such networking—and blacks—with a somewhat reduced opportunity— used these channels to disseminate threat information.

In Mount Vernon, the two ethnic groups were residentially interspersed and consequently each group had an approximately equal chance to receive first warning from any of the three sources. White warning recipients are about equally split between an authority as first source (42 percent) and relatives or friends (44.3 percent). Whites cited the mass media as initial warning sources fairly infrequently. The most frequent source of first warning among Mexican-Americans was relatives or friends (44.4 percent), followed by the mass media (30.6 percent) and authorities (25 percent). It is interesting to note that in Mount Vernon the majority of each ethnic group reported relatives or friends as first warning source. This relatively high level of networking among both ethnic groups is probably related to the characteristics of the community and the type of environmental threat involved. The Abilene flood represented a familiar, slow-developing threat in a semirural setting with a history of similar threats. Under those circumstances we found that Mexican-Americans relied to a greater extent on social networks than either whites or blacks. This finding is consistent with the results of other flood-threatened communities with similar characteristics (cf. Perry, Lindell, and Greene, 1981; Perry and Mushkatel, 1984). Mount Vernon is a semirural community facing a technological threat that had recently affected neighboring communities. Two factors distinguished the Mount Vernon case from Abilene: (1) the precise nature of the threat—a derailed tank car carrying liquid propane—was unfamiliar to warning recipients, and (2) the onset of the threat was rapid and unexpected by the public and the time available for citizens to comply with the warning was short. One would expect Mexican-Americans in Mount Vernon to engage in a relatively high level of networking contacts, because kin and friendship networks are commonly used channels of information exchange among these citizens during nonemergency times (Moore, 1976:102–113; Alvirez and Bean, 1976). Under the circumstances described above, however, the level of social network contacts among whites also increases, in the case of Mount Vernon, to levels approximating those of minority citizens.

   The patterns of first warning source among Denver respondents approximate those seen in the Mount Vernon data. Among blacks, 46.5 percent of the respondents were first warned by relatives or friends, 32.6 percent by an authority, and 20.9 percent via the mass media. A rank ordering of the first warning sources for whites duplicates the order for blacks: 53.8 percent were warned initially by relatives or friends, 25.6 percent by an authority, and 20.5 percent by mass media. The majority of Mexican-Americans (71.4 percent) were warned by relatives or friends, with much smaller but equal proportions citing an authority (14.3 percent) and the mass media (14.3 percent). It is interesting to note that the proportions of blacks and whites first warned via mass media are virtually identical, with an only slightly smaller proportion of Mexican-Americans citing radio or television as first warning source. Consequently, in Denver the mass media were cited as initial warning source less often than authorities and relatives or friends by all three ethnic groups and by similar proportions of respondents within each ethnic group. Blacks received an initial warning message from authorities more often than whites, who in turn cited this source more often than Mexican-Americans.

Finally, in Denver the greatest proportion of respondents in each ethnic group cited relatives or friends as their first warning source. Furthermore, a considerably larger proportion of Mexican-Americans (than whites or blacks) were initially warned by relatives or friends. These findings suggest some general conclusions regarding the use of social network contact in relaying warning messages among the three ethnic groups that can be interpreted in terms of differing characteristics of the three warning events studied.

An examination of the data on citizens of different ethnicity warned first by relatives or friends shows several general patterns across the three communities. First, a greater proportion of Mexican-Americans were first warned via social networks in Denver (71.4 percent) than in either Mount Vernon or Abilene, where the proportions are approximately equal (44.4 and 42.1 percent, respectively). Second, the proportion of whites first warned by relatives or friends increases substantially as we move from Abilene to Mount Vernon (from 28 to 44.3 percent) and increases moderately when we move from Mount Vernon to Denver (to 53.8 percent). Third, the proportion of blacks first warned via social networks increases substantially from Abilene to Denver. Fourth, the proportion of whites warned by relatives and friends in Denver is similar to the proportion of blacks first warned by the same source in Denver.

From these empirical patterns, by taking into account characteristics of the disaster threat, we can make three general inferences about the use of social networks to relay warning information by different ethnic groups. First, Mexican-Americans tend to rely upon social networks to relay warning information to a greater extent than blacks or whites. This assertion is consistent with our data on the Abilene flood and seems to hold true generally when the threat agent is familiar to the public and characterized by gradual onset and when the community involved is semirural or a small town (cf. Perry, Lindell, and Greene, 1981; Perry and Greene, 1982b). Second, when response time is relatively short and the public is unfamiliar with the nature of the threat agent, the proportion of whites who relay warning information via social networks increases, while the proportion of Mexican-Americans (who normally have a higher base rate for such exchanges) stays about the same. This interpretation is supported in our data when the proportions of citizens first warned by friends or relatives are compared between Abilene and Mount Vernon, where the principal structural differences between events relate to response time and threat agent. Finally, communication of warning information via social networks is highest among all three ethnic groups when the threat agent is unfamiliar, response time is short, environmental cues of pending danger are present, and the endangered area is urban. Furthermore, the increase in levels of warning information exchange among Mexican-Americans is likely to be greater than that observed among blacks and whites.

These statements summarize the empirical patterns reflected in our data across the three study sites. In all cases, the frequency of social network contacts was higher among Mexican-Americans than among either blacks or whites. Also, the increase in proportion of network contacts among Mexican-Americans is higher than among blacks and whites as we compare the Abilene threat with those in Mount Vernon and Denver. Other warning response data also support the thesis that when the public is unfamiliar with the threat (Perry, Lindell, and Greene, 1981) and when environmental cues representing danger are present (Perry, 1985; Gruntfest, Downing, and White, 1978), warning recipients tend to accelerate the extent to which they seek information regarding the recommended protective measures. Our data suggest that urban-dwelling citizens, particularly Mexican-Americans, engage in higher levels of warning information exchange than do those who live in semirural or small town settings. This finding must be interpreted cautiously, however, because of the paucity of rural-urban warning response comparisons available in the empirical literature (Drabek, 1983).

Research suggests that a first step toward obtaining citizen compliance with a warning message is accomplished when the individual is warned by a source perceived to be credible (Perry, 1979a; Mileti, 1975:210; Anderson, 1969a:299; Williams, 1964:94; Janis, 1962:59). Studies of the differential credibility of warning sources provide feedback regarding whether or not the official emergency response system itself is credible, whether the way in which a particular warning was handled affected credibility, and to what extent other sources already viewed as highly credible might be incorporated into the emergency response system. Understanding the differential credibility of sources also allows authorities to evaluate which ones are most useful for delivering immediate warning information regarding a disaster in progress.

Table 2.2 shows the proportion of respondents who classified their first warning source as highly reliable by ethnicity for each study site. Concern here is with citizen rankings of the source of their initial warning message on a reliability dimension. Respondents were asked to rank the credibility of their first warning source as "highly reliable," "usually reliable," or "sometimes not reliable." (To obtain the proportion of respondents ranking a given source in the latter two categories, one can subtract the proportion entered in the table from 1.0.) The data presented here are more specific than general ratings of sources citizens believe to be reliable. Instead, the proportions in Table 2.2 reflect the credibility attributed to a single source from whom the respondent has just received a danger message. Thus the proportions do not represent abstract rankings but describe citizen confidence in the source at a crucial point in the warning response process.

Most citizens first warned by an authority rated the source as highly reliable. With one exception, this claim holds true across all three ethnic groups and all three disaster events. All Mexican-Americans warned by authorities of the Abilene flood and the Denver nitric acid spill and 89 percent of those in the Mount Vernon propane gas threat rated this source as highly reliable. Among whites, 86 percent of those in Abilene, 97 percent of those in Mount Vernon, and 90 percent of those in Denver rated authorities as highly reliable. In Denver, 86 percent of black warning recipients also rated authorities as a highly reliable source. The only exception is to be found among black flood warning recipients, where only 60 percent rated authority as a highly reliable source. In Abilene, blacks warned by an authority were concentrated at the two ends of the reliability continuum: the remaining 40 percent rated this source as sometimes not reliable. No compelling explanation readily suggests itself to account for the lower confidence ratings by blacks in Abilene. Mexican-Americans and whites show similar proportions across all three sites and blacks in Denver were similar to whites and Mexican-Americans. It appears likely that situational factors specific to blacks warned in Abilene—perhaps a neighborhood antipathy regarding police—account for the lower ratings of authorities among this ethnic group.

When the mass media were the initial warning source, consistently

Table 2.2
Proportion of respondents ranking source as highly reliable by ethnicity

First warning source	Abilene			Mount Vernon		Denver		
	Blacks	Whites	Mexican-Americans	Whites	Mexican-Americans	Blacks	Whites	Mexican-Americans
Authority	.60 (44)	.86 (7)	1.00 (4)	.97 (37)	.89 (9)	.86 (14)	.90 (10)	1.00 (7)
Mass media	.49 (18)	.65 (52)	.94 (18)	.50 (12)	1.00 (11)	.56 (9)	.50 (8)	.88 (8)
Relatives/friends	1.00 (4)	.59 (22)	1.00 (12)	.41 (38)	.31 (16)	.85 (20)	.80 (21)	.82 (35)

Note: The number of cases upon which the proportion of respondents was calculated is given in parentheses.

smaller proportions of blacks and whites rated them as highly reliable than was the case when an authority was the first source. Approximately one-half of the whites first warned by the mass media in all three sites rated the source as highly reliable. Forty-nine percent of black respondents in Abilene and 56 percent of those in Denver rated mass media as highly reliable. Significantly higher proportions of Mexican-Americans in Abilene (94 percent), Mount Vernon (100 percent), and Denver (88 percent) rated mass media as highly reliable. Thus, while blacks and whites placed less confidence in the media, large proportions of Mexican-Americans rated this source as highly reliable across types of disaster threat (flood versus propane gas versus nitric acid spill) and across community settings (semirural, small town, and large city). Records of interviewer debriefings show that Mexican-American respondents tended to listen to Spanish language broadcasts and expressed the belief that both English and Spanish radio and television broadcast content was governed by standards that would forbid airing false statements about a pending disaster. Moore (1976:96–100) has commented on the role of communication within the Mexican-American community, indicating the importance of institutions such as Spanish radio broadcasts as representing ethnic community solidarity and culture, to be distinguished from communication links dependent upon the Anglo community. Given this ethos, namely, that Spanish language broadcasts are part of a positive cultural pattern and that all broadcasts are screened for accuracy, the higher proportions of Mexican-Americans describing the mass media as a highly reliable first warning source are readily interpretable.

Therefore, in terms of issuing disaster warnings to Mexican-Americans, the mass media—particularly Spanish language broadcasts—are apt to be treated as reliable sources. This was not the case with blacks and whites in our sample; both ethnic groups tended to be skeptical of mass media warnings. A predominant objection raised by whites regarding media warnings was that "reporters are always looking for a story—they make everything sound bad so you never know what's really happening." Black respondents expressed reservations about media consistent with a variety of research on the behavior of black Americans: mass media tend to be controlled by the white majority and rarely deal with issues relevant to blacks or to the preservation of a black community (Altshuler, 1970:66–69; Staples, 1976:38–39).

The reliability ratings of relatives and friends as a first warning source show some differences by ethnicity and among different disaster events. In

Abilene, a small town setting confronted by a familiar flood threat, all of the minority citizens first warned by relatives or friends rated this source as highly reliable. Comparatively, only 59 percent of whites rated relatives and friends as highly reliable. This pattern is compatible with what one would expect based upon the race relations literature (cf. Jackson, 1973:437; Staples, 1976; Pinkney, 1975:161; Blackwell, 1975). That is, minority citizens are more likely to attribute higher levels of credibility to same-ethnicity contacts from kin and friendship networks than white citizens. An important qualifier here is that we are observing differential attributions of reliability between majority and minority group citizens prevalent in response to a familiar threat in a small town setting.

The data from Mount Vernon allow examination of credibility attributions of whites and Mexican-Americans also in a small town who are also facing an unfamiliar environmental threat. In this setting, the proportions of whites (41 percent) and Mexican-Americans (31 percent) ranking relatives or friends as highly reliable are very low. In Mount Vernon the danger about which citizens were warned was a potential propane gas containment breach—an unfamiliar threat, accompanied by no visible environmental cues, thereby making it difficult for citizens to evaluate it. In similar situations, particularly those involving technological disaster agents, citizens have tended to place less confidence in social network contacts, which have the same faculties for threat evaluation as the warning recipients, and greater confidence in warnings from authorities, who are presumed to have access to specialized threat information (cf. Perry, 1985). The Mount Vernon data show this same pattern and demonstrate that the argument applies to at least two ethnic groups: whites and Mexican-Americans.

The Denver data add still another dimension to understanding the credibility of relatives or friends as warning sources. Two features distinguish the Denver disaster from Abilene and Mount Vernon: the nitric acid produced numerous visible cues that something was amiss, and warning recipients lived in a large urban area. In this setting, large proportions of blacks (85 percent), whites (80 percent), and Mexican-Americans (82 percent) first warned by a relative or friend described that source as highly reliable. It can be argued that the attribution of credibility to relatives or friends is a function of two primary factors. First, even though citizens were unfamiliar and inexperienced with nitric acid threats, visible cues (fire, odor, vapor cloud, and presence of police, fire, and emergency services personnel and vehicles) definitely estab-

lished the existence of danger. Second, because the urban setting was characterized by multiple opportunities for citizens to obtain threat-relevant information, warning recipients could reasonably assume that a relative or friend
delivering a warning message possessed some special information (perhaps as
a function of being warned themselves by authorities at an earlier time or
simply collecting information from other sources or by having observed the
threat itself). Under these specific conditions, it became plausible for citizens,
regardless of ethnicity, to view a relative or friend from whom first warning
was just received as a highly reliable source.

In summary, the data in Table 2.2 may be interpreted as supporting five
general conclusions regarding attributions of credibility of authorities, mass
media, and relatives or friends as first warning sources among blacks, whites,
and Mexican-Americans. First, warning recipients tend to regard authorities
(police, fire fighters, uniformed emergency personnel) as highly reliable
warning sources; this conclusion holds across all three types of disaster events
for blacks, whites, and Mexican-Americans. Second, blacks and whites
viewed the mass media as less reliable warning sources in all three sites.
Third, Mexican-Americans rated the mass media as highly reliable sources in
all three disaster settings. Fourth, when the threat involved is familiar to the
public and the setting is semirural or a small town, minority citizens are more
likely than whites to regard relatives or friends as reliable first warning
sources. When the setting is a small town but the threat is unfamiliar, both
minority and white warning recipients tend to define relatives or friends as
less reliable warning sources. Finally, when the threat is unfamiliar but accompanied by visible environmental cues and the setting is urban, blacks,
whites, and Mexican-Americans regard relatives or friends as credible warning sources.

Warning content

The content or information contained in a disaster warning message constitutes the basic data upon which warning recipients must act to understand
the pending threat (Williams, 1964:94; Fritz, 1957:6–9). The content of the
first warning message is particularly important for two reasons. From a theoretical point of view, first message content forms the cue for warning recip-

ients to begin the evaluative phase of the warning response process that culminates in the development of a warning belief and an assessment of personal risk. From the standpoint of managing emergency operations, the more specific the content of first warning, the greater the probability that citizens will believe the message and define themselves as being at risk and the quicker they will comply with protective actions suggested by authorities (Moore et al., 1963:31–33; Mileti and Beck, 1975:28). Before examining the correlation of warning content with warning belief and perceived personal risk, we will review the extent to which message content varies among different warning sources.

Research on disaster warning message construction has shown that the most effective warning messages contain several elements: a brief description of the threat, impact location, likely severity, and a suggested action for protection (cf. Gruntfest, Downing, and White, 1978:73; Mileti and Harvey, 1977:6; Williams, 1957:17). Table 2.3 shows warning message content by source and ethnicity for each site. Two levels of warning content have been identified. The most vague of the two message forms contained a statement that a danger existed and described the likely impact location. The more specific message described the danger and impact area *and* included information or severity with a suggestion to evacuate. This latter message is abbreviated in Table 2.3 as "Danger: Action." In these data our classification of content of the first warning message is based upon citizen self-reports. This means that our classifications represent not necessarily what the source communicated but instead what the warning recipient remembers hearing. In analyzing the content of disaster warnings these perceptual data are important because citizens act upon parts of the message that they recall (subject to "noise" effects in transmission) and not necessarily upon the message that the sender transmits (cf. Mileti, 1974).

The Abilene flood data show that all whites and Mexican-Americans and 59.1 percent of the blacks who were first warned by an authority recalled hearing the most specific warning message. This finding is consistent with the results of other research on flood warning content (cf. Drabek and Boggs, 1968), although our data suggest that the magnitude of the association between warnings from authorities and specificity of message is weaker among blacks than in the other two ethnic groups. Message content for citizens first warned via mass media varies considerably among the ethnic groups. Approximately 40 percent of blacks warned via the mass media recalled hearing a

Table 2.3

Warning message content by first warning source and ethnicity

Message content	Abilene						Mount Vernon[1]						Denver					
	Authority		Mass media		Relatives/ friends		Authority		Mass media		Relatives/ friends		Authority		Mass media		Relatives/ friends	
	N	%	N	%	N	%	N	%	N	%	N	%	N	%	N	%	N	%
Blacks																		
Danger	18	40.9	11	61.1	0	0.0	—	—	—	—	—	—	4	14.3	4	44.4	4	20.0
Danger: action	26	59.1	7	39.9	2	100.0	—	—	—	—	—	—	12	85.7	5	55.6	16	80.0
Whites																		
Danger	0	0.0	25	48.1	13	56.5	5	13.5	2	16.7	15	39.4	2	20.0	3	37.5	7	33.3
Danger: action	7	100.0	27	51.9	10	43.5	32	86.5	10	83.3	23	60.6	8	80.0	5	65.0	14	66.7
Mexican-Americans																		
Danger	0	0.0	6	33.3	6	35.2	3	33.3	4	36.4	13	81.2	3	42.9	3	37.5	10	28.5
Danger: action	4	100.0	12	66.7	11	64.8	6	66.7	7	63.6	3	18.8	4	57.1	5	62.5	25	71.5

[1] There were no blacks in the Mount Vernon sample.

specific message, and whites were about evenly split between the vague and specific messages. Mexican-Americans, on the other hand, more often heard a specific message (66.7 percent) from the mass media. Too few blacks in Abilene were warned first by relatives or friends to make reliable inferences about comparative warning content. Whites, however, were about evenly split between vague and specific content when the warnings came from relatives or friends, and the majority of Mexican-Americans (64.8 percent) heard a specific message. These flood data, representing a small community facing a relatively slow-developing threat, suggest two general observations: (1) citizens first warned by uniformed authorities tend to recall higher levels of specific warning content, and (2) Mexican-Americans first warned via mass media or relatives or friends recall more specific elements than either blacks or whites warned by the same source.

The Mount Vernon data also show that whites and Mexican-Americans first warned by an authority were more likely to receive the most specific message than citizens first warned by mass media or relatives or friends. In turn, citizens of both ethnic groups first warned via mass media were more likely to hear a specific message than those warned by relatives or friends. Two interesting points should be made regarding these data. First, the difference between the proportion of citizens receiving a specific warning from authorities and mass media is small for whites (86.5 percent versus 83.3 percent) and Mexican-Americans (66.7 percent versus 63.6 percent). This pattern is different from the case for Abilene, where mass media warnings tended to be much less specific than those from authorities. The greater relative precision of the mass media warnings in Mount Vernon is probably a function of the short time of forewarning. Because there was little time available, fewer mass media sources operated (only radio, in fact) and media had less opportunity to edit messages—for the most part radio stations tended to simply relay the message given them by county authorities. The second point that deserves comment is that Mexican-Americans whose first warning message came from relatives or friends were far less likely to hear a specific message than whites. This phenomenon appears for the most part to be related to the aforementioned higher levels of warning message relay among Mexican-American social networks. Interviewer debriefings indicate that Mexican-American respondents frequently reported high levels of concern over the unfamiliar nature of the threat and consequently relayed the briefest possible message to the greatest number of social contacts before beginning to evacuate their own households. Under the circumstances, this phenomenon resulted in brief and apparently vague messages being disseminated among the Mexican-American community.

Finally, the Denver data for blacks and whites first warned by an authority are consistent with the other communities in that these respondents were most likely to hear a specific message. The majority of Mexican-Americans warned by an authority also heard the most specific message, but in absolute terms the proportion of Mexican-Americans in this category was smaller than that observed for blacks or whites. Citizens of all three ethnic groups first warned via the mass media were less likely to hear a specific message than those warned by an authority or through relatives or friends. This pattern more closely approximates the media warning content results in Abilene than Mount Vernon. In Denver, unlike either of the other communities, blacks, whites, and Mexican-Americans warned by relatives or friends were very likely to hear a specific message. It is probable that the urbanized setting in Denver accounts for both the greater frequency of citizens warned by relatives or friends and the greater specificity of messages received via this source compared with the mass media. Denver experienced the same short forewarning period encountered in Mount Vernon (where media warnings tended to be specific), but the population warned lived in closer proximity to one another, resulting in higher levels of face-to-face contacts among warning recipients and between authorities issuing warnings and warning recipients. There were also visible cues consistent with the disaster warning and regarding which citizens could assemble information directly (without interpretation by authorities). Under these circumstances, there was less dependence upon mass media for threat information generally and citizens were able to relay detailed threat information among themselves.

In summary, one must remember to exercise great caution in the interpretations offered for our data on message specificity. The numbers of cases in some subcells are very low, particularly in the Abilene and Denver samples. For the most part, low cell counts are a function of the warning context described in chapter 1. In Abilene, for example, most blacks were warned by authorities, most whites via mass media, and most Mexican-Americans by friends and relatives; this left few warning messages to be classified as either vague or specific that could come from different sources. In effect, there is a correlation between warning source and ethnicity that restricts our ability to make between-source assessments of message content. With this caution in mind, and treating the data as indicative rather than conclusive, there are three patterns identifiable in Table 2.3. First, across all three events and all three ethnic groups, citizens first warned by an authority were most likely to hear the most specific warning message. Second, in small town or semirural settings where forewarning is short, citizens of all ethnic groups warned via mass media were more likely to hear specific messages than those warned by relatives or friends. Third, when forewarning is short but the population warned is urbanized, the proportion of all ethnic groups warned via mass media is smaller, and those warned through relatives or friends are more likely to hear specific warning messages.

The research literature on warning response behavior suggests that warning message content should be correlated with the extent to which citizens believe that the warning accurately portrays a valid or real environmental threat (cf. Perry, Lindell, and Greene, 1981:60–62). That is, the more specific the warning message, the more likely it is that citizens will develop a high level of warning belief. Table 2.4 shows the level of warning belief associated with the first warning message heard by message content for each study site. Citizens who reported that they felt certain the warning message accurately described a pending environmental threat were characterized as showing high warning belief; all others were included in the low warning belief category.

The Abilene flood data generally support the contention that the proportion of citizens characterized by a high level of warning belief increases as we move from the less specific to the more specific warning message. This relationship is strongest among blacks and whites and also holds for Mexican-Americans, though the magnitude of the correlation is smaller. It is interesting to note that almost all Mexican-Americans, without regard to the specificity of the warning message, developed a high level of warning belief.

The correlation between message content and warning belief is also positive in the data from Mount Vernon, representing a situation where citizens were unfamiliar with the environmental danger. Among whites, 56.6 percent of those hearing the vague message developed a high warning belief compared with 81.6 percent of those who heard the more specific message. Similarly, 50 percent of the Mexican-Americans exposed to the less specific message developed a high warning belief versus 93.8 percent of those receiving the more specific message. In general, Mount Vernon warning recipients given a specific warning message were more likely to show high warning belief than were Abilene respondents who also heard a specific message. This supports the hypothesis that citizens facing an unfamiliar threat accompanied by no visible environmental cues are far more likely to develop high levels of

Table 2.4

Initial warning belief by message content and ethnicity

Initial warning belief	Abilene				Mount Vernon[1]				Denver			
	Danger		Action		Danger		Action		Danger		Action	
	N	%	N	%	N	%	N	%	N	%	N	%
Blacks												
Low	20	69.0	11	31.4	—	—	—	—	3	37.5	4	12.1
High	9	31.0	24	68.6	—	—	—	—	5	62.5	29	87.9
Whites												
Low	16	42.1	15	34.0	10	43.4	12	18.4	4	33.3	5	18.5
High	22	57.9	29	66.0	13	56.6	53	81.6	8	66.7	22	81.5
Mexican-Americans												
Low	1	8.3	1	3.8	10	50.0	1	6.2	2	12.5	4	11.7
High	11	91.7	25	96.2	10	50.0	15	93.8	14	87.5	30	88.3

[1]There were no blacks in the Mount Vernon sample.

warning belief when given specific warning messages. Thus, to promote higher levels of citizen attention to and compliance with such warnings, emergency managers should devote special attention to constructing warning messages that include descriptions of the threat and likely impact area, severity and timing of impact, and suggestions for protective actions.

Among blacks and whites in the Denver data there is also a positive correlation between increasing message specificity and higher levels of warning belief. The proportion of blacks expressing high warning belief increases from 62.5 percent among those hearing the less specific warning to 87.9 percent of those exposed to the more specific message. Likewise, 66.7 percent of whites who received the vague message versus 81.5 percent who received the specific message reported high warning belief. Mexican-Americans in the Denver sample responded similarly to Mexican-Americans in the Abilene sample. That is, the majority of Mexican-Americans developed a high warning belief whether the message was vague (87.5 percent) or specific (88.3 percent). In fact, this finding constitutes one ethnicity effect that persists across all three events studied here. Greater proportions of Mexican-Americans than blacks or whites develop high levels of warning belief even when given a less specific warning message. We must again temper our interpretations of these data by noting that we obtained little variance on the warning belief dimension for Mexican-Americans; the small cell sizes indicate that very few Mexican-American respondents reported low belief.

Our final question concerning the impact of warning content focuses upon people's levels of perceived personal risk. Presumably, the more specific the warning message, the more effectively recipients can evaluate the personal risk posed by the environmental threat. Citizens who reported, after hearing the first warning, that the environmental threat might result in moderate or severe damage to their person or property were classified as believing personal risk to be high. Those who felt that damages would not result or that such injury would be slight were said to perceive personal risk as low.

Table 2.5 shows perceived personal risk after the first warning by warning content for each ethnic group. Among all three ethnic groups, in all three community disasters, the proportion of citizens who initially perceived personal risk as high *increases* as we move from the vague to the more specific message content. In Abilene, 31 percent of blacks given a vague message perceived risk as high, compared with 51.5 percent of those given a specific message. Among whites, 10.5 percent of those who heard the less specific

Table 2.5
Initial perceived personal risk by message content and ethnicity

Initial personal risk	Abilene				Mount Vernon[1]				Denver			
	Danger		Danger: action		Danger		Danger: action		Danger		Danger: action	
	N	%	N	%	N	%	N	%	N	%	N	%
Blacks												
Low	20	69.0	17	48.5	—	—	—	—	7	70.0	13	39.3
High	9	31.0	18	51.5	—	—	—	—	3	30.0	20	60.7
Whites												
Low	34	89.5	29	67.4	18	78.3	46	70.7	9	75.0	14	51.8
High	4	10.5	14	32.6	5	20.7	19	29.3	3	25.0	13	48.2
Mexican-Americans												
Low	11	91.7	22	84.6	18	90.0	13	81.2	9	56.3	14	41.1
High	1	8.3	4	15.4	2	10.0	3	18.8	7	43.8	20	58.9

[1]There were no blacks in the Mount Vernon sample.

message versus 32.6 percent of those hearing the more specific message developed a perception of personal risk as high. Mexican-Americans who defined risk as high increased from 8.3 to 15.4 percent as we move from the less detailed to the more detailed warning message. Likewise, in the Mount Vernon data the proportion of whites who define personal risk as high increased from 20.7 to 29.3 percent as message content increased from low to high specificity. Mexican-Americans who perceived high risk increased from 10 percent when given a vague message to 18.8 percent when given a specific message. Finally, at the Denver site, the proportion of citizens who perceived risk as high increased among blacks (30 to 60.7 percent), whites (25 to 48.2 percent), and Mexican-Americans (43.8 to 58.9 percent) as message content increased from vague to specific.

In concluding this discussion, note that the data presented in Tables 2.4 and 2.5 show that as warning content becomes more specific, citizens' initial warning belief and perception of personal risk increase. Thus, warning content is an important tool through which emergency managers may influence warning belief and personal risk assessments. This task is important because it is known that ultimately warning belief and risk assessment are correlated with the extent to which citizens comply with the suggested protective measures in disaster warnings. Before examining the extent to which warning recipients' first actions are related to risk and warning belief, we will briefly examine the role of prior experience with disasters relative to those latter variables.

Past disaster experience

Formulations from social science theory support the contention that past experience with disaster events plays an important role in the process through which warning recipients arrive at a situational definition of danger (Perry and Greene, 1982b). In this context, an individual's past experience can be said to provide information that he or she may treat in much the same way as information from a warning message. The distinction is that a warning message affords current information about the pending disaster (and is controlled by emergency managers), while past experience yields general information about environmental dangers derived from the individual's idiosyncratic history of exposure to disasters (cf. Perry, Lindell, and Greene, 1981:68–70; Drabek and Boggs, 1968:445–447; Windham et al., 1977:49). The theoretical arguments are strong and intuitively make it difficult to ignore the concept of past experience in formulating explanations of warning belief and personal risk assessment. The empirical record, however, is at best equivocal in describing the relationship between past experience and warning belief and risk assessment. Perry, Lindell, and Greene (1981:71) reported that past experience with disasters was positively correlated with warning belief in three communities that experienced seasonal floods, but the magnitude of the correlation was low.

The data analyzed here are interesting because past experience was measured in terms of the total history of respondents' experience with all types of disasters. Furthermore, experience was recorded as any experience with a disaster agent; there was no stipulation that respondents had to have sustained personal injury or property damage in connection with the disaster. This more general measurement strategy was employed on the assumptions that citizens generalize disaster experiences across different events and that social psychological processes favoring recall of more recent events usually operate. Table 2.6 shows initial warning belief by past experience with natural or man-made disasters by ethnicity. The data for the Abilene flood show that 54.8 percent of the whites with no prior disaster experience developed a high warning belief, compared with 70.3 percent of those with disaster experience. This positive correlation between experience and level of warning belief replicates the results of other studies of white warning recipients facing a flood threat. Among minority citizens in Abilene, there is only a very low magnitude relationship between experience with disasters and level of warning belief. Statistically, it is appropriate to argue that among blacks and Mexican-Americans prior experience has no impact on level of warning belief. That is, blacks with and without experience are approximately evenly split between low and high levels of warning belief. Mexican-Americans, on the other hand, tend to develop a high level of warning belief whether they have prior disaster experience or not. Thus, the Abilene flood data confirm the results of previous studies that show a positive link between experience and warning belief for whites and reveal that this relationship does not hold for blacks and Mexican-Americans.

The Mount Vernon data, in sharp contrast to Abilene, represent a warning setting wherein the public was unfamiliar with the threat, forewarning was short, and there were no visible cues that an environmental threat existed.

Table 2.6

Initial warning belief by past experience and ethnicity

Initial warning belief	Abilene				Mount Vernon[1]				Denver			
	Experience		No experience		Experience		No experience		Experience		No experience	
	N	%	N	%	N	%	N	%	N	%	N	%
Blacks												
Low	17	56.7	14	46.7	—	—	—	—	0	0.0	7	17.1
High	13	43.3	16	53.3	—	—	—	—	2	100.0	34	82.9
Whites												
Low	11	29.7	19	45.2	9	36.0	13	22.8	1	5.0	8	42.1
High	26	70.3	23	54.8	16	64.0	44	77.2	19	95.0	11	57.9
Mexican-Americans												
Low	0	0.0	2	8.3	3	33.3	8	29.7	1	10.0	5	12.5
High	13	100.0	22	91.7	6	66.7	19	69.3	9	90.0	35	87.5

[1] There were no blacks in the Mount Vernon sample.

Under these conditions there was no relationship between past disaster experience and warning belief for either whites or Mexican-Americans. For the most part, the Mexican-American pattern duplicates the pattern in the Abilene data where most of these warning recipients developed a high warning belief whether or not they reported any prior disaster experience. Among whites, the correlation between experience and higher levels of warning belief changed from being strong and positive in Abilene to weak and negative in Mount Vernon, approximating no relationship. One can argue that the change in the relationship among whites is a function of the changed warning environment in Mount Vernon. Here, citizens had no prior experience with the potential disaster agent and there were no visible cues (such as fires, smoke, etc.) that allowed them to associate the propane gas threat with any previous disaster experience. Thus, it is appropriate to argue that when whites are faced with an unfamiliar threat that they cannot link up with previous threat experience, their levels of initial warning belief are controlled by variables other than prior experience.

The Denver setting provides an opportunity to test the condition described above for whites. In Denver the public was also confronted with an unfamiliar threat, but it was accompanied by visual cues—particularly fire and a vapor plume—that are associated with other types of potential disasters. Based upon the aforementioned reasoning, one would predict that a strong positive relationship should exist between prior disaster experience and higher levels of warning belief among whites. The data in Table 2.6 support this expectation: 57.9 percent of whites with no disaster experience developed a high warning belief versus 95 percent of those with prior experience. Unfortunately, only two blacks reported having any prior disaster experience in the Denver sample, making it impossible to draw any statistically reliable conclusions regarding this variable. This pattern for Mexican-Americans in Denver once again approximates the pattern observed in Abilene and Mount Vernon: 87.5 percent of those without disaster experience and 90 percent of those with experience developed a level of warning belief.

The data in Table 2.6 show four identifiable patterns of the importance of disaster experience across the three ethnic groups. First, when confronted with a familiar threat, whites with prior disaster experience exhibit higher levels of warning belief, while experience has no effect on warning belief among minority group warning recipients. Second, when whites are faced with an unfamiliar threat accompanied by visual cues allowing them to link the otherwise unfamiliar threat to other disaster experiences, prior experience is strongly correlated with high levels of warning belief. Third, when faced with an unfamiliar threat that is not accompanied by visual cues, prior disaster experience is not related to warning belief among either whites or Mexican-Americans. Finally, based on comparisons across three different warning settings, prior experience is uncorrelated with level of warning belief among Mexican-Americans.

It has been argued in the warning literature that citizens' initial assessments of personal risk should be related to their history of experience with disasters (cf. Stallings, 1967). The reasoning here is that people exposed to disasters are more likely to appreciate the kinds and extent of damage that can accrue and should therefore be more likely to initially assess personal risk as high. This contention has not been subjected to much empirical scrutiny, however, and scholars have counter-argued that initial risk assessments are more likely to be made based upon warning message content and that consequently there should be no relationship between prior experience and risk perception.

Table 2.7 shows initial personal risk assessment by prior disaster experience and ethnicity. The Abilene data show consistently no relationship between prior experience and initial risk perception in all three ethnic groups. That is, the proportion of respondents who perceive risk to be high is approximately the same between those with experience and those without among blacks (40 versus 43.3 percent), whites (21.6 versus 22 percent), and Mexican-Americans (15.4 versus 12.5 percent).

In Mount Vernon, the proportion of whites who perceived high risk does increase slightly for those with disaster experience, suggesting that a low positive relationship exists for these variables when the threat is unfamiliar and not accompanied by visual cues. In this setting there is also a slight increase in level of perceived personal risk among Mexican-Americans with prior disaster experience. The Denver data, representing an unfamiliar threat with visible cues, also show slight increases in level of perceived risk among whites and Mexican-Americans with prior disaster experience. Once again, with only two blacks reporting prior disaster experience, no statistically reliable comparisons can be made regarding its impact on risk assessment.

The data in Table 2.7 suggest that across all three ethnic groups prior disaster experience has no impact on initial risk assessment when the threat involved is familiar to warning recipients. The correlation between prior experience and perceived risk is somewhat equivocal when dealing with less famil-

Table 2.7

Initial personal risk assessment by past experience and ethnicity

Initial personal risk	Abilene				Mount Vernon[1]				Denver			
	Experience		No experience		Experience		No experience		Experience		No experience	
	N	%	N	%	N	%	N	%	N	%	N	%
Blacks												
Low	18	60.0	17	56.7	—	—	—	—	0	0.0	20	48.8
High	12	40.0	13	43.3	—	—	—	—	2	100.0	21	51.2
Whites												
Low	29	78.4	32	78.0	15	60.0	44	77.2	11	55.0	12	63.2
High	8	21.6	9	22.0	10	40.0	13	22.8	9	45.0	7	36.8
Mexican-Americans												
Low	11	84.6	21	87.5	7	77.8	24	88.9	4	40.0	19	47.5
High	2	15.4	3	12.5	2	22.2	3	11.1	6	60.0	21	52.5

[1] There were no blacks in the Mount Vernon sample.

iar threats. When the threat is unfamiliar and no visual cues are present, whites with prior experience do assess risk higher than those without experience. Under these same conditions, Mexican-Americans with experience also perceive risk as slightly higher than those lacking experience. Similarly, when visual cues accompany an unfamiliar threat, whites and Mexican-Americans reporting prior experience define personal risk to be slightly higher than their counterparts without experience. Unfortunately, except for the Mount Vernon whites, the magnitude of the relationship between disaster experience and perceived risk is relatively low. Thus, the most appropriate interpretation of these data is to note the differences between the Abilene data and the other two disaster settings and suggest that further studies of experience and risk assessment as response to unfamiliar threats is necessary to clarify the question of how the two variables are interrelated (if at all) in these latter settings.

Determinants of first action

A citizen's first action after hearing an initial disaster warning message has been shown to be a function of the extent to which the first message is believed and the associated initial assessment of risk (cf. Perry, Lindell, and Greene, 1981:47–49). Our concern here is with the action undertaken immediately after first warning receipt. We acknowledge that in almost any disaster citizens will hear multiple warnings, and that after a first warning is received most citizens will engage in some information gathering regarding the threat. However, with this in mind, we can conceive of the warning response process as a series of interdependent steps:

1. Receive first warning message.
2. Arrive at initial assessments of warning belief and personal risk (based on source credibility, warning content, and prior experience).
3. Undertake first action.
4. Gather further information regarding the environmental threat (proactively by contacting sources believed to have information and passively by receiving additional warning messages).
5. Arrive at final assessments of warning belief and personal risk;

make decisions regarding the opportunity for and feasibility of protecting oneself in view of the threat.

6. Make final decision to ignore warning, comply with protective action suggested in warning message, or innovate by adopting an alternate protective action.

The first sections of this chapter focused upon the first two steps of the process described above. In this closing section we will examine the types of first responses undertaken, attending closely to differences among ethnic groups, and examine the relationships among initial warning belief, risk assessment, and first action. Chapter 3 will deal with the last three steps in the warning response process.

The first action or first warning response undertaken by warning recipients is of particular interest because it marks a decision point that can profoundly affect the speed with which the individual completes the remaining steps and ultimately the decision regarding warning compliance. Four classes of first action are of interest here: (1) doing nothing, (2) beginning the warning confirmation process, (3) engaging in some family-oriented activities, and (4) engaging in some protective measures. Each of these options has implications for the likely outcome of the larger warning process. Citizens who choose at this point to do nothing in essence choose to start the process again with each subsequent warning they hear until disaster impact occurs or until some combination of source credibility, message content, and prior experience moves them to take action. Warning recipients who attempt to confirm the message are initiating the fourth step in the warning response process, thereby clarifying the nature of the threat and deciding what further actions might be undertaken to minimize the negative consequences of disaster impact. Citizens who undertake some family-oriented action, such as relaying warnings to relatives or accounting for the safety of household members, may be seen as having tentatively accepted the idea that a potentially harmful environmental threat exists and as taking positive steps relative to their families as a preface to or as part of gathering further information. Finally, citizens who prepare to undertake or begin undertaking some protective action have in effect already made the decisions described in steps three and four and are proceeding to engage in adaptive behaviors vis-à-vis the environmental threat.

Our initial hypothesis focused on only one of the four activities listed above: as warning belief and perception of personal risk increase, so does the probability of engaging in a protective action. Conversely, this also implies that as belief and risk increase, the probability of doing nothing decreases. Keeping these hypothesized relationships in mind, we can now examine the effects of warning belief and perceived risk upon all four categories of initial warning response.

Table 2.8 shows initial warning response by first warning belief and ethnicity. In Abilene, blacks and whites show similar response patterns that are consistent with our hypotheses regarding the correlation of warning belief with engaging in protective actions. The proportion of blacks whose first action was to do nothing declines substantially as we move from low (61.3 percent) to high (21.2 percent) levels of warning belief. Concomitantly, 9.7 percent of the blacks with low warning belief adopted a protective action, compared with 30.3 percent of those expressing a high warning belief. Indeed, the modal warning response category for blacks with low belief was to do nothing, while the largest single category among those with high belief was message confirmation. Relatively few blacks, whether warning belief was low or high, initially engaged in some family-oriented activity. Among Abilene whites, approximately the same proportions of those characterized by low belief (41.9 percent) and high belief (43.1 percent) chose to do nothing in response to their first warning message. The proportion engaging in a protective action, however, increases as we move from low (12.9 percent) to high (23.5 percent) belief. The largest proportion of whites expressing low belief engaged in warning confirmation behaviors, while the modal response category among those with high belief was to do nothing. Without regard to level of warning belief, relatively few whites engaged in family-oriented responses as an initial warning response. Only two of the Mexican-American respondents in Abilene reported a low warning belief and both chose to do nothing in response to the first warning messages. While this inhibits our ability to compare low versus high belief warning responses, it is important to note that most Mexican-Americans (69.4 percent) engaged in a family-oriented initial warning response.

Among whites in Mount Vernon, the proportion who engaged in a protective action increases from 13.6 percent of those with low warning belief to 48.5 percent of those with high warning belief. Although the absolute number of whites doing nothing is very low, the proportion increases slightly as we compare low belief (4.5 percent) with high belief (9.1 percent) respondents. Among whites with low warning belief, there is a tie for modal warning re-

Table 2.8

Initial warning response by first warning belief and ethnicity

Initial warning response	Abilene				Mount Vernon[1]				Denver			
	Low belief		High belief		Low belief		High belief		Low belief		High belief	
	N	%	N	%	N	%	N	%	N	%	N	%
Blacks												
Nothing[2]	19	61.3	7	21.2	—	—	—	—	3	42.9	6	16.7
Confirm	6	19.4	12	36.4	—	—	—	—	0	0.0	2	5.6
Family[3]	3	9.7	4	12.1	—	—	—	—	2	28.6	14	38.9
Protective[4]	3	9.7	10	30.3	—	—	—	—	2	28.6	14	38.9
Whites												
Nothing	13	41.9	22	43.1	1	4.5	6	9.1	3	33.3	5	16.7
Confirm	14	45.2	12	23.5	9	40.9	5	7.0	5	55.6	16	53.3
Family	0	0.0	5	9.8	9	40.9	23	34.8	0	0.0	3	10.0
Protective	4	12.9	12	23.5	3	13.6	32	48.5	1	11.1	6	20.0
Mexican-Americans												
Nothing	2	100.0	4	11.1	0	0.0	0	0.0	1	16.7	5	11.6
Confirm	0	0.0	4	11.1	3	27.3	3	12.5	0	0.0	6	14.0
Family	0	0.0	25	69.4	6	54.5	18	75.0	2	33.3	24	55.8
Protective	0	0.0	3	8.3	2	18.2	3	12.5	3	50.0	8	18.6

[1]There were no blacks in the Mount Vernon sample.
[2]Respondent continued his/her normal routine.
[3]Family-oriented actions include warning others and/or attempting to account for the safety of other household members.
[4]Protective actions are any effort to preserve personal safety or property.

sponse between the categories for warning confirmation and family-oriented behavior. The most frequently used warning response among high belief whites was to undertake some protective action. It is interesting to note that greater relative proportions of whites (at both levels of warning belief) in Mount Vernon chose a family-oriented action than did Abilene whites. None of the Mount Vernon Mexican-Americans chose to do nothing as an initial warning response. Also, among these respondents there is a slight decline in the proportion undertaking a protective action as we compare those expressing a low belief (18.2 percent) with those characterized by high belief (12.5 percent). The largest proportions of Mexican-Americans at both levels of warning belief chose to engage in some family-oriented action. There was apparently also a greater relative concern about warning confirmation by Mexican-Americans in Mount Vernon than in Abilene.

In the Denver sample, blacks who chose to do nothing declined significantly from 42.9 percent of those with low warning belief to 16.7 percent of those with high warning belief. There is also an increase in the proportion of respondents undertaking a protective action as level of warning belief increases from low to high. Most blacks expressing a low warning belief chose to do nothing, while the categories of family-oriented and protective actions are tied for the modal warning response among blacks with warning belief. It should also be observed that greater relative proportions of blacks in Denver chose family-oriented actions than was the case in Abilene. Like blacks, whites in Denver show a decrease in the proportions doing nothing and an increase in the proportion undertaking a protective action as we move from low to high levels of warning belief. Among whites, however, the modal category for initial warning response was warning confirmation for both low and high belief respondents. It should also be noted that fewer whites in Denver engaged in family-oriented actions than was the case in Mount Vernon. Among Mexican-Americans, the proportion of respondents doing nothing as well as the proportion undertaking a protective action decreases when we compare low versus high belief respondents. The modal warning response among Mexican-Americans with a low belief was to undertake a protective action, while the mode for those with high belief was to engage in a family-oriented activity. Finally, relatively fewer Mexican-Americans were concerned with warning confirmation in Denver (and in Abilene) than was the case in Mount Vernon.

We can summarize the relationships between warning belief and initial warning response, highlighting differences among ethnic groups and disaster events, by elaborating seven general conclusions. Caution must again be exercised in generalizing these findings, however, because of the relatively small numbers of respondents from all ethnic groups who developed a low warning belief, particularly in the Mount Vernon and Denver samples. First, across all three disaster settings, Mexican-Americans are more likely to engage in family-oriented actions (at both levels of warning belief) than blacks or whites. Second, across all disaster settings, there is a strong positive relationship between increasing levels of warning belief and the probability of undertaking a protective action among whites and blacks; this relationship does not hold for Mexican-Americans. Third, both whites and Mexican-Americans are less likely to do nothing as an initial warning response when the threat agent is unfamiliar and no visible cues are present than is the case when the threat is familiar or unfamiliar but accompanied by visible cues. Fourth, in settings where the threat is familiar or unfamiliar with visible cues, whites are less likely to engage in family-oriented actions than when confronted by an unfamiliar threat with no visible cues. Fifth, Mexican-Americans undertake relatively more warning confirmation actions when responding to first warning of an unfamiliar threat not accompanied by visual cues than is the case with either a familiar threat or an unfamiliar one with visual cues. As a sixth general conclusion, blacks are more likely to engage in family-oriented activities when the threat is unfamiliar (even when accompanied by visible cues) than when the threat is familiar. Finally, Mexican-Americans engage in warning confirmation behaviors less frequently in response to familiar or unfamiliar threats with cues than when facing unfamiliar threats lacking visible cues.

Table 2.9 shows initial warning response by first risk assessment for each ethnic group. Our primary concern with evaluating these data lies in testing the hypothesis that increases in level of perceived risk are accompanied by increases in the probability of undertaking a protective action. Among blacks and whites in Abilene there is a positive relationship between increases in perceived personal risk and increased likelihood of engaging in a protective action. The proportion of blacks who chose to do nothing decreases from 58.3 percent among those perceiving low risk to 18.5 percent among those who believed risk to be high. At the same time, the proportion undertaking a protective action increased from 8.3 percent to 33.3 percent as we moved from low to high personal risk. Among whites who did nothing in response to the first warning, 42.9 percent estimated risk as low while 38.9 percent saw risk

Table 2.9

Initial warning response by first risk assessment and ethnicity

Initial warning response	Abilene				Mount Vernon[1]				Denver			
	Low risk		High risk		Low risk		High risk		Low risk		High risk	
	N	%	N	%	N	%	N	%	N	%	N	%
Blacks												
Nothing[2]	21	58.3	5	18.5	—	—	—	—	7	35.0	2	8.7
Confirm	9	25.0	9	33.3	—	—	—	—	2	10.0	0	0.0
Family[3]	3	8.3	4	14.9	—	—	—	—	5	25.0	11	47.8
Protective[4]	3	8.3	9	33.3	—	—	—	—	6	30.0	10	43.5
Whites												
Nothing	27	42.9	7	38.9	6	9.4	1	4.2	6	26.1	2	12.4
Confirm	24	38.1	2	11.1	12	18.8	2	8.3	14	60.9	7	43.8
Family	3	4.8	2	11.1	22	34.4	10	41.7	0	0.0	3	18.8
Protective	9	11.5	7	38.9	24	37.5	11	45.8	3	13.0	4	25.0
Mexican-Americans												
Nothing	5	15.6	1	20.0	0	0.0	0	0.0	3	13.6	3	11.1
Confirm	4	12.5	0	0.0	6	20.7	0	0.0	5	22.7	1	3.7
Family	21	65.7	4	80.0	21	72.4	3	75.0	10	45.5	16	59.3
Protective	2	6.3	0	0.0	2	6.9	1	25.0	4	18.2	7	25.9

[1] There were no blacks in the Mount Vernon sample.
[2] Respondent continued his/her normal routine.
[3] Family-oriented actions include warning others and/or attempting to account for the safety of other household members.
[4] Protective actions are any effort to preserve personal safety or property.

as high. The proportion of whites who undertook a protective action increased from 11.5 percent when risk was believed to be low to 38.9 percent of those defining risk to be high. Among Mexican-Americans in Abilene there is no relationship between perceived risk and initial warning response; 68 percent of all Mexican-Americans (without regard to risk assessment) engaged in some family-oriented response.

Among both Mexican-Americans and whites in Mount Vernon there is a positive relationship between perceived risk and proportion of respondents undertaking a protective action. Most Mexican-Americans at both levels of risk assessment, however, still chose to engage in a family-oriented action as an initial warning response.

In Denver, perceived risk is positively correlated with the probability of undertaking a protective action among all three groups. Thirty-five percent of blacks who defined risk as low did nothing versus only 8.7 percent of those who believed personal risk was high. Conversely, 30 percent of blacks perceiving low risk undertook a protective action compared with 43.5 percent of those defining risk as high. Among whites there is a decrease in the proportion doing nothing from 26.1 percent of the low risk respondents to 12.4 percent of the high risk respondents. There is a corresponding increase in the proportion undertaking a protective action as we move from low risk (13 percent) to high risk (25 percent). Mexican-Americans in Denver also showed a decline in the proportion doing nothing (13.6 to 11.1 percent) and an increase in the proportion undertaking a protective action (18.2 to 26.9 percent) as we move from low to high perceived personal risk. Once again, however, large proportions of Mexican-Americans chose family-oriented actions independent of the level of perceived risk.

Four general inferences can be drawn to summarize our analyses of the interrelationships among warning belief, perceived risk, and initial warning response. First, among blacks and whites there is a positive relationship between higher levels of warning belief and increased likelihood of engaging in a protective action. Second, among Mexican-Americans, warning belief is unrelated to the likelihood of undertaking a protective action; these respondents tend to engage in family-oriented activities no matter what the level of warning belief. Third, in general, among blacks, whites, and Mexican-Americans as perceived personal risk increases so does the likelihood of adopting some protective action as an initial warning response. The fourth general conclusion serves as a caveat to the third conclusion: the link between risk and undertaking a protective action is very weak among Mexican-Americans faced with a familiar disaster threat; across all disaster types there is a strong tendency for Mexican-Americans to engage in family-oriented actions independent of the level of perceived risk.

3 Social processes following warning

Chapter 2 described the dissemination of a disaster warning as being both the product of several social processes and as the stimulus that initiates other social processes. Up to this point we have focused on variables related to individuals' first response to a warning message. We have examined the relationships among warning source, message content, and prior experience and the impact of these factors upon citizens' initial levels of warning belief and perceived personal risk. Subsequently we sought to examine the empirical relationship of warning belief and personal risk to people's first response to the first warning message. This chapter is aimed at understanding three important processes stimulated by receipt of first warning: warning confirmation patterns, warning compliance behavior, and post-compliance processes.

Warning confirmation patterns

When a warning message is delivered to a threatened population, research indicates that nearly without exception a process of information gathering is begun (Drabek, 1969:344; Drabek and Stephenson, 1971:195). As we pointed out in chapter 2, warning recipients tend to be skeptical of the first warning they hear. Thus, citizens attempt to confirm the elements of the warning message through some collection of other sources and in this fashion arrive at a personal definition of the situation as threatening or nonthreatening. Confirmation processes, then, are oriented to obtaining future threat-relevant information; the nature and number of sources contacted describe the confirmation pattern.

Table 3.1 shows the first source contacted for confirmation by ethnicity for each research site. An interesting first observation regarding these data is that most citizens—across disaster types and ethnic groups—did attempt to confirm the warning message. Also, among citizens who made no attempt at warning confirmation, two differentials emerge, one related to ethnicity and the other to the warning setting. Fewer whites made no attempt to confirm the warning when a familiar threat was involved (14.8 percent in the Abilene flood) or when visual cues were present (15.4 percent in Denver) than when an unfamiliar threat with no environmental cues was involved (30.2 percent in Mount Vernon). These data are consistent with the results of other studies of majority citizen warning confirmation patterns (cf. Perry and Greene, 1982a:68; Perry and Mushkatel, 1984; Perry, Lindell, and Greene, 1981:31). The reasoning behind this response pattern is (1) citizens faced with familiar threats (e.g., floods) or with unfamiliar threats accompanied by environmental cues (e.g., volcanic eruptions with fires, ash fall, or mudflows; earthquakes with fires; hazardous materials with fires or vapor plumes) believe that they can make a personal evaluation of the danger and tend to vigorously gather information to support such assessments, while (2) citizens confronted with an unfamiliar threat without environmental cues have no grounds upon which to base a personal evaluation and are consequently more likely to accept or reject the warning message based upon the plausibility of its content than to seek further sources for confirmation. This pattern fits whites in our data particularly well and also generally describes the confirmation behavior of Mexican-Americans, in that greater proportions of these latter respondents made no attempt at confirmation in Abilene and Denver than in Mount Vernon.

The above pattern notwithstanding, minority citizens tend to show confirmation differences by community size that we do not find among whites. In particular, both blacks (26.2 percent) and Mexican-Americans (7.9 and 2.8 percent) in rural or small town settings are more likely to *not* seek warning confirmation than is the case in an urban setting (51.2 and 28 percent, respec-

Table 3.1

First source contacted for confirmation by ethnicity

First source contacted	Abilene						Mount Vernon[1]				Denver					
	Blacks		Whites		Mexican-Americans		Whites		Mexican-Americans		Blacks		Whites		Mexican-Americans	
	N	%	N	%	N	%	N	%	N	%	N	%	N	%	N	%
Authority	7	10.8	2	2.5	0	0.0	16	18.7	3	8.4	3	7.0	6	15.4	4	8.0
Mass media	7	10.8	36	44.4	22	57.9	23	26.7	14	38.9	15	34.9	21	53.8	28	56.0
Relatives/ friends	34	52.3	31	38.2	13	34.2	21	24.4	18	50.0	3	7.0	6	15.4	4	8.0
No attempt	17	26.2	12	14.8	3	7.9	26	30.2	1	2.8	22	51.2	6	15.4	14	28.0

[1]There were no blacks in the Mount Vernon sample.

tively). Drabek (1983) has alerted disaster researchers to be aware of potential rural-urban differences in warning response behaviors. Apparently, one way in which such differences are manifest among minority citizens is that smaller proportions of urban dwellers attempt to confirm warning messages than in less urbanized areas. One qualification must be mentioned as an interpretive caution relative to limitations of the data being analyzed here. The generalization is based upon data from two sites: the Abilene flood experience, which involved a familiar threat, and the Denver nitric acid spill, which carried recognizable cues that a disaster was in progress. Consequently, the degree of urbanness of community is confounded with type of disaster threat. Therefore, it is at least possible that some part of what we have described as a rural-urban difference may be attributable to a difference between a familiar threat (flooding) and a less familiar threat accompanied by environmental cues. Also, we are really dealing with two urban areas, though Denver is much larger than Abilene, rather than comparing a truly rural site with an urban site. There were no data on blacks in Mount Vernon (an unfamiliar threat without visible cues in a rural area) upon which comparisons could be made with Abilene and Denver. The Mexican-American data are supportive of the rural-urban difference hypothesis, however, because the proportions of these citizens *not* seeking warning confirmation is considerably lower in both less urban sites (Abilene and Mount Vernon) than in Denver. More data must be examined involving different warning settings in both rural and urban areas across several ethnic groups before any final conclusions can be drawn regarding rural-urban differences.

Among citizens who did attempt to confirm the initial warning message received, relatively few sought to do so by first contacting an authority; across all three warning settings and for each ethnic group, the proportion of citizens first attempting confirmation through authorities does not reach 20 percent. Within the limits of this generalization, however, there are differences among the ethnic groups with regard to the use of authorities for warning confirmation in different warning settings. Blacks are approximately equally likely to use authorities for a first confirmation attempt in familiar (10.8 percent in Abilene) and unfamiliar (7 percent in Denver) threats. Mexican-Americans, on the other hand, infrequently contact authorities first in familiar threats (none in Abilene), but do so more frequently in unfamiliar threats (8.4 and 8 percent in Mount Vernon and Denver, respectively). Like Mexican-Americans, whites were less likely to seek first confirmation from authorities in the more familiar flood threat (2.5 percent) than when dealing with the less familiar threats in Mount Vernon (18.7 percent) and Denver (15.4 percent). Thus, both Mexican-Americans and whites behaved consistently with the hypothesis that "citizens are more likely to attempt warning confirmation with authorities when the threat is unfamiliar or when it can be assumed that authorities possess specialized knowledge or equipment needed for threat assessment" (Perry and Greene, 1982b:421).

In all three events, most citizens who made an attempt to confirm the warning message first contacted either the mass media or a relative or friend. While most "contacts" with the mass media probably involved only switching on the radio or television set, some of these contacts involved more committed searching on the part of citizens. This was evidenced by reports of heavier loads of telephoned information requests by local radio stations in all three sites. There is an interesting pattern in the use of mass media versus relatives or friends as first confirmation sources across the three types of warning settings. In Abilene, representing a less urban setting and a more familiar flood threat, the largest proportions of whites and Mexican-Americans first attempted confirmation through mass media; for each group, the next most frequently used confirmation source was relatives or friends. In the same setting, more than half of the blacks (52.3 percent) first contacted a relative or friend to confirm the warning message (relatively few—10.8 percent—used either mass media or authorities as a first confirmation source). In Denver, an urban area facing an unfamiliar threat, the bulk of blacks (34.9 percent), whites (53.8 percent), and Mexican-Americans (56 percent) first contacted mass media for warning confirmation. Also among all three ethnic groups, relatively small proportions of citizens attempted to confirm the warning by first contacting a relative or friend. Whites in Mount Vernon most frequently attempted confirmation first with mass media (26.7 percent) and secondarily through relatives and friends (24.4 percent). Mexican-Americans in Mount Vernon turned first to relatives or friends for confirmation (50 percent), followed by the mass media (38.9 percent).

These data may be summarized in the form of three general assertions. First, in all three settings, whites trying to confirm a warning message first contacted the mass media. Furthermore, whites used relatives or friends as a first confirmation source more often in familiar threats than in unfamiliar threats, whether visible cues were present or not. These patterns do not change as we move across the rural-urban continuum. Second, the greatest proportions of Mexican-Americans used mass media as a first confirmation source in familiar threats or unfamiliar threats accompanied by visible environmental cues. A rural-urban differential also exists among Mexican-Americans in that those living in less urban areas (whether the threat is familiar or unfamiliar) used relatives or friends as a first confirmation source less frequently than those living in urbanized areas. Finally, blacks are more likely to first contact a relative or friend to confirm a warning in rural settings than in an urban area, where mass media are more likely to be used as a first confirmation source.

One important index of citizens' perceived reliability of the first source contacted for confirmation is the number of additional sources subsequently contacted for further information. In this case, the concept of source reliability is also bound up with the idea of consistency of message content. That is, the more reliable the first source is believed to be and the more consistent subsequent messages are with the first, the lower the number of additional sources contacted.

Table 3.2 shows total number of sources contacted by first confirmation source and ethnicity for each research site. These data indicate that, although comparatively few citizens chose authorities as a first confirmation source, those who did—across all three sites and among blacks, whites, and Mexican-Americans—tended to contact a minimum number of additional sources. This suggests that when a message is confirmed by an authority, citizens feel confident enough about the reliability of the message to abbreviate the information-seeking process. This finding has important implications for the design of warning systems. The less time citizens spend in the confirmation- or information-seeking process the shorter the elapsed time between initial warning receipt and the time individuals make a decision to comply with (or reject) the warning message. Furthermore, the shorter this elapsed time, the faster the process of warning response will be, and consequently the period of time citizens are exposed to danger is reduced.

Since first confirmation of a warning message with authorities is correlated with a reduction in the number of additional sources contacted, thereby reducing total warning response time, measures aimed at enhancing the likelihood of official confirmation can produce shorter warning response times. One strategy for increasing the likelihood that citizens can obtain confirmation of warnings with authorities is to develop warning confirmation centers and incorporate them into community emergency response plans (cf. Perry,

Table 3.2

Number of additional sources contacted by first confirmation source and ethnicity

		First confirmation source					
		Authority		Mass media		Relatives/ friends	
	Number additional sources	N	%	N	%	N	%
Abilene							
Blacks	1–2	1	14.3	2	28.6	10	29.4
	3–4	6	85.7	4	57.1	18	52.9
	5+	0	0.0	1	14.3	6	17.7
Whites	1–2	2	100.0	20	55.6	16	51.6
	3–4	0	0.0	15	41.7	13	41.9
	5+	0	0.0	1	2.8	2	6.5
Mexican-	1–2	0	0.0	9	40.9	3	23.1
Americans	3–4	0	0.0	13	59.1	10	76.9
	5+	0	0.0	0	0.0	0	0.0
Mount Vernon[1]							
Whites	1–2	14	87.5	15	65.2	12	57.1
	3–4	2	12.5	8	34.8	9	42.9
	5+	0	0.0	0	0.0	0	0.0
Mexican-	1–2	1	33.3	10	71.4	8	44.4
Americans	3–4	2	66.7	3	21.4	9	50.0
	5+	0	0.0	1	7.1	1	5.6
Denver							
Blacks	1–2	3	100.0	13	86.7	1	33.3
	3–4	0	0.0	2	13.3	2	66.7
	5+	0	0.0	0	0.0	0	0.0
Whites	1–2	3	50.0	8	38.1	2	33.3
	3–4	3	50.0	13	61.9	3	50.0
	5+	0	0.0	0	0.0	1	16.7
Mexican-	1–2	4	100.0	15	53.6	2	50.0
Americans	3–4	0	0.0	12	42.9	2	50.0
	5+	0	0.0	1	3.6	0	0.0

[1] There were no blacks in the Mount Vernon sample.

1985:185). Such centers could be managed by authorities and accessed by one or more confirmation telephone numbers. By advertising the existence of such telephone numbers in the community, emergency managers can maximize citizens' opportunity to confirm a warning message with authorities. In the event of an acute emergency such confirmation centers disseminate accurate warning information and also serve a rumor control function.

Among citizens who contacted mass media as a first confirmation source, there are differentials in the number of additional sources contacted both by ethnicity and between disaster events. Minority citizens seek more additional warning confirmation sources than whites when the disaster agent is familiar and the setting is a small town. In response to the Abilene flood, 71.4 percent of the blacks and 59.1 percent of the Mexican-Americans who first confirmed the warning via mass media sought three or more additional sources. The majority of Abilene whites (55.6 percent) whose first confirmation source was the mass media followed up by contacting only one or two additional sources, while 41.7 percent contacted three or four new sources and only 2.8 percent sought five or more.

In general, citizens who first confirmed a warning about an unfamiliar threat (with or without visible cues) via mass media were less likely to seek additional confirmation sources than when the warning setting involved a familiar threat. In Mount Vernon, 65.2 percent of whites and 71.4 percent of Mexican-Americans using mass media as a source for initial confirmation sought further information from only one or two additional sources. In Denver, only one or two additional sources were contacted by 86.7 percent of blacks, 38.1 percent of whites, and 53.6 percent of Mexican-Americans. Thus, in a rural setting where the threat is unfamiliar and not accompanied by environmental cues, both whites and Mexican-Americans who first confirmed a warning message with mass media tended to contact relatively fewer additional sources. However, when confronted by an unfamiliar threat accompanied by cues in an urban setting, minority citizens tended to accept first confirmation by mass media and seek fewer additional confirmation sources than their white counterparts. As an interpretive caution, one should note that part of the reason Denver respondents sought fewer additional confirmation sources may be related to a structural issue: Denver warning recipients may have believed they had less time to protect themselves and consequently cut short the process of making contacts.

These findings, even cautiously interpreted, emphasize the importance of the mass media as a warning confirmation source in dealing with disaster threats that are largely unfamiliar to the public at risk. Emergency managers can potentially reduce citizen warning response time in unfamiliar threat situations by insuring that, as part of the warning dissemination process, local mass media also receive detailed warning information. This increases the chance that citizens who do use mass media as first confirmation sources will hear a warning compatible with the official message.

The data in Table 3.2 indicate that in general warning recipients in all three ethnic groups seeking first confirmation from relatives or friends tend to contact more additional sources when the threat is familiar than when it is unfamiliar. In fact, relatives or friends are rarely used as a first confirmation source by any ethnic group when the threat is unfamiliar. When relatives and friends are used as first confirmation sources in familiar threats, minority citizens are more likely to seek larger numbers of additional sources than whites. In Abilene, 70.6 percent of blacks and 76.9 percent of Mexican-Americans sought three or more additional sources, compared with only 48.4 percent of the whites. Similarly, 55.6 percent of the Mexican-Americans in Mount Vernon (an unfamiliar threat in a rural setting) contacted three or more additional sources after first confirming a warning with relatives or friends, versus 42.9 percent of the whites. Thus, the ethnic differential involving a greater likelihood of minorities seeking more additional sources among those who first confirmed a message with relatives or friends holds across familiar and unfamiliar threats in less urbanized settings. The relatively small number of Denver respondents who chose relatives or friends as a first confirmation source precludes any rural-urban comparisons.

Finally, in attempting to understand the warning confirmation process, it is important to consider the range of confirmation sources used by warning recipients. Table 3.3 shows, for people who confirmed the warning with more than one source, the frequency with which other sources were utilized. These data show the frequency of contacts with confirmation sources by respondents who attempted to confirm the warning with multiple sources. Unlike our previous analyses of choice patterns for first confirmation source or total number of additional sources, these data do not reflect citizen perceptions of the credibility or reliability of the sources named. Instead, they show the sources most often sought out by warning recipients engaging in the process of confirmation. Thus, these data tell us which confirmation sources are most often contacted by different ethnic groups in response to three different threats.

Table 3.3
All sources used for warning confirmation by ethnicity

Confirmation sources	Blacks		Whites		Mexican-Americans	
	N	%	N	%	N	%
Abilene						
Authority	16	24.6	10	12.3	0	0.0
Mass media	48	73.8	72	88.8	33	86.8
Relatives/friends	45	69.2	54	66.0	32	84.2
Mount Vernon[1]						
Authority	—	—	83	79.0	8	19.0
Mass media	—	—	32	30.4	29	69.0
Relatives/friends	—	—	43	40.9	41	97.6
Denver						
Authority	25	58.1	33	84.6	11	22.0
Mass media	24	55.8	36	92.3	39	78.0
Relatives/friends	8	18.6	10	25.6	17	34.0

Note: Percentages are calculated using total number of warning recipients as base.
[1]There were no blacks in the Mount Vernon sample.

There are two patterns of confirmation source usage represented in Table 3.3; one differential appears between familiar and unfamiliar disaster events, and the other deals with differences among ethnic groups. In response to the more familiar flood threat in Abilene, the greatest proportions of blacks used the mass media (73.8 percent) and relatives or friends (69.2 percent) as confirmation sources. Similarly, whites and Mexican-Americans also contacted the mass media (88.8 and 86.8 percent, respectively) and relatives or friends (66 and 84.2 percent, respectively) when seeking multiple sources for warning confirmation. Therefore, in response to a familiar threat, people of all three ethnic backgrounds using multiple confirmation sources turn in greatest proportion to the mass media, followed by relatives or friends.

When confronted by an unfamiliar environmental threat, however, blacks and whites shift their emphases for confirmation to authorities and mass media. Thus, in Denver, 58.1 percent of blacks and 84.6 percent of whites turned at some point to authorities for confirmation, and mass media were contacted by

92.3 percent of whites and 55.8 percent of blacks. Mexican-Americans in Denver retained the same pattern as Mexican-Americans in Abilene: the greatest proportion contacted the mass media (78 percent) followed by relatives or friends (34 percent). In response to the propane gas warning in Mount Vernon, the two confirmation sources used most often by Mexican-Americans were also mass media (69 percent) and relatives or friends (97.6 percent), although their relative order of use frequency is reversed. Mount Vernon whites shifted their pattern of confirmation seeking such that authorities were contacted by the majority of respondents (79 percent) followed by relatives or friends (40.9 percent).

These data can be summarized in four propositional statements. In response to familiar threats, blacks, whites, and Mexican-Americans engaged in warning confirmation with multiple sources contact the mass media most frequently, followed by relatives or friends. When dealing with an unfamiliar threat (in either an urban or rural setting), Mexican-Americans also use mass media and relatives or friends most frequently when contacting sources for warning confirmation. In connection with an unfamiliar threat in an urban area, blacks and whites most frequently contact authorities and mass media as warning confirmation sources. Finally, faced with an unfamiliar threat in a rural or small town setting, whites also confirm warnings most often with authorities, but relatives or friends displace the mass media in this setting as the second most frequently contacted confirmation source.

Warning compliance behavior

After a first warning message initiates warning confirmation, warning recipients will finalize their assessments of warning belief and personal risk based on information gained in the confirmation process. Conceptually, these are "considered" assessments revised from those originally made at the time the first warning message was received. Research indicates that it is these two latter assessments that figure most prominently in citizen decisions to comply with the protective measures suggested in the warning message (cf. Perry, Lindell, and Greene, 1981:25–30; Drabek, 1969). Thus, the higher the individual's levels of warning belief and perceived personal risk, the greater the likelihood of compliance with the warning.

In all three communities studied here, the target warning response promoted by authorities was evacuation. That is, as part of the official decision-making process, authorities determined that the most effective means of minimizing potential danger to the population at risk was to relocate them to a place outside of the projected disaster impact area. Based on this decision, our respondents in Abilene, Mount Vernon, and Denver were advised, as part of the warning message, to evacuate their homes. Citizens so warned could engage in any one of three types of behavior as a warning response. First, they could in essence ignore the evacuation request and do nothing; that is, continue their normal routine. Second, they could acknowledge that some danger existed and therefore undertake some protective action, but stop short of following official instructions to evacuate. In the communities studied here, protective actions to property or person included sandbagging, digging diversion ditches, moving personal property to high ground, and caulking doors in Abilene and turning off gas and electricity, sealing doors, windows, and/or fireplaces, and staying indoors in Mount Vernon and Denver. Finally, citizens' third option was to comply with the evacuation warning and relocate outside the danger area.

Table 3.4 shows warning response by level of warning belief for each ethnic group. The Abilene data support the hypothesis that as warning belief increases so does the proportion of citizens who comply with the target warning response. Among blacks, 48.1 percent of those with low warning belief opted to continue a normal routine compared with 2.6 percent of those with high warning belief. Alternatively, 11.1 percent of blacks whose warning belief was low evacuated, versus 86.8 percent of those exhibiting high warning belief. Although the strength of the correlation is weaker than that among blacks, both whites and Mexican-Americans with high warning belief were more likely to evacuate (thereby fully complying with the warning message) than those with low levels of warning belief. Whites with low warning belief were more likely to do nothing in response to warnings (51.4 percent) than those with high warning belief (27.7 percent). Only 20 percent of whites with low belief evacuated, compared with 48.9 percent of those with high warning belief. This pattern also persists among Mexican-Americans, where 30 percent of low belief respondents did nothing versus 22.3 percent of those with high belief, and 25 percent of those with low warning belief evacuated compared to 44.4 percent of those with high warning belief.

Before examining the warning response patterns in Mount Vernon and

Table 3.4

Warning response by warning belief and ethnicity

Warning response	Blacks				Whites				Mexican-Americans			
	Low belief		High belief		Low belief		High belief		Low belief		High belief	
	N	%	N	%	N	%	N	%	N	%	N	%
Abilene												
Nothing	13	48.1	1	2.6	18	51.4	13	27.7	6	30.0	4	22.3
Protective measures	11	40.7	4	10.5	10	28.6	11	23.4	9	45.0	6	33.3
Evacuation	3	11.1	33	86.8	7	20.0	23	48.9	5	25.0	8	44.4
Mount Vernon[1]												
Nothing	—	—	—	—	5	35.7	16	21.6	7	50.0	9	40.9
Protective measures	—	—	—	—	2	14.3	0	0.0	2	14.3	0	0.0
Evacuation	—	—	—	—	7	50.0	58	78.4	5	35.7	13	59.1
Denver												
Nothing	0	0.0	0	0.0	1	14.2	1	3.1	2	18.2	2	5.1
Protective measures	2	40.0	7	18.4	3	42.9	0	0.0	1	9.1	1	2.6
Evacuation	3	60.0	31	81.6	3	42.9	31	96.9	8	72.7	36	92.3

[1] There were no blacks in the Mount Vernon sample.

Denver, three observations should be made regarding warning belief in connection with these two relatively unfamiliar threat agents and the more familiar flood threat in Abilene. First, proportionately fewer citizens in all three
ethnic groups developed a low warning belief in the two unfamiliar threats
than was the case in Abilene. Second, among those citizens with low warning
belief, greater proportions evacuated anyway when the threat was unfamiliar
than when the threat was familiar. Finally, even greater proportions of citizens
with high warning belief evacuated in unfamiliar threats than in the flood
threat. Thus, in general—and across all three ethnic groups—fewer citizens
developed a low warning belief and more complied with the target warning
response at both levels of warning belief when faced with an unfamiliar threat
than when the threat was familiar.

In spite of these differences between familiar and unfamiliar threats, the
correlation between increasing warning belief and warning compliance still
holds in Mount Vernon and Denver across all three ethnic groups. In Mount
Vernon, 35.7 percent of whites and 50 percent of Mexican-Americans showing
low warning belief did nothing in response to warning messages, while only
21.6 percent of high belief whites and 40.9 percent of high belief Mexican-
Americans continued a normal routine. Conversely, 50 percent of whites with
low belief evacuated, compared to 78.4 percent of those with high warning
belief. Likewise, only 35.7 percent of Mexican-Americans expressing low
warning belief complied with the evacuation warning, versus 59.1 percent of
those with high warning belief.

In Denver, the proportion of evacuees increased as we move from low to
high levels of warning belief within each ethnic group. Thus, 60 percent of
low belief blacks evacuated, versus 81.6 percent of those with high warning
belief. Among whites, 42.9 percent of those exhibiting low levels of warning
belief evacuated, compared with 96.9 percent of those with high warning
belief. Finally, 72.7 percent of Mexican-Americans with low belief versus
92.3 percent of those with high warning belief complied with the evacuation
warning. One qualifier should be repeated regarding the observed positive
correlation between increasing levels of warning belief and warning compliance in Denver. Comparatively few blacks, whites, or Mexican-Americans
chose to do nothing (6 or 4.5 percent) or to engage in protective measures (14
or 10.6 percent) as opposed to evacuation (112 or 84.8 percent) *no matter
what the level of warning belief.* Interestingly, this pattern is also present to a
lesser extent among whites and Mexican-Americans in Mount Vernon, where

29.8 percent of the respondents did nothing, 3.2 percent took some protective measures, but 66.9 percent evacuated whether warning belief was low or high.

In interpreting these data, one must remember that two patterns exist relative to warning belief, both of which persist across all three ethnic groups. First, there is a positive relationship between level of warning belief and warning compliance; this is true for each ethnic group and each disaster setting. Second, relatively speaking, the importance of high warning belief is slightly less in unfamiliar threats, where citizens are more likely to comply with the target warning response at both levels of warning belief. This latter conclusion suggests that other variables—such as perceived personal risk—may be more important than warning belief in explaining warning compliance in unfamiliar threats. Support for this interpretation can also be found in the very high levels of compliance at the Three Mile Island nuclear reactor accident, which certainly represented an unfamiliar threat (Perry, 1985).

Table 3.5 shows warning response by perceived risk and ethnicity in each study community. These data are consistent with the hypothesis that there is a positive relationship between increasing levels of personal risk and warning compliance. Indeed, our data show that this assertion holds for blacks, whites, and Mexican-Americans in all three warning settings. In response to the Abilene flood, 46.7 percent of blacks who perceived risk as low did nothing; none of the blacks who believed risk was high chose this response option. In fact, all of the high risk blacks evacuated, while only one (3.3 percent) of those who assessed risk as low evacuated. Among whites, 51.9 percent of those believing risk to be low did nothing, compared to 10.7 percent of those seeing risk to be high. On the other hand, 78.6 percent of high risk whites complied with the evacuation warning, versus 14.8 percent of the low risk whites. A greater proportion of Mexican-Americans who believed risk was low (46.7 percent) did nothing, compared to those who believed risk was high (9.1 percent). High risk Mexican-Americans were slightly more likely to evacuate (36.4 percent) than those perceiving low risk (33.3 percent). Interestingly, the majority of these citizens who believed risk was high (54.5 percent) undertook protective measures short of full warning compliance (i.e., evacuation).

As we found when analyzing warning belief patterns, there are distinct differences in risk perception and warning response behaviors between the more familiar flood threat and the less familiar hazardous materials threats in Mount Vernon and Denver. The important common pattern in the two types of

Table 3.5
Warning response by risk perception and ethnicity

Warning response	Blacks				Whites				Mexican-Americans			
	Low risk		High risk		Low risk		High risk		Low risk		High risk	
	N	%	N	%	N	%	N	%	N	%	N	%
Abilene												
Nothing	14	46.7	0	0.0	28	51.9	3	10.7	7	46.7	2	9.1
Protective measures	15	50.0	0	0.0	18	33.3	3	10.7	3	20.7	12	54.5
Evacuation	1	3.3	35	100.0	8	14.8	22	78.6	5	33.3	8	36.4
Mount Vernon[1]												
Nothing	—	—	—	—	21	35.6	0	0.0	14	63.6	2	14.3
Protective measures	—	—	—	—	2	3.4	0	0.0	2	9.1	0	0.0
Evacuation	—	—	—	—	36	61.0	29	100.0	6	27.3	12	85.7
Denver												
Nothing	0	0.0	0	0.0	2	15.4	0	0.0	4	20.0	0	0.0
Protective measures	9	57.9	0	0.0	3	23.1	0	0.0	2	10.0	0	0.0
Evacuation	8	47.1	26	100.0	8	61.5	26	100.0	14	70.0	30	100.0

[1] There were no blacks in the Mount Vernon sample.

warning settings is that among blacks, whites, and Mexican-Americans the proportion of citizens who evacuate increases as perceived risk increases from low to high. However, the magnitude of the correlation between risk and warning compliance is much greater in the unfamiliar threat settings (Mount Vernon and Denver) than when a more familiar threat was involved. In fact, with the exception of two high risk Mexican-Americans in Mount Vernon (representing 1.6 percent of the total), all respondents in the two unfamiliar threats who perceived risk as high complied with the evacuation warnings. Furthermore, even among citizens who believed personal risk was low, those responding to a warning that involved an unfamiliar threat were more likely to evacuate than those faced with a comparatively familiar flood threat. That is, a total of 55 percent of low risk respondents (seventy-two people) in Mount Vernon and Denver evacuated, compared with 14.1 percent (fourteen people) in Abilene.

Part of the over-representation of evacuees among citizens defining risk as low in Mount Vernon and Denver may be an empirical artifact. It is known that citizens faced with an unfamiliar threat are less able to identify a range of different protective measures than those facing more familiar threats, particularly floods (Perry and Mushkatel, 1984:231). Consequently, citizens facing unfamiliar threats may have relatively fewer protective options to choose among than people confronted with a more familiar environmental danger. Under these conditions one would expect citizens to undertake officially recommended warning responses (in these data, evacuation) in greater proportions as a default means of reducing the likely negative consequences of disaster impact. Our data on citizens who perceive personal risk to be low support this interpretation: 36.4 percent (thirty-six people) of those confronted with a familiar threat ignored the evacuation warning to undertake protective measures they devised, compared with only 13.7 percent (eighteen people) of those facing an unfamiliar threat.

In summarizing our analyses of the relationships of warning belief and perceived risk with warning compliance, the most striking finding is the absence of differentials by ethnic group membership. Thus, among blacks, whites, and Mexican-Americans, as the levels of warning belief and perceived risk increase, so does the probability of warning compliance. Although these fundamental relationships hold across warning settings, three differentials were detected according to the relative familiarity of the public with the threat agent. First, the correlation between warning belief and warning compliance is stronger in unfamiliar threats. Second, citizens who perceive risk as low are more likely to undertake protective measures different from the target warning response in familiar as opposed to unfamiliar threats. Finally, citizens who believe personal risk is high almost always comply with the target warning response when the threat agent is unfamiliar.

It also appears that, at least in some cases, perceived risk is a more important determinant of warning compliance than level of warning belief. This hypothesis can be examined by looking at the probability of evacuation under different combinations of warning belief and personal risk by ethnicity and warning setting (see Table 3.6). The probability of evacuation is the simple ratio of the number of evacuees in a given category to the total number of warning recipients in the category. The probability varies from 0.00 (no one evacuates) to 1.0 (everyone evacuates).

The data in Table 3.6 generally confirm the conclusions drawn in our previous analyses. In cases where the probability of evacuation is not 1.0, for both levels of perceived risk the probability of evacuation increases as we move from low to high levels of warning belief. Likewise, at both levels of warning belief, increases in perceived risk from low to high are accompanied by increases in the probability of evacuation warning compliance. Furthermore, for all combinations of warning belief and perceived risk, the probability of evacuation is higher when the threat is unfamiliar than when the threat is familiar. These data also confirm the hypothesis that perceived risk is of relatively greater importance in the decision to comply with an evacuation warning than level of warning belief. This conclusion is derived from three observations. It is only under conditions of high perceived risk that the probability of evacuation reaches 1.0. In all but three cases, when personal risk is high, all respondents, both low and high warning belief, evacuate.

Post-compliance processes

Up to this point we have followed citizen warning compliance decision making from its beginning at first warning receipt, through the warning comfirmation process, to the final decision to ignore the message, adopt an alternative protective measure, or comply with the officially suggested warning response. When evacuation is the target warning response, the behavior of citizens fol-

Table 3.6

Probability of warning compliance (evacuation) by warning belief, perceived risk, and ethnicity

	Low risk		High risk	
	Low belief	High belief	Low belief	High belief
Abilene				
Blacks	.04	.00	1.00	1.00
	(25)	(5)	(2)	(33)
Whites	.04	.23	.55	.44
	(24)	(30)	(11)	(17)
Mexican-				
Americans	.29	.33	.23	.56
	(7)	(9)	(13)	(9)
Mount Vernon[1]				
Whites	.30	.67	1.00	1.00
	(10)	(49)	(4)	(25)
Mexican-				
Americans	.36	.18	.33	1.00
	(11)	(11)	(3)	(11)
Denver				
Blacks	.50	.46	1.00	1.00
	(4)	(13)	(1)	(25)
Whites	.20	.88	1.00	1.00
	(5)	(8)	(2)	(24)
Mexican-				
Americans	.40	.80	1.00	1.00
	(5)	(15)	(6)	(24)

Note: The number in parentheses gives the base number of cases upon which the probabilities were calculated.
[1] There were no blacks in the Mount Vernon sample.

lowing a decision to comply with the warning is of special interest. In this closing section we will examine three post-compliance responses: the decision to seek shelter, knowledge of shelter availability, and choice of transportation to shelter. All three of these issues have special implications for logistical planning for community evacuation. These analyses are based on questions asked only of respondents who successfully evacuated before disaster impact.

The nature of shelter facilities provided to evacuees by authorities has been the source of some argument among disaster researchers and emergency managers. It has often been reported that evacuees tend not to use public shelters. Stiles (1957) found that about 20 percent of flood-related evacuees reported to public shelters. Similarly, Perry, Lindell, and Greene (1981:140) reported shelter use in four flood disasters ranging from 2.5 to 29 percent of those complying with the evacuation warning. Moore et al. (1963:92) found that 58 percent of the evacuees in a hurricane disaster stayed with friends and relatives rather than visiting public shelters. While some researchers have interpreted these findings to mean that public shelters are of minimal importance, it should be emphasized that the literature on public shelter utilization is by no means entirely consistent. Emergency managers in particular must remember that no matter how great the proportion of evacuees that stay with friends and relatives, there still remain at least some citizens who depend on public shelters in every disaster event.

Table 3.7 shows evacuees' shelter destinations by ethnicity and warning setting. In Abilene, greater proportions of blacks (59.7 percent) and Mexican-Americans (46.2 percent) sought shelter in the homes of relatives than whites (38.5 percent). This is somewhat balanced by the fact that whites more often found refuge in friends' homes than minority citizens. In general, public shelter utilization was low, with blacks (12.9 percent) and whites (15.4 percent) about equal and Mexican-Americans infrequently using such facilities (7.7 percent). Although the absolute number is small, the proportion of Mexican-Americans who took shelter at the first safe place (high ground) was substantially larger than that among blacks and whites.

In Mount Vernon, the majority of both whites and Mexican-Americans sought shelter at a safe place. In this case, safe location was characterized by distance from the site of the derailed tank car carrying propane gas. There is some difficulty, too, in distinguishing safe place from public shelter. Shelter facilities were provided by the local Red Cross and their location was carried in warnings disseminated by authorities and mass media. Both these warning sources, however, also identified two city parks as a designated safe destination for evacuees. This latter information was obtained only after our interviewing process had begun, however. Consequently, many respondents who said they went to a park were classified as having sought out a "safe place." In this case, though, either park may also have been designated a "public shel-

Table 3.7

Shelter destination by ethnicity and warning setting

Shelter	Blacks N	Blacks %	Whites N	Whites %	Mexican-Americans N	Mexican-Americans %
Abilene						
Friends	14	22.6	15	38.5	2	15.4
Relatives	37	59.7	15	38.5	6	46.2
Public shelter	8	12.9	6	15.4	1	7.7
Safe place	3	4.8	3	7.7	4	30.8
Mount Vernon[1]						
Friends	—	—	13	18.3	3	16.7
Relatives	—	—	21	29.6	1	5.6
Public shelter	—	—	6	8.5	1	5.6
Safe place	—	—	31	43.7	13	72.3
Denver						
Friends	4	11.8	4	11.8	4	8.9
Relatives	14	41.2	17	50.0	29	64.4
Public shelter	16	47.0	5	14.7	7	15.6
Safe place	0	0.0	8	23.5	5	11.1

[1]There were no blacks in the Mount Vernon sample.

ter" in the sense that it was identified in warnings given by authorities as a place outside of the likely disaster impact area.

The most conservative interpretation for these data, then, is probably to combine the public shelter and safe place response categories and point out that the greatest proportions of whites and Mexican-Americans used one of these officially suggested options in seeking shelter. It should also be indicated that the sheltering situation in Mount Vernon was rather unique in that the evacuation was known in advance to be a short-term protective measure. That is, authorities knew that replacing the tank car on the tracks would take a short time and that the threat to public safety would exist only during this time. It is also likely that authorities and mass media issuing warnings included the short-term nature of the evacuation. Thus, a properly qualified conclusion to be drawn from the Mount Vernon data is: When the period of evacuation is known in advance to be short, both majority and minority group evacuees tend to utilize officially sanctioned shelter areas in preference to the homes of friends and relatives.

The largest proportions of evacuees in Denver, across all three ethnic groups, found shelter in the homes of friends or relatives. Blacks and whites depended upon friendship networks for shelter in slightly greater proportions than Mexican-Americans, while these latter evacuees depended more often upon relatives than either blacks or whites. Blacks were considerably more likely than whites or Mexican-Americans to use public shelters. Whites more often evacuated to a "safe place" than Mexican-Americans or blacks.

In summary, based on the data in Table 3.7, four inferences can be drawn. In general, without regard to ethnicity, evacuees tend to seek shelter in the homes of friends or relatives. Three qualifications of this conclusion are necessary. When the period of evacuation is known in advance to be short, minority and majority group evacuees will use shelter areas suggested by authorities in preference to staying with friends or relatives. In less urban settings, Mexican-Americans are less likely to use public shelters than blacks or whites. In highly urbanized areas, blacks utilize public shelters more often than whites or Mexican-Americans.

Another issue raised in the research literature is the question of how people who go to a given shelter learn of its availability. It is often argued that the warning message is the appropriate medium to communicate information regarding shelter availability (cf. Mileti, 1974:28). In practice, however, different officials usually have responsibility for warning dissemination and shelter provision. In some cases it is probable that personnel disseminating warnings may have only a general understanding of shelter arrangements.

The data in Table 3.8 reinforce this impression of differing responsibilities, showing that comparatively small proportions of evacuees cited the warning message as the place they learned about a shelter. The only exception is in the Denver data, where 44.1 percent of black evacuees reported hearing about shelter in the warning message. The proportions of whites and Mexican-Americans who learned of shelter from the warning in Denver are similar to the proportions in the other sites. The high figure for Denver blacks is no doubt related to our previous finding of higher levels of public shelter use among these citizens. Indeed, Table 3.7 shows that sixteen blacks reported to public shelters and we know that fifteen blacks heard about shelter availability

Table 3.8

Knowledge of shelter availability by ethnicity and warning setting

	Blacks		Whites		Mexican-Americans	
Knowledge of availability	N	%	N	%	N	%
Abilene						
Destination initiated by contact	10	16.1	10	25.6	1	7.7
Evacuees made contact	42	67.7	21	53.8	8	84.7
Warning message	7	11.3	1	2.6	0	0.0
First safe place	3	4.8	7	17.9	4	30.8
Mount Vernon[1]						
Destination initiated by contact	—	—	9	12.5	1	5.9
Evacuees made contact	—	—	30	41.7	9	52.9
Warning message	—	—	10	13.9	2	11.8
First safe place	—	—	23	31.9	5	29.4
Denver						
Destination initiated by contact	9	26.5	7	20.6	10	22.2
Evacuees made contact	8	23.5	15	44.1	24	53.3
Warning message	15	44.1	4	11.8	7	15.5
First safe place	2	5.9	8	23.5	4	8.9

[1]There were no blacks in the Mount Vernon sample.

through the warning message. Since public shelters are most usually mentioned in official warnings as evacuation destinations, one can infer that the preponderance of Denver blacks was warned by authorities, advised to relocate to a public shelter, and complied with the request.

The majority of evacuees, however, in all three sites and including majority and minority citizens discover the shelter facilities they eventually use by making the first contact themselves. Thus, locating shelter, particularly with friends or relatives, tends to be a process in which the evacuees themselves take the initiative and make first contact, usually through use of the telephone. There are two interesting departures from this pattern that account for relatively smaller but nonetheless noticeable proportions of shelter seekers. First, in Mount Vernon, characterized by a projected short period of absence for evacuees, larger and approximately equal proportions of whites

(31.9 percent) and Mexican-Americans (29.4 percent) located shelter by simply stopping at the first safe location they came upon. This tactic for determining shelter availability was less frequently used by all three ethnic groups in the Abilene and Denver evacuations, where the term of absence was not known in advance and presumed to be longer.

The second variation on finding shelter relates to a process that has been designated "evacuation by invitation." More than a decade ago, Drabek (1969:345) found that warning recipients in a flood disaster were contacted by relatives or friends who invited them to come to their homes. Drabek speculated that "in localized disasters [where forewarning is sufficient] this process could be highly important" (1969:346). The existence of this process of evacuation by invitation has since been reported in flood threats (Perry, Lindell, and Greene, 1981:141) and in connection with volcanic eruptions (Perry and Greene, 1982b:94). The data in Table 3.8 indicate that invitations to evacuate were issued in all three warning settings to members of all three ethnic groups; in Denver such invitations accounted for 26.5 percent of blacks, 20.6 percent of whites, and 22.2 percent of Mexican-Americans. These findings support Drabek's initial finding and introduce the qualification that the effect exists in urban areas even when the period of forewarning is relatively short.

From the perspective of the emergency manager, the preceding discussions of shelter utilization and knowledge of shelter availability have yielded at least two important observations. First, when given an opportunity to choose, people tend to prefer to evacuate to the homes of friends and relatives rather than to public shelters. Second, the warning message is not necessarily where most people hear about the availability of shelter.

These points argue strongly for the development and use of reasonable flexible shelter plans for evacuees, particularly in communities that are part of or close to large metropolitan areas. It may, for example, be both cost effective and efficient to use temporary "shelter checkpoints" where evacuees could report to obtain additional information about the evacuation effort and then either depart to stay with friends or relatives or be assigned to stay in a public facility (Fritz and Mathewson, 1957). Such a plan would minimize the need for elaborate and extensive shelter facilities, permit evacuees their choice of arrangements, and allow for a more careful accounting of those who do evacuate. Shelter checkpoints would also offer an ideal place for recording evacuees' names and their shelter destinations to facilitate the operation of family message centers, where concerned relatives or friends from outside the disaster area could quickly find data on evacuees. This kind of shelter accounting also allows officials to keep careful track of who evacuated, how many evacuated, and where they went. Note that a shelter checkpoint should be a specified destination in a safe area that could probably also be a public shelter. It should therefore not be confused with "roadside checkpoints," which tend to snarl traffic and generally impede the flow of evacuees from the threatened area.

Another alternative to traditional public sheltering might involve distributing information to residents of frequently threatened areas that would describe in advance safe areas as well as routes to these areas for potential evacuees. Residents then could be instructed to make contact with friends or relatives in the safe area and arrange in advance for shelter in that home in the event of disaster impact. In this way as soon as an evacuation warning was issued, evacuees could depart, arrive at their host's home, and simply call an official checkpoint to indicate that they were safely out of the area. Residents of threatened areas who could not locate family or friends in designated safe areas could either stay at a public shelter or perhaps through local civic organizations arrange to meet with residents of the safe area and discuss the possibility of potential shelter. It is acknowledged that this strategy is more useful in the case of riverine floods or civil defense evacuations; its utility with hurricanes or other disasters where scope of impact is great and direction and place of impact vary widely is probably limited.

Finally, our data indicate that people did not often report that the warning message was the source of information about the availability of the place to which they evacuated. In general, the modal pattern seems to involve a citizen's receiving a warning message and then making phone calls to (1) confirm the message and (2) find a place to go. One way of incorporating this behavior pattern into the emergency evacuation management process would involve developing warning and evacuation information centers. Citizens could be instructed to contact these centers for warning confirmation and/or more detailed instructions regarding shelter. Such a system could be based on telephone or radio contact and could also serve a rumor-control function. Furthermore, since confirming instructions could be somewhat standardized, such centers would minimize problems that traditionally arise when citizens receive contradictory or conflicting warning messages and instructions while seeking confirmation or specific evacuation information.

An alternate strategy that combines both warning and confirmation processes could involve using initially a telephone call warning system whereby preselected key residents in different geographic zones would be warned by telephone by an emergency response official and the residents in turn would assume the responsibility of warning other citizens in their area. This approach is feasible only in small communities that experience localized disaster impacts. All residents could have available the telephone number of a center so that after the initial warning they could call for detailed information.

It should be noted here that a difficulty frequently cited with strategies such as the preceding that involve the use of telephones is the problem of snarled communications. Fritz and Mathewson (1957) discussed telephone convergence on a disaster area as a significant problem. In fact, many disaster-planning handbooks emphasize that community officials should never advise citizens to use their telephones (Leonard, 1973; Healy, 1969). It is also well known that such rules are systematically violated; people call into an area to check on relatives, and residents call out to issue reassurance to friends and relatives and to seek official confirmation of warnings. Since the late fifties and early sixties, when many of the studies that suggested avoiding telephones were conducted, technical advances have been made in the telephone industry. Quarantelli and Taylor (1977) argue that technical innovation coupled with the fact that people disobey the request not to use telephones anyway is sufficient to suggest that evacuation incentives (such as those described previously) that utilize some telephone contacts are not at all infeasible.

An additional option that does not depend exclusively on telephones involves broadcasting, on a continual basis, relevant information about the hazard and about evacuation procedures and destinations. The broadcast medium could be either radio or television (assuming the local availability of both), but it is important that the station be officially designated as the community's source for disaster information and that the public be aware of this designation. Establishing credibility of the warning source can be nearly as important as the information disseminated. It should be mentioned that in recent years the Emergency Broadcast System (EBS) "has been expanded so that it can also be used during day-to-day emergencies at the state and local levels" (Defense Civil Preparedness Agency, 1978). Thus it may be possible to administratively simplify this warning and evacuation information strategy by working within EBS.

The coordination and use of evacuation plans also involve logistics issues resulting from the movement of people. When a warning message calls for evacuation, local authorities are requesting that citizens undertake a specific adaptive action where timing is often critically important and effective adaptation of the community as a whole depends upon a coordinated exodus. Under such circumstances, the question of how citizens exit the area to be evacuated arises.

Table 3.9 shows mode of transportation by ethnicity for each research site. In general, among blacks, whites, and Mexican-Americans across all three sites, the majority of evacuees departed the danger area in a family-owned vehicle. In the less urbanized sites (Abilene and Mount Vernon), a slight ethnic differential exists: minority citizens were less likely to evacuate in a family car and more likely to use some form of officially provided transportation. In Denver, almost all whites (97.1 percent) and Mexican-

Table 3.9
Mode of transportation by ethnicity and warning setting

Transportation	Blacks		Whites		Mexican-Americans	
	N	%	N	%	N	%
Abilene						
Family vehicle	47	74.6	40	90.9	7	46.7
Friend's vehicle	7	11.1	0	0.0	0	0.0
Official's vehicle[1]	7	11.1	1	2.3	5	33.3
Walked	2	3.2	3	6.8	3	20.0
Mount Vernon[2]						
Family vehicle	—	—	67	89.3	12	66.7
Friend's vehicle	—	—	6	8.0	1	5.6
Official's vehicle	—	—	1	1.3	1	5.6
Walked	—	—	1	1.3	4	22.2
Denver						
Family vehicle	16	47.1	33	97.1	43	95.6
Friend's vehicle	5	14.7	1	2.9	0	0.0
Official's vehicle	12	35.3	0	0.0	1	2.2
Walked	1	2.9	0	0.0	1	2.2

[1]An official's vehicle refers to transportation via any mode supervised by authorities.
[2]There were no blacks in the Mount Vernon sample.

Americans (95.6 percent) evacuated in a family car. On the other hand, only about half of the blacks used a family vehicle and 35.3 percent used some official transportation.

These data highlight two important issues. First, most evacuees leave in a family car and consequently the number of existing vehicles in almost any evacuation is large enough to merit careful attention from emergency managers. Second, official transportation is needed and used by evacuees, particularly ethnic minorities. Thus, there are a large number of cars on the road at about the same time that must somehow be channeled out of the area to be evacuated. Numerous studies have indicated that evacuations can be more effectively accomplished if the people involved have a plan—a route of egress and a safe destination. Having advance plans also helps to minimize traffic-coordination difficulties and lowers the number of families either not evacuating at all or evacuating to an even more dangerous location (Hamilton, Taylor, and Rice, 1955; Drabek, 1969; Sillar, 1975; Lachman, Tatsuoka, and Bonk, 1961).

Since available research findings do suggest that people who are not given an evacuation plan are slow to take action, it can be recommended that emergency managers could establish safe destinations and plausible routes that could be distributed to citizens in advance as part of general community emergency preparation. Such a plan need not be particularly elaborate and could be made available to the public in the form of a labeled map. The Federal Emergency Management Agency is planning to communicate such maps via newspapers in connection with its Crisis Relocation Planning (Defense Civil Preparedness Agency, 1978), but the same kind of maps could be printed on index cards for public distribution. Particularly in the case of riverine floods, where floodplains and patterns might be known, such a plan would put important information on how to leave into the hands of the population to be evacuated. More important, however, specific instructions on routes and destinations could help to minimize traffic coordination problems by taking into account road capacities and other traffic-flow variables.

An alternative strategy that would minimize the material citizens must maintain until an evacuation is necessary involves making detailed route and destination information available at the time of warning. This could be accomplished using either of two strategies. As we suggested in the preceding section, citizens could be given a telephone number, either in advance or as part of the warning message, to call for detailed evacuation instructions. Upon calling the number, citizens could report their location and be given appropriate evacuation instructions for their location. Note that especially when warnings are delivered via mass media, this telephone-in strategy serves numerous functions simultaneously: (1) the call confirms the warning message, (2) the call helps the individual to determine whether he or she is in an area to be evacuated (that is, the individual can assess personal risk), and (3) the call helps the individual obtain information on safe destinations and exit routes. This type of plan has the disadvantage that it would probably involve special—and expensive—modifications to telephone equipment to handle the volume of calls.

In some communities, evacuation warnings are usually issued on a face-to-face basis; designated emergency officials—often fire fighters or police officers—issue the warning to each household in the threatened area. In such cases, officials could explain the warning and hand residents a single sheet of paper with a map and other appropriate instructions. In itself, this procedure would speed and simplify the evacuation process since details (to which the citizen could refer later) would be supplied in written form and only a minimum verbal explanation would be needed. The amount of lead time and the number of personnel available for delivering warnings serve as limiting factors when this strategy is used.

Another emergency management tactic involves the transportation of evacuees to shelter in official vehicles. Most evacuation plans assume that the majority of evacuees will supply their own transportation, but limited official transportation is routinely made available to allow for citizens who have no vehicle and cannot otherwise arrange transportation. Authorities can systematize and publicize the available official transportation. This action can be accomplished by specifying departure times and locations for official transportation either as part of a community emergency plan or within the warning message itself. While it is known that most families tend to transport themselves, those unable to do so would be given an opportunity to evacuate in an orderly fashion, even on short notice (Drabek and Stephenson, 1971:200). Furthermore, if evacuees can be transported in designated official vehicles, the number of cars on the road is reduced, increasing the ease with which an area can be evacuated.

4 Citizen involvement in threat management

We have devoted considerable attention to the ways people behave when they receive a warning message. Earlier chapters have traced this process from responses to the initial warning, through the compliance decision-making process, to shelter-seeking behavior. We pointed out in chapter 1, however, that the behavior of both authorities and citizens during the response phase is shaped by what goes on before a threat is imminent, that is, during the preparedness phase.

In this chapter we will specifically examine differentials among blacks, whites, and Mexican-Americans relative to their involvement in community emergency response and planning. Three general issues regarding citizen involvement in community hazard management are addressed. First, we will consider citizen perceptions of the nature of and need for engaging in adaptive responses to official warnings. This involves reviewing reasons given for complying and not complying with evacuation warnings as well as describing the kinds of protective actions undertaken and reasons given for so doing. Second, we will examine the channels through which minority and majority citizens obtain information regarding community hazards. These analyses include descriptions of information sources believed to be valuable as well as those channels that have been used in the past. Finally, citizen perceptions of various outreach and participation techniques are discussed. This includes a review of citizen reports of desired participation modes and the most effective means for emergency managers to disseminate information as well as a discussion of the extent of language problems encountered.

Engaging in adaptive behaviors

In chapters 2 and 3 we analytically examined citizen adoption of different adaptive behaviors in terms of theoretical models of evacuation warning response. These analyses explained adaptive behavior in the language of social scientists, devoting special attention to concepts learned from the empirical literature of disaster research, including notions of perceived personal risk and warning belief. The goal was to predict citizen warning response using the conceptual and analytic tools available to social science. The outcomes of these analyses were encouraging because the variables included in our model collectively accounted for a large proportion of the variance in citizen warning response.

In the first part of this section we will turn to a review of citizen answers to general, unstructured inquiries about why they did or did not comply with the evacuation warning message. Thus, we are not here interested in variables reputed to be important by social scientists, but with reasons given by citizens for engaging in particular behaviors. In this way we have an opportunity to consider citizens' perceptions of their motivations for obeying or ignoring the instructions of emergency management authorities. From these data we can obtain insights into the way citizens reason when confronted with warnings of environmental threats.

Table 4.1 shows the most important reason for evacuating given by citizens who complied with the evacuation warnings in each site. These data include only those citizens who both reported hearing some warning and who subsequently evacuated. Among whites in Mount Vernon, the most frequently chosen reason for evacuating was that officials warned them to do so (50.8 percent). This reason was followed by receipt of warnings from friends and relatives (18.5 percent), watching neighbors evacuate (12.3 percent), and seeing the derailed propane tank car (10.7 percent). Mass media warnings (radio in this case) were least frequently mentioned as the most important

Table 4.1
Most important reason for evacuating by ethnicity

Reason	Mount Vernon Whites		Mount Vernon Mexican-Americans		Abilene Blacks		Abilene Whites		Abilene Mexican-Americans		Denver Blacks		Denver Whites		Denver Mexican-Americans	
	N	%	N	%	N	%	N	%	N	%	N	%	N	%	N	%
Neighbors and friends left	8	12.3	3	18.8	9	14.8	9	23.7	0	0.0	6	17.6	10	29.4	10	22.2
Media warnings	5	7.7	0	0.0	0	0.0	4	10.5	0	0.0	3	8.8	0	0.0	8	17.7
Officials' warnings	33	50.8	5	31.2	24	39.3	5	13.2	2	15.4	16	47.0	14	41.1	9	20.0
Warnings from friends and relatives	12	18.5	3	18.8	13	21.3	7	18.4	2	15.4	8	23.5	5	14.7	17	37.7
Past experience	0	0.0	0	0.0	15	24.6	13	34.2	9	69.2	0	0.0	1	2.9	1	2.4
Saw impact site[1]	7	10.7	5	31.2	0	0.0	0	0.0	0	0.0	1	2.9	4	11.8	0	0.0

Note: Only those who received a warning and evacuated were asked the most important reason they did so.

[1] In Mount Vernon this referred to seeing the derailed tank car. In Abilene it referred to seeing high water. In Denver reference is made to seeing the damaged tank car or fire, smoke, or the associated vapor plume.

reason for evacuating (by 7.7 percent of the respondents) and none of the citizens cited past experience with disasters as a reason for leaving.

Mount Vernon Mexican-Americans cited with equal frequency officials' warnings and seeing the impact site as the most important factors in evacuating warning compliance (31.2 percent). These citizens also mentioned warnings from friends and relatives and the departure of neighbors less often but with equal frequency as important reasons for evacuating (18.8 percent). None of the Mexican-American respondents mentioned media warnings or past disaster experience as reasons for evacuating. The majority of whites cited warning information from officials as the most important reason for deciding to evacuate; warnings from friends and relatives trailed at some distance as the second most frequently given reason. Among Mexican-Americans, officials' warnings and seeing the impact site were most frequently given as the primary reason for evacuation compliance. Consequently, when faced with an unfamiliar threat, citizens will seek out sources perceived to have relevant expertise upon which to base a warning compliance decision, and in most cases such expertise will be attributed to emergency authorities. These citizen perception data suggest that for minority respondents, witnessing the impact site (that is, assembling personal evidence of danger) is equally important or at least perceptually equivalent to officials' warnings.

The Abilene flood response data reveal different patterns of behavior probably attributable to the different characteristics of the threat agent. Among blacks, the largest proportion of respondents identified officials' warnings as the most important reason for evacuating (39.3 percent). Although chosen by substantially smaller proportions of citizens, past experience with floods (24.6 percent) and warnings from friends and relatives (21.3 percent) were also perceived as significant factors in evacuation decision making. The departure of neighbors was cited by 14.8 percent as the most important reason for evacuation compliance. None of the black respondents mentioned either media warnings or sight of high water as reasons for leaving their homes. Most Mexican-Americans cited past flood experience most often as the primary reason for evacuating (69.2 percent). This was followed by officials' warnings and warnings from friends and relatives (each chosen by 15.4 percent) as bases for evacuation compliance. Media warnings, the departure of neighbors, and sighting high water were not chosen by any of the Mexican-American respondents as important reasons for evacuating.

Like Mexican-Americans, the greatest proportion of whites in Abilene reported that past experience with floods formed the single most important reason for evacuating (34.2 percent). For whites, however, the warning compliance of neighbors also weighed heavily as a factor in evacuating (chosen by 23.7 percent of the respondents). Following these two reasons, whites endorsed warnings from friends and relatives (18.4 percent), officials' warnings (13.2 percent), and media warnings (10.5 percent) as important reasons for complying with the evacuation warning message.

With respect to flood evacuation warning compliance, the two groups of minority citizens identified the same three reasons for evacuating—officials' warnings, past experience, and warnings from friends and relatives—although the relative order of importance differs. It remains, however, that taken together past experience and officials' warnings account for nearly 65 percent of the blacks and nearly 85 percent of the Mexican-Americans. Past experience with flooding was also an important motivation for whites to comply with the evacuation warning, but these citizens endorsed a wider range of reasons for evacuating than the two minority groups. Among whites, the evacuation of neighbors and mass media warnings assumed positions of greater relative importance than among blacks or Mexican-Americans. Even acknowledging these differences, however, the same combination of factors that accounted for most minority citizens—past experience, officials' warnings, and warnings from friends and neighbors—also accounts for more than 65 percent of the whites. These findings support the contention that, across the three ethnic groups, when dealing with a familiar (or recurrent) threat, past experience is an important factor in evacuation compliance. One may add to this that warning information supplied by officials and friends and relatives also has a positive impact on compliance.

The Denver data are similar to Mount Vernon in that the threat involved was unfamiliar to the public but distinguished by the urban environment (compared to the rural or small town setting of Mount Vernon). Interestingly, although the relative ordering differs, the same three reasons given for evacuating predominate the choices expressed by blacks, whites, and Mexican-Americans: warnings from officials, warnings from relatives and friends, and the departure of neighbors and friends. As we found in Mount Vernon, officials' warnings were important in the evacuation decision-making process in Denver. In fact, warnings from officials were cited as the most important reason for evacuating by the largest proportions of blacks (47 percent) and whites (41.1 percent) and the third largest proportion of Mexican-Americans (20 percent).

These data support our previous argument that in unfamiliar threat settings citizens from all ethnic backgrounds tend to look to authorities as a leading source of threat-relevant information. In contrast to the more familiar flood threat in Abilene, past experience was not often cited as a reason for warning compliance by blacks, whites, or Mexican-Americans in Denver. But unlike their more rural counterparts in Mount Vernon, Denver urban dwellers emphasized the role of social networks in their decisions to evacuate. Among blacks, warnings from friends and relatives was the second most frequently mentioned compliance reason (23.5 percent), followed by the departure of neighbors and friends (17.6 percent). Whites cited neighbors and friends evacuating as the most important reason for leaving with the second greatest frequency (29.4 percent) and warnings from friends and relatives next most often (14.7 percent). The largest proportion of Mexican-Americans (37.7 percent) gave warnings from friends and relatives as the most important reason for evacuating, followed by the departure of neighbors and friends (22.2 percent). Thus, urban-based blacks, whites, and Mexican-Americans tended to emphasize the importance of social networks in warning compliance decisions and in so doing distinguished themselves from their less urban counterparts who faced either familiar or unfamiliar threats.

Finally, an important observation may be made regarding officials' warnings and citizen evacuation compliance. In all three threat settings, none of the respondents (regardless of ethnicity) completely or even largely disregarded officials' warnings in making evacuation compliance decisions. This finding emphasizes the idea that information from emergency management officials is a significant motivating factor for citizens coping with both familiar and unfamiliar types of environmental threat. Furthermore, while emergency managers can have no influence over a citizen's past disaster experience and little influence over such things as warnings from friends and relatives, they exercise considerable control over officially disseminated warning information. Aside from underscoring the significance of careful warning message construction and dissemination, these data demonstrate that officials' warnings also contribute to warning compliance indirectly to the extent that they motivate the neighbors of potential evacuees to leave the threatened area. The communication of warning information by authorities is therefore an important emergency management tool that should be cultivated.

Having reviewed reasons given as important in decisions to evacuate, we can now change perspectives and examine citizen beliefs about important reasons for *refusing* to comply with an evacuation warning. In all three sites, comparatively few warning recipients chose not to evacuate: twenty-four in Mount Vernon, eighty-one in Abilene, and nineteen in Denver. Interestingly, in all three communities the same reason was given by most respondents for not evacuating: the belief that they were in no serious danger. This reason accounts for 66.7 percent of both Mount Vernon and Abilene respondents and 78.9 percent of Denver respondents. When these data are subdivided into ethnic groups, this finding still holds. For blacks, whites, and Mexican-Americans in each community, the majority of respondents who did not evacuate claimed that they chose not to because they were in "no serious danger." Very small proportions of respondents justified not evacuating because they felt that evacuating would not protect them, because they wanted to stay and protect their property, and because their family was not together when the warning was received. The frequencies with which these reasons were offered are so small, however, as to preclude meaningful discussion of patterns between ethnic groups.

Although they must be interpreted cautiously, the data on evacuation noncompliance support the idea that, as a condition for evacuating, citizens must believe that the level of personal risk as a function of the environmental threat is such that a serious danger is posed. It is consequently noteworthy that the *modal* category of most important reasons for noncompliance is "no serious danger" *for all ethnic groups in all three threats*. From an applied emergency management perspective, there are two messages here. Once again we see that the structure of the warning message can be of critical importance to citizen response. In particular, the message needs to accurately communicate information that allows recipients to estimate personal risk or make inferences about likely danger. Specifically, in as brief a form as possible, the warning message should identify the likely place and time of projected disaster impact and carry some statement about the likely severity of the impact.

The second point to be made is that citizens will evaluate any protective measure suggested by authorities in a warning message. When a suggestion to evacuate is given, citizens appear to consider the question: Is my physical safety sufficiently threatened that I should abandon my property? In cases where citizens believe that there is little or no risk to physical safety *and* that they might be able to save or protect some of their belongings or property, they tend to ignore evacuation warnings. When authorities have carefully measured the risks according to the best available information and decided that evacuation is called for, an effort should be made to include some of the reasoning in the warning message. If immediate evacuation is necessary due to the potential life-threatening nature of the pending disaster, then that information should be available to citizens.

We have seen that many citizens will undertake adaptive behaviors at the request of authorities with little apparent hesitation. This kind of response appears to occur in situations where the emergency managers have established themselves in the eyes of the community as visible, credible authorities with special knowledge of emergencies and with access to special technical information. In cases where an emergency services department is in the process of establishing itself, or in the case of an established department trying to enhance an already positive citizen rapport, an explanation of why the suggested protective measure was chosen will tend to build additional respect among citizens. When evacuation is the target response, an explanation of the nature and extent of personal safety dangers is likely to increase the level of citizen compliance.

We have considered why citizens do and do not comply with the target warning response. It is widely known that either as an adjunct or alternative to evacuating citizens who receive disaster warnings engage in protective actions. It is therefore instructive to consider the types, frequency, and underlying reasons given by citizens for the protective actions they undertake. Table 4.2 shows protective actions undertaken by ethnicity for each study site. The Mount Vernon data show that a greater proportion of whites engaged in protective actions than Mexican-Americans. Among whites, 55.4 percent claimed to have engaged in no such actions, while 12.5 percent said they did something but couldn't recall what. No protective actions were reported by 78 percent of the Mexican-Americans and 9.8 percent could not remember what protective action they undertook. At least in Mount Vernon, the high proportions of citizens who reported no protective actions are related to the low levels of familiarity with the threat. These citizens expressed concern with the emergency, but many voiced the opinion that, aside from evacuating, it was not clear what measures could be taken to protect either themselves or their property from the propane gas threat. Among whites, 34.6 percent did report that they took some measure to protect their homes. The measure most frequently mentioned was to close windows and doors, but respondents also reported closing off chimneys and pushing towels around doors and windows to achieve a better sealing effect. Protective measures to the dwelling were reported by 14.6 percent of the Mexican-Americans; almost all of these were to close windows and doors.

Table 4.2

Protective actions undertaken by ethnicity

Protective action	Mount Vernon[1] Whites		Mount Vernon[1] Mexican-Americans		Abilene[2] Blacks		Abilene[2] Whites		Abilene[2] Mexican-Americans		Denver[3] Blacks		Denver[3] Whites		Denver[3] Mexican-Americans	
	N	%	N	%	N	%	N	%	N	%	N	%	N	%	N	%
None	58	55.4	32	78.0	52	77.6	43	53.1	15	39.5	10	23.3	7	17.9	15	30.0
Can't remember	13	12.5	4	9.8	0	0.0	3	3.7	5	13.2	0	0.0	0	0.0	0	0.0
Brought things inside	0	0.0	0	0.0	10	14.9	26	32.1	14	36.8	1	2.3	9	23.1	3	6.0
Protect dwellings[4]	36	34.6	6	14.6	2	3.0	18	22.2	15	39.5	30	69.8	29	74.4	34	68.0
Disconnect utilities	9	8.7	0	0.0	11	16.4	25	30.9	3	7.9	6	14.0	15	38.5	14	28.0

Note: All respondents were asked what protective actions they took.

[1] Percentages are given for all citizens in each category: whites calculated on base n = 104; Mexican-Americans on base n = 41.

[2] Percentages are given for all citizens in each category: blacks calculated on base n = 67; whites on base n = 81; Mexican-Americans on base n = 38.

[3] Percentages are calculated for blacks on base 43; whites on base 39; Mexican-Americans on base 50.

[4] Abilene protective measures included sandbag, tie down trailer, dig diversion ditch, caulk doors, empty basement, raise furniture and equipment on blocks. Mount Vernon and Denver protective measures included seal chimney, close windows, seal doors.

Among members of both ethnic groups, the expressed purpose of these measures was to keep gas out of the house. Some of the Mexican-American respondents reported that their objective was to avoid having the house smell like propane if anything went wrong. This reason was also given by some white respondents, while others felt that keeping gas out of the house would minimize the risk that it could be ignited by a water heater or household appliance and result in a fire. Among the 8.7 percent of whites who reported disconnecting utilities, the most frequently expressed concern was with fire.

In Abilene, the flooding phenomenon was considerably more familiar to residents and a wider range of protective actions was reported. The lowest levels of undertaking no protective actions are observed among whites (53.1 percent) and Mexican-Americans (39.5 percent). A greater proportion of blacks (77.6 percent) reported undertaking no protective actions, but this is probably inflated due to the high proportions of blacks who reported that they evacuated immediately after being warned and the relatively higher proportion of renters among these citizens, who felt little need to engage in property protection.

In connection with patterns of protective actions in the Abilene flood, there are three findings of interest in Table 4.2. First, whites and Mexican-Americans attended to bringing property stored outside into the home as a means of preserving it in far greater proportions than blacks. Second, 39.5 percent of the Mexican-Americans took measures to protect their house, compared with 22.2 percent of the whites and 3 percent of the blacks. Among all three ethnic groups the most frequently mentioned protective measures were to raise furniture and equipment on blocks above likely water levels, caulk doors, and tie down trailers or secure sheds in the yard. Finally, 30.9 percent of the whites reported that they disconnected utilities (gas and/or electricity) as a protective measure, versus 16.4 percent of blacks and 7.9 percent of Mexican-Americans.

In response to the nitric acid spill in Denver, the majority of blacks (69.8 percent), whites (74.4 percent), and Mexican-Americans (68 percent) chose to undertake measures to protect their houses or apartments. Since the majority of our respondents did not own the dwelling in which they lived, it may be reasonably assumed that the motivation for these protective efforts was more to preserve the contents rather than the building itself. More minority citizens—22.3 percent of blacks and 30 percent of Mexican-Americans—reported undertaking no protective measures than whites (17.9 percent). Also, greater proportions of whites remembered to disconnect utilities and bring belongings indoors (38.5 and 23.1 percent, respectively) than blacks (14 and 2.3 percent) or Mexican-Americans (28 and 6 percent).

Table 4.3 shows the total number of protective actions undertaken by ethnicity. These data are probably a conservative (low) estimate of the extent to which protective actions were engaged in because we have combined those who claimed to have done something but couldn't remember what with those who reported doing nothing. We do not impugn the reliability of citizens who couldn't remember, but felt it appropriate to not count them among citizens to whom the protective actions were sufficiently important to merit specific recall. There are two important inferences to be drawn from these data, both of which are related to ethnic differentials. The first point is that in all three study communities, whites were more likely to engage in multiple (two or more) protective measures than minorities. The Mount Vernon data show that 10.6 percent of the whites undertook two or more protective actions, while none of the Mexican-Americans did so. In Abilene, 29.6 percent of whites versus

Table 4.3
Total number of protective actions undertaken by ethnicity

Site	Number of actions	Blacks		Whites		Mexican-Americans	
		N	%	N	%	N	%
Mount Vernon[1]	None or can't recall	—	—	71	68.3	36	87.8
	One	—	—	22	21.2	5	12.2
	Two or more	—	—	11	10.6	0	0.0
Abilene	None or can't recall	52	77.6	45	55.6	20	52.6
	One	6	9.0	10	12.3	11	28.9
	Two or more	9	13.4	24	29.6	7	18.4
Denver	None or can't recall	11	25.6	7	17.9	15	30.0
	One	25	58.1	11	28.2	19	38.0
	Two or more	7	16.3	21	53.9	16	32.0

[1] There were no blacks in the Mount Vernon sample.

18.4 percent of Mexican-Americans and 13.4 percent of blacks reported undertaking multiple protective actions. Two or more protective actions were undertaken by 53.9 percent of Denver whites, compared with 16.3 percent of blacks and 32 percent of Mexican-Americans.

A seond general finding relates to a difference among research sites as well as between minority and majority citizens. The majority of all citizens in the less urban settings of Mount Vernon and Abilene undertook *no protective actions*. This is in sharp contrast to urban Denver, where much smaller proportions of blacks, whites, and Mexican-Americans engaged in no protective actions. A related point is that in all three sites greater proportions of whites undertook multiple protective measures when compared with minority group citizens.

Table 4.4 enumerates reasons given for undertaking protective actions by ethnicity for each community studied. In response to the hazardous materials emergency in Mount Vernon, the largest proportion of whites (60.5 percent) claimed that the specific protective actions undertaken were done as a personal choice. That is, when asked to explain why they took protective actions they replied that they analyzed the situation and took the measures that seemed appropriate to them in light of what they believed to be the threat. The next largest proportion of whites (31.6 percent) reported undertaking protective actions on the basis of advice given them by authorities. Respondents were classified here whether they said that authorities volunteered the protective action information or that the information was given only after questioning.

Most Mexican-American respondents (45.5 percent) reported that they engaged in protective actions at the suggestion of relatives. However, nearly an equal number (36.4 percent) of these citizens cited authorities' advice as the reason for engaging in protective actions. In Mount Vernon, then, approximately equal proportions of whites and Mexican-Americans cited the advice of authorities as an important motivation for protective actions, and for both ethnic groups this was the second most frequently given reason. The greatest proportion of whites relied on personal choice, while Mexican-Americans listened to suggestions from relatives in deciding whether to undertake protective measures.

In Abilene, the majority of citizens from all three ethnic groups reported personal choice as the primary reason for engaging in protective actions. This response accounted for 72.7 percent of the blacks, 78.8 percent of the whites, and 66.7 percent of the Mexican-Americans. Thus, approximately three-

Table 4.4

Reasons for undertaking protective actions by ethnicity

| | Mount Vernon | | | | Abilene | | | | | | Denver | | | | | |
| | Whites | | Mexican-Americans | | Blacks | | Whites | | Mexican-Americans | | Blacks | | Whites | | Mexican-Americans | |
Reason	N	%	N	%	N	%	N	%	N	%	N	%	N	%	N	%
Authorities advised it	12	31.6	4	36.4	0	0.0	1	3.0	0	0.0	8	25.0	5	16.1	2	5.7
Past actions in disasters	1	2.6	0	0.0	1	9.1	3	9.1	0	0.0	0	0.0	3	9.7	0	0.0
Personal choice	23	60.5	1	9.1	8	72.7	26	78.8	10	66.7	22	68.8	22	70.9	31	88.6
Friends' and neighbors' suggestions	2	5.3	1	9.1	0	0.0	3	9.1	3	20.0	2	6.2	1	3.3	0	0.0
Relatives' suggestions	0	0.0	5	45.5	2	18.2	0	0.0	2	13.3	0	0.0	0	0.0	2	5.7

fourths of the blacks and whites claimed that they identified and used protective measures on the basis of their own analysis of the threat and how to best protect themselves from it. A few blacks relied on suggestions from relatives and past experience with floods, and some whites cited past experience and suggestions of friends and neighbors, but on the whole these citizens claim to have reposed most confidence in their own judgment. The bulk of Mexican-Americans also cited personal choice as a prime motivation, but they also depended slightly more heavily than the other two ethnic groups upon suggestions drawn from social networks (13.3 percent cited relatives, 20 percent cited friends and neighbors).

It should be mentioned here that in a flood threat there is probably a thin line between personal choice and past experience. It is likely that citizens who reported analyzing the situation and doing what seemed appropriate structured their reasoning in terms of their own past experience with floods as well as information they had accumulated over time from various sources regarding what to do in floods. Hence, one who cites personal judgment in a flood is not necessarily saying that "independent of past experience, I thought about the threat and protected myself from dangers I identified." It is more likely that such an interpretation would be appropriate for the Mount Vernon or Denver data or in connection with an infrequently experienced environmental threat. Therefore, among the Abilene respondents, past experience is not entirely independent of personal judgment.

In Denver, personal choice was the reason cited for undertaking protective actions by 68.8 percent of the blacks, 70.9 percent of the whites, and 88.6 percent of the Mexican-Americans. Blacks also credited the advice of authorities (25 percent) and the suggestions of friends and neighbors (6.2 percent) as reasons for undertaking protective measures. Like blacks, whites also cited authorities (16.1 percent) as the basis for protective actions, but emphasized past experience (9.7 percent) over the suggestions of friends and neighbors (3.3 percent). The few Mexican-Americans who did not rely on their personal choice for protective actions were evenly split between the advice of authorities (5.7 percent) and relatives' suggestions (5.7 percent).

The series of cross-tabulations of data on citizens who undertake protective actions yields several important conclusions that need to be placed in perspective. We have seen that citizens faced with a relatively more familiar flood threat engage in a wider range of protective actions with greater frequency than citizens who attempt to cope with an unfamiliar threat. An important implication of this finding is that if citizens know about specific protective measures, they will use them. Also, in some cases, particularly blacks and whites faced with flooding, people who undertook any protective action at all tended to use multiple measures rather than just one. Finally, especially with unfamiliar threats, citizens did cite authorities as one important source of advice in choosing whether to adopt some protective action.

These findings all point to the idea that citizens do engage in protective actions and that emergency management authorities can influence citizen behavior. By operating some type of hazard information dissemination program, emergency managers can tell citizens about desirable protective actions. Obviously such programs should not and could not cover all types of hazards, but the three or four primary environmental threats to any given community could certainly be covered. The objective of such programs should be to pack citizens' protective action repertoires with measures deemed appropriate by emergency managers. Assuming that measures devised by authorities will in fact be technically appropriate and effective, this strategy allows emergency managers to provide information in sufficient quantity that in an emergency citizens will choose an appropriate measure. Thus, even though a citizen may believe that the protective action was his or her own idea, the repertoire or "store" of potential activities from which it was drawn can be influenced by authorities. Furthermore, by disseminating information on various protective actions, emergency managers can introduce ideas for protection that compete with other less appropriate measures citizens may devise on their own or hear from others. Indeed, if authorities pursue an active campaign of dissemination there is less reason for citizens to seek out information on protective measures (which may or may not be correct) from other sources.

This discussion raises an important issue about disseminating protective action information to the public that no doubt bothers many emergency managers. That is, if we tell people about a variety of protective measures, might it not confuse them? Would people engage in the wrong protective action at the right time? For example, what if people sandbagged their houses instead of evacuating in a flood? The answer to the question is not really difficult if one visualizes emergency management as a profession dedicated to helping the public live in harmony, or at least coexist, with the natural and man-made environment. There is no reason to believe that citizens cope better with dangers about which they are ignorant or regarding which they must rely upon folk wisdom to manage. As Murton and Shimabukuro (1974:157) report, sacrificial offerings to prevent volcanic eruptions provided comfort to some residents of Puna District, Hawaii, but they had little effect on reducing vulnerability even though 88 percent of their respondents acknowledged this strategy as a coping mechanism. Certainly this is an extreme example, but the important point is that for optimal effectiveness emergency managers and citizens must work in concert to achieve protection from environmental threats. This means that an important part of managing emergencies depends upon educating the public.

With respect to the question of citizens engaging in alternatives to an officially desired protective action (if they know of several), the answer is yes. Two qualifications follow, however. First, it is probably better for citizens to engage in some protective action than none, if they ultimately choose not to engage in the protective response authorities have in mind (the "target" response). Second, and more important, is the idea that one of the tasks of effective emergency management is to induce people to engage in the most appropriate protective action. Citizens are likely to always consider alternatives to officially advised actions. It is directly, through the structure of the warning message, and indirectly, through their demeanor and reputation, that emergency managers must convince threatened citizens that the recommended protective action is most appropriate.

Furthermore, one should not rule out the idea of multiple protective measures in connection with any given disaster event. Certainly helping citizens protect themselves from physical injury should be foremost among emergency management goals. However, there are situations in which circumstances permit emergency managers to allow for citizens' propensities to preserve property as well as personal safety. For example, in connection with floods, where there is usually some advance warning relative to the timing of the event, authorities might advise that there are so many hours available for certain protective measures and then name them, but that at a specified time evacuations must begin. The key is in understanding the time available, identifying the risks, and communicating this information to the endangered public. It may be necessary to say that a flood is expected immediately, there is no time for protective measures for property, and citizens must evacuate immediately to insure personal safety. In either of the above cases emergency managers must act upon the best information available to them and communicate both their decision regarding appropriate protective actions and the reasons behind the decision to the public. Research has shown that citizens will reevaluate emergency response information no matter what authorities do. It is argued here that by providing the logic behind the decision authorities at least increase the chance that citizens will arrive at the same, or at least a similar, conclusion regarding the environmental threat.

Hazard information

In the preceding discussion we examined the question of citizens' perceptions of their own actions in response to a community emergency. At several points it was argued that what citizens do during the emergency period is a function both of the immediate information given them (usually in a warning message) and of more general information that they accumulate over a longer period of time, independent of any specific disaster event. A prime function of emergency management outside the context of an active disaster event is to inform citizens about the existence and nature of environmental threats and involve them in the process of public protection.

In the discussions of hazards information sources that follow, we are using mass media as sources, not channels, following our discussion in chapter 2. Certainly there is more inevitable overlap, but we are interested in reporting on citizen perceptions of sources utilized. Thus, even if a respondent read a newspaper article written by an emergency manager and believed the information source was the newspaper, that is important feedback for emergency managers who wish to use mass media channels. It would suggest that care should be taken to establish an independent identity for emergency managers.

Table 4.5 shows primary source of emergency response information by ethnicity for each study site. These data are community specific in that they were assembled by asking citizens to name the source they would contact if they wanted to know more about the community plan for dealing with floods or hazardous materials emergencies. In Mount Vernon the largest proportions of both whites (49 percent) and Mexican-Americans (52.5 percent) identified authorities—police and fire fighters—as the source they would contact to learn more about emergency response planning for hazardous materials incidents. This finding is consistent with studies that show that citizens tend to identify uniformed and highly visible community social control agents as pro-

Table 4.5
Primary source of community emergency response information by ethnicity

Source	Mount Vernon				Abilene						Denver					
	Whites		Mexican-Americans		Blacks		Whites		Mexican-Americans		Blacks		Whites		Mexican-Americans	
	N	%	N	%	N	%	N	%	N	%	N	%	N	%	N	%
Authorities[1]	51	49.0	21	52.5	19	28.4	17	21.0	15	44.1	18	41.9	11	28.2	23	46.0
Mass media[2]	3	2.9	3	7.5	8	11.9	11	13.6	9	26.5	1	2.3	1	2.6	6	12.0
Social networks[3]	6	5.8	10	25.0	0	0.0	3	3.7	5	14.7	3	7.0	3	7.7	3	6.0
City officials[4]	0	0.0	2	5.0	9	13.4	11	13.6	1	2.9	7	16.3	6	15.4	4	8.0
Railroad officials[5]	5	4.8	0	0.0	—	—	—	—	—	—	6	14.0	10	25.6	1	2.0
Emergency services[6]	39	37.5	4	10.0	31	46.3	39	48.1	4	11.8	8	18.6	8	20.5	13	26.0

[1] Authorities includes police and fire departments.
[2] Mass media includes both local television and radio.
[3] Social networks includes relatives, friends, and neighbors.
[4] City officials includes mayor, city council, planning office, and city manager.
[5] This category was not relevant to the Abilene flood threat.
[6] Emergency services includes city civil defense director, county emergency services department, and city office of emergency preparedness.

viders of emergency information. This outcome is also probably related to the fact that in Mount Vernon the evacuation warning was disseminated by police officers and citizens would be expected to look to these personnel as sources of further information. Another expected finding is that the second largest proportion of Mexican-Americans (25 percent) reported that they would seek further emergency response information through social network contacts. Our other warning response data suggested that Mexican-Americans draw more on social networks either directly for emergency-related information or indirectly for referrals to appropriate persons or agencies than either whites or blacks.

The Mount Vernon data show two response patterns that were not anticipated. First, neither ethnic group perceived the mass media (radio, in this community) as a source of emergency response information in any large proportions. Although both whites and Mexican-Americans reported hearing warnings via radio, each group apparently correctly perceived that the media have no technical role in the design of emergency response plans for hazardous materials accidents. This perception may be a function of the technological nature of the threat. In connection with natural hazards, where mass media disseminate what appears to the public to be continous threat-relevant information, citizens are somewhat more likely to identify the media as repositories of emergency information (cf. Perry and Greene, 1982a). This is also consistent with the Abilene flood data wherein relatively larger proportions of citizens identified mass media as points of contact for emergency response information. Another point of interest is that relatively few whites and Mexican-Americans identified city officials or railroad officials as sources of emergency response information.

The second unanticipated finding in the Mount Vernon data is the relatively high proportion of whites (37.5 percent) who specifically identified the county emergency services office as the appropriate place to gain information regarding hazardous materials emergency response plans. Indeed, for whites this office was the second most frequently identified source behind local authorities. It is equally remarkable that even 10 percent of the Mexican-Americans were aware of the function of the county emergency services office. This finding was unanticipated because disaster studies have only infrequently reported that citizens are sensitive to the operations of emergency services personnel other than those routinely visible in the community, usually police and fire fighters.

The relevant county emergency services office (for Mount Vernon) has been waging public information campaigns for approximately one year and has been cited in the news regarding emergencies in nearby communities. Just a few weeks prior to the incident at Mount Vernon, a similar derailment occurred in a community less than 10 miles distant and was managed by the county emergency services office working in conjunction with local authorities. Local newspaper coverage of this incident was substantial and the role of the county office was clearly identified. County emergency services staff had also made efforts to have emergency related interviews published in local papers. The relatively high proportions of citizens who identified the emergency services office as an important information source suggest that these visibility-enhancing efforts were successful.

The Abilene data show an even stronger tendency to identify emergency services officers as a primary source of flood response information. Nearly half of the blacks (46.3 percent) and whites (48.1 percent) reported that the place to obtain flood emergency response planning information was the office of the city civil defense director. A smaller proportion (11.8 percent) of the Mexican-Americans also reported that the appropriate place for obtaining flood response advice was the civil defense office. This finding is no doubt a function of information dissemination efforts on the part of the civil defense office. Although the staff is small, the director has been active in the production and dissemination of protective information on seasonal hazards; he has publicized the routine duties of his office (for example, by inviting print and broadcast media to be present at tests of civil defense sirens) and submitted to the local radio station and newspaper interviews regarding various topics related to emergency management. Furthermore, the civil defense director has promoted a policy of close coordination and response linkage between his office and the relatively visible operations of the police and fire departments. By making these linkages clear to the public as part of the emergency information dissemination process, the office of civil defense has come to be identified—particularly by blacks and whites—as occupying a coordinating role in cooperation with police and fire fighters in the management of emergencies in Abilene. At this point one should recall that an important goal for emergency managers is to achieve identification in the eyes of the public as the controllers of emergency response information. We suggested that intensive attention to dissemination practices was one technique for accomplishing this, and the data from both Mount Vernon and Abilene indicate that the technique can yield considerable success.

The second most frequently mentioned source of emergency response information among Abilene blacks and whites was the authorities (28.4 percent and 21 percent, respectively). This was the most frequently cited flood response information source among Mexican-Americans (44.1 percent). As we pointed out in our discussion of the Mount Vernon data, citizens frequently identify police and fire fighters as sources of information on how to respond to community emergencies because of their high visibility and because citizens are accustomed to seeing these personnel respond to most community crises. Also, as we anticipated, Mexican-Americans were more likely than blacks or whites to look to social network contacts for response information regarding floods. On the other hand, blacks and whites were more likely than Mexican-Americans to cite city officials as sources for emergency response information.

As we found in the Mount Vernon data, the most often cited source of emergency preparedness information among Denver respondents was local authorities—41.9 percent of blacks, 28.2 percent of whites, and 46 percent of Mexican-Americans. This tends to support the hypothesis that in unfamiliar threats, citizens of all ethnic backgrounds tend to seek information from the most visible official sources. In this regard, however, the Denver data show a slight ethnic differential not seen in Mount Vernon. Smaller proportions of Denver whites than minority citizens endorsed public sector authorities as the source for emergency preparedness information. Instead, a relatively greater proportion of whites (25.6 percent) identified a private sector agency—railroad authorities—as the repository of emergency planning information, compared to blacks (14 percent) and Mexican-Americans (2 percent). These two sources account for about 50 percent of all respondents, but minority citizens emphasized local authorities, while whites were more evenly divided among public and private sector officials. Another ethnic differential in Denver that was also found in Mount Vernon and Abilene is the tendency for greater proportions of Mexican-Americans, versus blacks or whites, to name the mass media as a primary source of emergency planning information.

There is one difference among sites that is apparently related to the more urbanized setting in Denver. Larger proportions of blacks (16.3 percent), whites (15.4 percent), and Mexican-Americans (8 percent), identified city officials as the appropriate people from whom to obtain emergency preparedness information. Interestingly, this appears to fit into a trend: as we move across our sites from least urban (Mount Vernon) to most urban (Denver) the proportion of respondents identifying city-level elected or appointed officials as information sources increases. Finally, consistent with our findings in Mount Vernon and Abilene, Denver respondents identified local emergency managers as sources of preparedness planning information; this source was named by 18.6 percent of blacks, 20.5 percent of whites, and 26 percent of Mexican-Americans.

Perhaps the most important finding in Table 4.5 should be seen in light of the relatively high levels of emergency preparedness and active emergency services offices in all three communities. That is, if we combine authorities and emergency services figures as sources of emergency response information, these categories account for more than 80 percent of the whites and 60 percent of the Mexican-Americans in Mount Vernon, nearly three-fourths of the blacks and whites and more than half of the Mexican-Americans in Abilene, and half of the Denver blacks and whites and two-thirds of the Mexican-Americans. Therefore, most citizens are identifying appropriate sources for accurate emergency response information and this appears to be related to the proactive approach to emergency management practiced in each community.

After discussing citizen answers to the question of the appropriate source for specific emergency response information it is interesting to consider where citizens obtain more general information on both natural and man-made threats. The purpose here is to identify the channels through which citizens routinely receive information about the nature of environmental threats and what they can do to protect themselves. These data allow emergency managers to assess the information needs of their communities and choose dissemination channels with respect to their coverage among subgroups of the community population.

Table 4.6 shows sources of environmental hazards information by ethnicity. Note that these data refer to general information about man-made and natural threats, and citizens were asked to confine the sources mentioned to those from which they definitely recalled obtaining some information in the past. In terms of data interpretation, these responses represent citizen perceptions of the places that they recall having seen disaster-relevant information. It would be inappropriate to make inferences about the likely content of the information, particularly its technical accuracy. These data are also probably subject to recency effects relative to recall as well as the effects of cumulative exposure; that is, those sources from which citizens remember getting information over a long period of time are more likely to be mentioned. For our purposes, however, these qualifications do not compromise the usefulness of

Table 4.6

Sources of past information on environmental hazards by ethnicity

| | Mount Vernon[1] | | | | Abilene[2] | | | | | | Denver[3] | | | | | |
| | Whites | | Mexican-Americans | | Blacks | | Whites | | Mexican-Americans | | Blacks | | Whites | | Mexican-Americans | |
Source	N	%	N	%	N	%	N	%	N	%	N	%	N	%	N	%
Local newspapers	78	75.0	18	43.9	35	52.2	55	67.0	20	52.6	13	30.2	37	94.8	24	48.0
Radio	52	50.0	21	51.2	29	43.3	32	49.5	15	39.5	18	41.8	28	71.7	26	52.0
Television	50	48.1	7	17.1	46	68.7	54	66.7	29	76.3	17	39.5	22	56.4	36	72.0
Speaker at organization	10	9.6	0	0.0	4	6.0	10	12.3	0	0.0	3	6.9	11	28.2	6	12.0
Social networks[4]	34	32.7	18	43.9	22	32.8	25	30.9	27	71.1	20	46.5	11	28.2	39	78.0
Local emergency authorities[5]	13	12.5	0	0.0	4	6.0	6	7.4	2	5.3	5	11.6	6	15.3	5	10.0
Local political official[6]	0	0.0	2	4.9	7	10.4	5	6.2	0	0.0	1	2.3	1	2.5	1	2.0
Magazine articles	39	37.5	2	4.9	9	13.4	22	27.2	2	5.3	7	18.6	24	61.5	20	40.0

Note: Respondents were asked about response information for natural and man-made disasters.

[1] Percentages are given for all respondents in each category: whites on base n = 104; Mexican-Americans on base n = 41.

[2] Percentages are given for all respondents in each category: blacks on base n = 67; whites on base n = 81; Mexican-Americans on base n = 38.

[3] Percentages based on n n = 43 for blacks, n = 39 for whites, n = 50 for Mexican-Americans.

[4] Social networks includes neighbors, friends, and relatives.

[5] Emergency authorities includes police, fire fighters, civil defense, and emergency services personnel.

[6] Political officials includes mayor, city council, city manager, and planning office.

the data. We are in fact interested in where citizens *think* they received information and their *perceptions* of the frequency with which different sources provided information.

Among whites in Mount Vernon, the most frequently reported sources of hazard information were newspaper articles (75 percent), radio (50 percent), and television (48.1 percent). Behind this constellation of most often used channels, whites identified magazine articles (37.5 percent) and social networks (32.7 percent) as information sources tapped with moderate frequency. Sources least often cited by whites were local emergency authorities, speakers at organizational meetings, and local political officials (listed in descending order of reported contact frequency). The information sources reported by Mexican-Americans also show natural breaks by frequency into three groupings. The most frequently cited sources were radio (51.2 percent), social networks (43.9 percent), and newspapers (43.9 percent). Television was cited as a source of information on environmental threats by 17.1 percent of the Mexican-Americans. The sources least frequently used by Mexican-Americans were magazine articles, local political officials, speakers at organizational meetings, and local emergency authorities.

With regard to the use of traditional or established channels for communicating information about environmental hazards to citizens, we can derive four conclusions from the Mount Vernon data. First, newspapers and radio are two channels that are very likely to reach both ethnic groups. Each of these media were among those most frequently cited by whites as well as Mexican-Americans as sources of hazard information in the past. Both of these channels are comparatively easily accessed by emergency managers, particularly through press releases and focused interviews on particular hazard issues.

Television, local magazine articles, and social networks are channels that whites cited with moderate frequency as hazard information sources. Television and magazines are tools for information dissemination that are less susceptible to use by emergency managers. Aside from news releases, public service announcements, and coverage of response to specific community disasters, uses of television to disseminate emergency response and planning are highly limited and require substantial resources and, in some cases, technical skills. An emergency manager might use television coverage, however, in its public service capacity to bring to the public's attention things such as the availability of specific seasonal hazard brochures or the time and place of public meetings. Like television, regional and local magazines are comparatively complicated channels for disseminating hazard information, even though this source has some appeal to whites. Preparation of short hazard awareness or response articles or participation in a focused interview constitute the primary modes of access to magazines available to emergency managers. It should be mentioned that when considering the use of magazines and television—or any other channel, for that matter—emergency managers should carefully weigh the benefit of the coverage obtained against the cost of using the channel. Hence, unless a department of emergency services has access to special resources or skills, television and magazines should probably not be targeted as primary channels for disseminating hazard information.

The data in Table 4.6 show that among Mexican-Americans television and social networks were frequently used sources of hazard information. Although less so than for Mexican-Americans, whites too reported that social networks were important channels for receiving hazard information. In this case, referring to social networks is another way of describing the process of obtaining information about hazards on a word-of-mouth basis from important people in the individual's social sphere. While it is true that there is little that emergency managers can do to affect or use this channel, it is important that they be aware of its existence and its special significance for Mexican-Americans. Some information can be "inserted" into this channel by developing neighborhood contacts or involving citizens in planning or advisory groups and allowing these people to carry information back into the community. Also, some information will circulate among social networks as a function of dissemination activities via other channels. Social networks should not be seen as a channel through which to disseminate specific hazard information; the difficult and complex aspects of gaining access and the high likelihood that information will become garbled in transmission mediate against such uses. Information that passes through social networks is probably most usefully conceived of in terms of the support-building function of citizen participation. That is, information about the perceived reliability of emergency services personnel can be expected to pass within social networks and, ideally, inquiries by citizens of their social network contacts would result in appropriate references to emergency managers for additional or specific information. Active cultivation of social networks, however, is likely to be a resource-consuming and relatively low-yield endeavor.

Finally, the Mount Vernon data show that local political authorities, local emergency authorities, and speakers at local civic and voluntary organizations are the established channels used least frequently by both ethnic groups. Of course this does not mean that these channels are undesirable, only that in the past they have enjoyed little utilization by citizens. In fact, it should be acknowledged that each is a limited coverage channel by definition. The coverage obtained by a speaker depends upon the organization to which he or she is dispatched and the attendance at the particular meeting when the presentation is made. Furthermore, historically, public contact with emergency services personnel has been largely confined to the response period of any given disaster event.

The emergence of emergency managers, as we now conceive the role, is a very recent phenomenon and the public at large is still in the process of adjusting to the presence of such officials and developing expectations for their performance. Future use of speakers or direct dissemination of information by emergency services personnel is a matter very much open to the creative inclinations of individual role incumbents. In any use of speakers or some other direct dissemination strategy, emergency managers should keep the technique's primary weak point in mind: the coverage obtained by any single effort will be limited. While speakers can disseminate very specific hazard information, conveying the message to any significant portion of the population requires many separate contacts with different organizations or groups.

The Abilene data show basic patterns similar to those observed in Mount Vernon; the frequency of citizen utilization across different channels is approximately the same for each community. Interestingly, blacks and whites in Abilene show similar use patterns for the five most frequently mentioned sources, and the use distribution for these two ethnic groups is similar to that observed for Mount Vernon whites. The use pattern for Abilene Mexican-Americans is different from that for blacks and whites but similar to Mount Vernon Mexican-Americans.

Among blacks the three most frequently cited channels for receiving information on environmental hazards were television (68.7 percent), newspapers (52.2 percent), and radio (43.3 percent). Likewise, 67 percent of the whites reported that they received hazard information through newspapers, 66.7 percent cited television, and 49.5 percent mentioned radio. Magazines and social networks were the next most frequently cited information sources by both blacks and whites. One should note that while the proportion of blacks and whites citing social networks was about the same (32.8 and 30.9

percent, respectively), a greater proportion of whites than blacks reported receiving hazard information through magazines.

Finally, the sources from which blacks and whites have received hazard information least often in the past are local political officials, local emergency authorities, and speakers at organizations. Again there are slight variations by ethnicity: whites are more likely to have received information from a speaker and blacks are more likely to have received information from a local political official. These differences at the low level of contact sources, however, should not divert attention from the similarities between blacks and whites with respect to sources that have been frequently used, particularly newspapers, television, and radio.

Among Abilene Mexican-Americans, the most frequently cited sources of hazard information were television (76.3 percent), social networks (71.1 percent), and newspapers (52.6 percent). The next most commonly cited source was radio (39.5 percent). This hierarchy of source utilization is the same as that reported by Mount Vernon Mexican-Americans, except that Abilene citizens used television more often than radio (the reverse order held in Mount Vernon). Channels through which information infrequently or never flowed to Abilene Mexican-Americans included magazines, local emergency authorities, local political officials, and speakers at organizations.

As a preface to examining the Denver data, several observations can be made regarding urban-rural differences in the source utilization data. These differentials generally hold across ethnic groups. Although they are still used relatively infrequently when compared to other sources, Denver urbanites were more likely to have obtained information from speakers at organizational meetings than citizens in less urban settings. Urban dwellers also reported higher levels of past contacts with local emergency authorities than observed in Mount Vernon or Abilene. Furthermore, slightly greater proportions of Denver respondents claimed to have obtained emergency response information from newspapers, magazines, and social networks. Like their less urban counterparts, Denver respondents reported that they rarely had obtained information regarding environmental hazards from local political officials.

The most frequently cited sources of past information among all three ethnic groups in Denver were social networks, radio, television, newspapers, and magazines. There are ethnic differentials regarding the relative frequency with which these sources were named. Minority citizens tended to emphasize social networks (46.5 percent of blacks and 78 percent of Mexican-Americans) as sources of past hazards information to a greater extent than whites (28.2 percent). Both blacks and Mexican-Americans identified the broadcasting media (radio and television) as the second most frequently used sources of past information as well as designating newspapers as the third most frequently used source. Most whites (94.8 percent) reported newspapers were a source of hazard information in the past. Radio was named by the next largest proportion of whites (71.7 percent), followed by magazine articles (61.5 percent) and television (56.4 percent).

The high degree of overlap in source utilization patterns at Mount Vernon, Abilene, and Denver increases our confidence in the findings. It also means that the conclusions drawn (with appropriate qualifiers) regarding channels through which to disseminate hazard information apply equally well to the three communities. Furthermore, with regard to ethnic group differences, we found that blacks and whites draw upon similar channels (historically at least) in gaining information about environmental threats. Mexican-Americans across the three sites were similar to each other but distinct from blacks and whites in their more frequent use of social networks as information sources. In general, across all three sites and ethnic groups, radio and newspapers are the traditional or established communication channels that reach the largest proportions of local community residents.

Citizen participation and outreach

In the preceding section we examined citizen reports of the channels through which they had received hazard information in the past. The focus was upon already existing or established communication channels through which emergency managers might choose to disseminate information. In this section we will change perspectives. Instead of asking citizens to identify past information sources, we asked our respondents to name the single best method that emergency managers could use to convey hazard information. Hence, these data carry an anticipatory or future orientation. In effect we have asked citizens to identify their preferences regarding communication modes. Table 4.7 summarizes citizen responses to the question of which channels constitute the best way to communicate hazards information.

As one might expect, Table 4.7 shows that citizen preferences for com-

Table 4.7

Best way to communicate environmental hazard information by ethnicity

	Mount Vernon				Abilene						Denver					
	Whites		Mexican-Americans		Blacks		Whites		Mexican-Americans		Blacks		Whites		Mexican-Americans	
Method	N	%	N	%	N	%	N	%	N	%	N	%	N	%	N	%
Mail letter or brochure	34	33.0	3	7.3	13	20.0	21	24.8	4	13.3	7	16.3	14	35.9	15	30.0
Speakers at organizations	8	7.8	0	0.0	2	3.1	4	5.4	0	0.0	2	4.7	0	0.0	2	4.0
Newspaper articles	38	36.9	12	29.3	9	13.8	22	29.7	3	10.0	8	18.6	11	28.2	4	8.0
Local radio	13	12.6	17	41.5	15	23.1	17	23.0	7	23.3	8	18.6	10	25.6	10	20.0
Local television	4	3.9	1	2.4	19	29.2	10	13.5	5	16.7	2	4.7	4	10.3	11	22.0
Neighborhood meetings	6	5.8	8	19.5	7	10.8	8	10.8	11	36.7	16	37.2	0	0.0	8	16.0

munication channels are different from the past sources of information discussed above. In Mount Vernon, white respondents preferred to receive hazard information through newspapers (36.9 percent) and through the mail (33 percent). With regard to the type of mailed information, almost all respondents felt that short brochures or typed information sheets were most appropriate. Whether information was to be mailed or published in newspapers, respondents expressed preferences for brevity and stressed the utility of seeing information on seasonally relevant threats just before the appropriate season. This latter suggestion was often justified by comments to the effect that protective information can easily be lost or forgotten during off-seasons. Based on these remarks, emergency managers might appropriately infer that repetition of information is more likely to be appreciated than treated as a problem. Fewer whites (12.6 percent) preferred to receive hazard information via radio. The smallest proportions of whites reported preferences for speakers at organizations (7.8 percent), block or neighborhood meetings (5.8 percent), and television (3.9 percent). In Mount Vernon (and Abilene as well) whites expressed clear preferences for written information that could be kept for future reference.

The most frequently cited preferred communication channel among Mount Vernon Mexican-Americans was radio (41.5 percent). Newspapers were a distant second choice, preferred by 29.3 percent of the respondents. The third most frequently named alternative among Mexican-Americans was a block or neighborhood meeting (19.5 percent), a choice that was rated as considerably less desirable by whites. When asked to elaborate, respondents most often described a neighborhood meeting as an event, advertised in advance, that could be held in a local union hall or church. Respondents also commonly expressed the opinion that the meeting place should be in the neighborhood, preferably within walking distance for most residents. The least preferred communication modes among Mexican-Americans were mailed information (7.3 percent), television (2.4 percent), and speakers at organizations (0 percent). Many of the Mount Vernon Mexican-Americans were agricultural workers and most were poor. Seen in this light their preferences for radio and newspaper communications (which are available at low cost) and for neighborhood meetings (which are more likely to reach relatively mobile agricultural workers when they are in town) are not difficult to understand.

Whites in Abilene chose the same three most preferred communication channels as those in Mount Vernon: newspapers (29.7 percent), mailed information (24.8 percent), and radio (23 percent). However, a comparatively larger proportion of Abilene than Mount Vernon whites chose radio as the best means of sending hazards information to citizens. Television and neighborhood meetings were selected as preferred communication modes by 13.5 percent and 10.8 percent, respectively, of the respondents. The least preferred mode, or the one these citizens felt was least likely to reach them, was sending speakers to organizational meetings (5.4 percent).

Large proportions of Abilene blacks, like the whites, felt that radio (23.1 percent) and mailed information (20 percent) formed acceptable communications channels, but these respondents most frequently endorsed television (29.2 percent). Newspapers and neighborhood meetings received a moderate proportion of endorsements (13.8 percent and 10.8 percent, respectively), and only 3.1 percent of blacks felt that speakers at organizations were the best way to communicate. Perhaps the most interesting aspect of communication mode preferences among Abilene blacks is that they almost perfectly match communication mode preferences among Abilene whites. If we order the six communication modes in terms of the proportion of citizens who endorsed each, both ethnic groups included mail and radio as top preferences, with neighborhood meetings in the middle group and speakers last. The only differences in priority ranking are that blacks included television in the top group while whites placed it with neighborhood meetings, and whites assigned newspapers to the top group while blacks rated newspapers with neighborhood meetings.

Abilene Mexican-Americans showed strong preferences for neighborhood meetings (36.7 percent) and radio (23.3 percent) as communications channels through which to receive information regarding environmental hazards. Television was rated somewhat lower; 16.7 percent of the respondents endorsed this mode. Mail (13.3 percent) and newspapers (10 percent) were seen as even less acceptable and none of the Mexican-American respondents endorsed speakers at organizations as a preferred means of acquiring information. Thus, Abilene Mexican-Americans were similar to those in Mount Vernon in that they both rated radio and neighborhood meetings among their most preferred communications modes and mailed information and speakers among the least preferred modes. Abilene citizens showed a preference for television over newspapers, however, while residents of Mount Vernon rated these two channels in the opposite order.

Like whites in Mount Vernon and Abilene, the three most frequently mentioned preferred dissemination channels among Denver whites were mailed information (35.9 percent), newspaper articles (28.2 percent), and radio (25.6 percent). Television was mentioned as a preferred source by only 10.3 percent of whites in Denver and none of these citizens endorsed speakers or neighborhood meetings. Minority citizens also rarely mentioned speakers as a preferred communication channel, but in contrast to whites, Denver blacks and Mexican-Americans more often endorsed neighborhood meetings as a preferred communication forum. Blacks also indicated a preference for newspapers and radio, while Mexican-Americans more frequently endorsed television and radio.

These data regarding citizen perceptions of the best ways to communicate hazard information have several important implications for emergency managers who are planning dissemination programs. Radio was the one channel that was rated as a desirable dissemination mode among all three ethnic groups at all three research sites. This finding is significant because local radio is a high coverage, low cost communication channel that is readily available to emergency managers. Furthermore, radio is a versatile channel in that an emergency manager (perhaps in the form of a structured interview or a public service spot) can disseminate specific hazard relevant information and/or simply raise a particular hazard issue and advise interested listeners where additional information can be acquired (for example, by picking up a brochure at a police or fire station or the local emergency services office). To a limited extent, an emergency manager can also participate in dialogues with citizens via this medium, perhaps by arranging to participate in a call-in program designed to solicit questions from listeners.

Amid these virtues, one must keep in mind the principal vices of radio: different stations will have different audiences and broadcasts at different times of day will have different audiences. Fortunately, for purposes of selling advertising, most radio stations are aware of what audience they serve and who is likely to be listening at different hours. Hence, an emergency manager planning an effective dissemination campaign must be aware of these limitations and probably will be forced to include several radio stations in the plan as well as broadcasts at different times.

With regard to ethnic variations, whites and blacks showed a preference for information received via the mail and through newspapers. These communication channels have the advantage of providing citizens with hazard information in written form that can be kept and referenced by those sufficiently motivated to do so. Mailed brochures have the advantage that emergency managers retain complete control of the content and style of information presentation. However, mailed brochures have a disadvantage: to attain maximum effectiveness the amount of information in any single message must be kept to a minimum and concisely presented. On the other hand, newspapers share with radio the problem of audience variation and require more of an emergency manager's time and resources for effective utilization.

Minority respondents rated neighborhood meetings higher than whites as a preferred communication channel. While conducting neighborhood meetings may be an effective way of reaching some segments of the community, this communication mode is by far the most taxing relative to emergency management time and resources. Neighborhood meetings have the advantages of allowing two-way communication and face-to-face contact, and the information to be disseminated can be tailored to the specific audience. Such meetings carry the disadvantages of requiring much advance preparation of material, locating and advertising a suitable meeting time and place, and demanding that at least one emergency manager work outside normally prescribed hours. Also, it should be remembered that while the opportunity to build positive rapport with citizens is great, the risk of alienating the participants is equally great if the neighborhood meeting is not carefully planned in advance. This is certainly not to say that neighborhood meetings should be avoided. If run well, they have many advantages over other communication channels and in fact may allow emergency managers to disseminate information to population segments who might otherwise be very difficult to reach. The key concern here is that emergency managers realistically inventory their available time and resources and only use such meetings as a communication channel when appropriate preparations can be made to insure success.

The above discussion of preferred communication channels addresses the issue of how emergency managers can disseminate hazards information to citizens. An equally important question relates to the ways in which emergency managers can involve citizens in community disaster response and planning. It has been argued that community emergency management should be seen as an activity guided by and drawing upon the technical expertise of emergency managers but accomplished jointly with the citizens to be protected. The rationale here is that citizens are more likely to comply with emergency measures they believe they have had a hand in devising. Also, and perhaps more important, having citizens involved in emergency planning affords emergency managers the chance to obtain immediate feedback on citizen perceptions of the acceptability or workability of different management strategies.

It would be inappropriate to expect that large numbers of citizens would be inclined to seek to participate as volunteers in emergency services organizations. Emergency managers considering this option for citizen involvement should not worry that their offices would become filled with volunteers who might obstruct the process of emergency management. On the other hand, volunteers can be useful for the reasons mentioned above as well as to help reduce chronic personnel shortages, particularly during the response period for any given disaster. To better understand how citizens might conceive their own involvement in emergency management, we asked our respondents about their willingness to participate in each of four activities.

The first option was to serve on a task force dealing with a specific emergency response issue such as the design of an evacuation protocol or the structure of emergency shelters. A second activity was to serve on an advisory committee dealing with general issues such as which community hazards should be managed or the need for special equipment or personnel. In both of these cases, respondents who asked about scope of effort were told that the service might involve one meeting per month for a year. The third option respondents were asked to comment on was service as auxiliary police or fire personnel. Again, citizens who inquired were told that such participation would demand two weeks of intensive training with one day of work per month for a year. The last option suggested to respondents was periodic work as an office helper in an emergency services department.

Table 4.8 shows the proportions of citizens who claimed they would work in each of the volunteer capacities by ethnicity for each study community. Interestingly, in both Abilene and Mount Vernon, so few Mexican-Americans volunteered for any of the activities that very little interpretation of the data is possible. The two most appropriate conclusions are that in general these choices for involvement were not appealing to the Mexican-Americans in these communities, but among those who did indicate a choice, work as auxiliary police or fire personnel seemed to be preferred. Larger proportions of blacks and whites indicated a willingness to work in some volunteer capacity, but in most cases only about one-fourth of the members of either ethnic group volunteered for a given activity. As expected, then, most citizens would not choose to do volunteer work in an emergency management capacity.

Among whites in Mount Vernon and Abilene, the most popular choices were participation on a task force or advisory committee. Whites reported less

Table 4.8

Preferred volunteer activity related to emergency services by ethnicity

Method	Mount Vernon[1] Whites		Mexican-Americans		Abilene[2] Blacks		Whites		Mexican-Americans		Denver[3] Blacks		Whites		Mexican-Americans	
	N	%	N	%	N	%	N	%	N	%	N	%	N	%	N	%
Citizen task force on specific issue	30	28.8	1	2.4	24	35.8	23	28.4	3	7.9	16	37.2	12	30.8	23	46.0
Advisory committee on general issues	27	26.0	1	2.4	12	17.9	24	29.6	2	5.3	8	18.6	9	23.1	14	28.0
Auxiliary police or fire personnel	18	17.3	5	12.2	17	25.4	11	13.6	1	2.6	14	32.6	11	28.2	22	44.0
Office help in an emergency services department	2	1.9	0	0.0	2	3.0	8	9.9	0	0.0	0	0.0	2	5.1	0	0.0

[1]Percentages are given for all respondents in each category: whites on base n = 104; Mexican-Americans on base n = 41.

[2]Percentages are given for all respondents in each category: blacks on base n = 67; whites on base n = 81; Mexican-Americans on base n = 38.

[3]Percentages are given for all respondents in each category: blacks on base n = 43; whites on base n = 39; Mexican-Americans on base n = 50.

interest in serving as auxiliary fire or police personnel and least interest in working in an emergency services office. Respondent comments indicated the perceived commitment and time involved in working as auxiliary police or fire fighters were too great. Some respondents also mentioned that volunteering for office work was inappropriate because they believed they lacked necessary skills (those most often mentioned included the ability to type and operate radio equipment). The attractiveness of serving on committees from the whites' point of view was that the task appeared to have definite parameters; particularly, a defined work commitment and completion time.

The largest proportion of blacks volunteered for service on a task force dealing with a specific emergency management problem. The next most endorsed volunteer activity among blacks was the option to work as auxiliary personnel in a police or fire department. Work on a general advisory committee was less often endorsed by blacks and very few agreed to volunteer as office help in an emergency services department.

The Denver data are noteworthy because there are no differences by ethnicity in the rank ordering of the four types of volunteer activity by frequency of citizen endorsements. The volunteer activity preferred by the largest proportions of blacks (37.2 percent), whites (30.8 percent), and Mexican-Americans (46 percent) was membership on a task force charged with addressing a specific problem. Work as an auxiliary police officer or fire fighter was favored by 32.6 percent of blacks, 28.2 percent of whites, and 44 percent of Mexican-Americans. It should be noted that greater relative proportions of minority citizens than whites in Denver endorsed these two options for participating in emergency management. Participation on an advisory committee was the third most frequently chosen mode of involvement among all three ethnic groups in Denver.

Three variations among the study communities should also be mentioned. The urban Mexican-Americans in Denver were far more willing to be involved in volunteer capacities than Mexican-Americans in the less urbanized sites at Mount Vernon and Abilene. The proportions of blacks opting for volunteer involvement in Abilene and Denver are similar; for these citizens the urban/less urban dimension has little impact on participation levels. Whites resemble blacks in that their desired participation levels are similar across all three communities. Finally, serving as volunteer office help was the least frequently endorsed participation mode among all three ethnic groups at all three sites.

The differences in proportions among blacks and whites in the data shown in Table 4.8 are not large enough to argue that any particular ethnic differentials exist. Two points appear to be worth comment. First, in the less urban settings, Mexican-Americans show little inclination to be involved in any of the four capacities mentioned; in Denver the desired participation levels were much higher. Second, blacks seem slightly more open to participation as auxiliary police or fire personnel than whites. In general, with regard to these data we should also keep two qualifications in mind. It is known that low income citizens tend to volunteer less often than higher income citizens. Because the Mexican-Americans in our samples represent the lower income categories, their apparent reticence to participate may be due to an income difference rather than to ethnic group membership. Furthermore, we have asked citizens about participating in only four fairly constrained kinds of activity. It would not be appropriate to assume that because the proportions of volunteers were fairly low when asked about these activities, volunteers would be equally slow to participate in other capacities. The mode and success of any citizen involvement effort depend upon the imagination and resourcefulness of the emergency manager who implements the program.

Finally, the last point to be mentioned in this chapter deals with the problem of language. We have pointed out that language barriers were potentially substantial obstacles to emergency management. In our samples of Mexican-Americans, none of those in Mount Vernon reported that they had any trouble understanding either the warning message or any other information imparted in English. Only four of the Mexican-Americans in Abilene reported any trouble understanding the flood evacuation warning. Two of these citizens reported that the first message they heard was in Spanish and two were warned in English. Those warned in English reported that they coped with the problem by having a bilingual family member translate. The two citizens warned in Spanish apparently received garbled messages because both claimed to have reached an understanding of the message by contacting police. Among Mexican-Americans in our samples, language barriers posed no difficulties with respect to emergency responses. This should not necessarily be interpreted to mean that all Spanish speakers would experience no disaster response related difficulties; considerable research is necessary to make such an assertion. It does seem likely, however, that Spanish speakers would experience relatively fewer interpretative problems than more recent immigrant ethnic groups, particularly those from Southeast Asia.

5 Emergency management policy and the local community

Our data analyses have focused upon the behavior of individuals—black, white, and Mexican-American citizens coping with disaster threats. We have traced citizens' decision-making processes from the time of first warning, through deliberations aimed at warning confirmation, to their warning compliance actions. We have also examined ethnic differences in hazard awareness, in the channels used to receive and send disaster-relevant information, and in desired levels of participation in the emergency management process.

Throughout our discussions of citizen behavior, there is implicit the idea that citizens act within an emergency management context created by authorities. That is, the structure or organization that identifies threats, constructs and disseminates warning messages, supervises evacuation exodus, and shelters evacuees is a part of local government. More accurately, it is a blend of local government, state government, federal government, and private organizations. Emergency management or the delivery of disaster services to citizens may consequently be conceived in terms of public policy.

The purpose of this chapter is to explicitly address this emergency management context in which citizens must operate. We begin by sorting out the intergovernmental system, attempting to make clear the nature of the linkages among the various actors. Particular attention will be given to emergency management strategies (comprehensive emergency management and inte-

grated emergency management) developed at the federal level and the consequences of the intergovernmental system for the likely implementation of
such approaches. Finally, after laying out the role of the community in emergency management, we will again focus upon citizens. In our closing section
we will explore ways in which majority and minority citizens can participate
in and contribute to community emergency management.

Public policy and the intergovernmental system

Before discussing the roles of the various governmental actors in emergency
management, it is necessary to examine the nature of the policy system within
which disaster planning occurs. Federal, state, and local government actors all
play important parts in managing disasters. These roles are best understood in
terms of the policy and intergovernmental system. The policy system or perspective is an analytic device that is used to divide policy into component
parts. The intergovernmental network is a function of the type of governmental system in the United States, namely, federalism. An understanding of the
policy system will permit us to differentiate the tasks that various governments and agencies execute in the performance of their legislated functions. A
better understanding of the intergovernmental system provides us with insights into the kinds of activities each level of government must perform to
successfully manage disasters. The policy system is a conceptual tool, while
the intergovernmental system is a characteristic of our governmental processes that provides constraints on and opportunities for those individuals
vested with policy-making responsibilities.

The policy system is often described as consisting of a series of stages
(Anderson, 1979). The stages taken as a whole delineate the various activities
involved in making and implementing public policy. These activities may be
grouped into four stages: policy formulation, adoption, implementation, and
evaluation (Mushkatel and Weschler, 1985a:52). Policy formulation consists
of planning and information gathering that are necessary for the development
of policy options and gaining the attention of decision makers. Policy adoption involves the endorsement of one or more of the options by a legitimate
authority (for example, Congress, the executive, and the courts), which then
transforms the option into a law or policy. The third stage of policy implemen-

tation refers to the actual execution of the policy. This stage involves the administration of the policy, including the development of the rules and regulations by which the policy will be administered. Finally, policy evaluation involves determining the effectiveness of the policy as it is being carried out in meeting the goals and objectives of the policy. This evaluation permits managers and governmental actors to make various adjustments in the policy to permit better performance.

All policy, including emergency management policies, may be viewed as consisting of these stages. Our previous discussion of evacuation planning fits into the policy formulation stage, while the data on evacuations themselves constitute implementation. From this discussion it should be clear that the formulation and implementation of evacuation plans reflect only a portion of the policy system.

The intergovernmental system

The formulation and implementation of public policy related to natural hazards is an exercise in intergovernmental relations (Gortner, 1977; Mushkatel and Weschler, 1985b; May and Williams, 1985). The mixture of policy tasks among the federal, state, and local governments prevents an a priori answer to the question of which level should undertake what tasks. The different levels of government have different responsibilities and different devices to carry out their mandates. There is an increasing amount of attention by scholars focusing upon emergency management in an intergovernmental context (Mushkatel and Weschler, 1985a; May and Williams, 1985). What seems clear from this research is that, first, some form of shared governance is desirable, and, second, while the federal government cannot and should not dictate activities to other jurisdictions, it must take the lead in emergency management development (May and Williams, 1985; Williams, 1980a; Mushkatel and Weschler, 1985a).

While May and Williams' recent work on the shared governance framework in emergency management deals primarily with the implementation of policy, much of it may be generalized to the simplified policy process being utilized here. Shared functions indicate that at least one of the following conditions is being met:

1. In the policy formulation stage a significant amount of decision-making power "is exercised both by those in the federal government and those in state and local governments" (May and Williams, 1985:22).
2. Shared governance also may be said to exist when actors from different levels of government are invested with significant responsibilities in the administration and/or formulation of policy.
3. Where officials "of all governments exercise significant influence over the operations of a given program, it will be considered a form of sharing" (Grodzins, 1966:11).

There are different modes or forms of shared governance that may characterize the implementation of different policies. The primary point to be derived here is that the intergovernmental policy system is fragmented among the levels of government not only with regard to policy implementation but also in the other policy stages. Because of this fragmentation, governmental units must share responsibility in the development and implementation of hazards policy. No single level of government possesses the ability, resources, or authority to successfully develop and implement policy. Instead, governments must acknowledge their mutual interdependence if successful policy is to be formulated, adopted, and implemented in this area. This interdependence of governmental levels is not a characteristic that is idiosyncratic only to emergency management policy. This characteristic has led Mushkatel and Weschler (1985a) to describe the sharing as constituting an "intergovernmental policy" system.

One important implication of this interdependent system is that no single level of government can hierarchically control policy outcomes. That is, it is beyond the scope of any governmental actor to centrally dominate the policy system. While the federal government is certainly a powerful actor in emergency management policy, it cannot and does not implement all hazards policy. Hence, it will be seen that the actual implementation and formulation of evacuation plans is primarily a local function. Similarly, the development of building codes with seismic provisions is a state function, yet the implementation of these codes is the responsibility of local governments.

Before examining the current functions of these various levels of government a brief discussion of the role of citizens in this policy process is necessary. In some areas of emergency management policy, the role citizens play in policy formulation or implementation is probably not large. For example, some policies tend to be constituent policies; that is, developed by experts in the field and requiring technical expertise to be implemented (Olson and Nielson, 1982). Policies that establish lateral load levels for buildings in earthquake-prone areas or the establishment of standards relating to various toxic wastes tend to be constituent types of policies. Yet, other policies clearly require citizen input at the formulation stage and cooperation during the implementation stage. In large part those hazards policies in which an actual service is delivered to the public demand some degree of citizen participation for success. Evacuations are one such policy area.

The federal government through the Federal Emergency Management Agency (FEMA) has attempted to take the lead in emergency management policy. Just as the intergovernmental system is fragmented, so is the responsibility for emergency management divided among a multitude of federal agencies. Only recently, with the establishment of FEMA, has an effort been made to centralize the management and policy functions in one agency. This effort to centralize has several problems, however.

FEMA was created largely from Presidential Reorganization Plan Number 3 and implemented first through Executive Order 12127 of March 31, 1979, and later Executive Order 12148 of July 20, 1979. Prior to its creation, emergency management in the United States could be characterized as myriad agencies housed in a conglomeration of different departments and offices (Mushkatel and Weschler, 1985a; May, 1985). FEMA replaced several smaller agencies housed in different parts of the federal government as the lead agency responsible for disaster relief, preparedness, and civil defense. The reorganization following from the executive orders transferred several other responsibilities and functions from such federal agencies as the Department of Commerce (the National Fire Academy for Fire Prevention and Control), the Federal Insurance Administration (federal flood, riot, and crime insurance programs), the Office of Science and Technology (Federal Emergency Broadcast System oversight), and the Department of Defense (functions of the Defense Civil Preparedness Agency) to FEMA. As comprehensive as this reorganization appears at first glance, several important functions were still controlled by other agencies.

To name just a few of these functions, the Department of Agriculture, the Federal Highway Administration, and the Small Business Administration all retained some operational responsibilities in the event of a disaster (Giuffrida,

1983). In short, the reorganization clearly led to some centralization of the emergency management functions, but it was an incomplete effort. Several of the potential and real problems with this type of reorganization have been discussed elsewhere (Mushkatel and Weschler, 1985a).

A listing of the various responsibilities and activities that the federal government must address through FEMA and other agencies clearly establishes the magnitude of the challenge confronting this newly created agency. The federal government is the primary source of preparedness planning grants, personnel and administrative support funds, special services, research and technical information regarding hazards and emergency management, and long-range recovery resources for all types of disasters. In addition, it also sponsors research directed toward developing mitigation measures and is the major source of much preparedness information, research, and development. Finally, FEMA is the lead federal agency for implementing the Earthquake Hazard Reduction Act of 1977. Clearly, other federal agencies assist in carrying out these functions and observers have noted that FEMA probably does not possess the organizational resources to fulfill its mission (Mushkatel and Weschler, 1985a; May and Williams, 1985). In addition, it is clear that FEMA and other federal agencies invested with emergency management functions will by necessity need to rely upon other levels of government to succeed in meeting these charges.

How then has FEMA attempted to meet these responsibilities? In 1984 FEMA adopted an implementation strategy referred to as the Integrated Emergency Management System (IEMS) to meet these responsibilities and to improve hazard and disaster management (Drabek, 1985; McLoughlin, 1983; Giuffrida, 1983). There has been considerable confusion concerning IEMS and how it differs from the earlier Comprehensive Emergency Management (CEM) systems. Drabek (1985) made a very useful distinction between these two types of systems. CEM refers to the attempt to develop the capacity for handling all phases of activity—mitigation, preparedness, response, and recovery—in all types of disasters. It is a generalized approach to disaster management that attempts to identify common or generic functions in all disasters and manage them through the four phases. IEMS is the implementation strategy being used by FEMA to have all levels of government adopt this approach (Drabek, 1985; Mushkatel and Weschler, 1985a).

Some of the challenges confronting these approaches have been discussed elsewhere in depth, but the principal obstacles consist of the following:

localism, lack of standardization, unit diversity, and fragmentation (both vertical and horizontal), all inherent in the American system of government and culture (Drabek, 1985; Mushkatel and Weschler, 1985a). Our purpose is not to scrutinize the CEM or IEMS developed by FEMA. Rather, it is to link specific activities, especially mitigation and preparedness planning, to what specific levels of government are doing in these areas. This examination may best be accomplished by viewing the heart of the CEM and IEMS.

Central to both systems are the four analytically discrete but interconnected categories distinguished by time phases relative to disaster impact: mitigation, preparedness, response, and recovery. Mitigation activities are directed at eliminating the causes of disaster, significantly reducing the chances a disaster will occur, or reducing the losses to life and property in the event of a disaster. When possible the focus is upon elimination of threat-posing agents. In this sense, mitigation activities have been most effectively employed in connection with technological hazards, where, once the threat has been identified, it is sufficiently subject to human control that steps may be taken to minimize the probability of an incident. For example, one can minimize the risks associated with transportation of hazardous material by highway or rail by establishing public health and safety rules regarding the strength of construction of containers, maintaining safety checks on transport vehicles, routing vehicles through low density population areas, and timing shipments to coincide with low activity periods in urban areas.

Another type of mitigation strategy is to acknowledge the existence of a hazard and attempt to manipulate human use patterns in a way that minimizes the consequences of the impact. Land use management strategies that restrict residential construction in flood plains is a mitigation measure against riverine flooding. Building codes and other land use plans may be used to mitigate the effects of hurricanes, earthquakes, and other hazards.

All these mitigation activities have the common characteristic of being long-range measures; they are taken well in advance. Often these types of measures are either a response to a specific disaster and are aimed at hazard reduction or at minimizing the chance that an incident will become a disaster. Interestingly, in the history of federal attempts at emergency management in the United States, the smallest proportion of funds and resources has been traditionally devoted to mitigation activities. At least one recent work associates the rising interest in mitigation activities to the creation of FEMA (May and Williams, 1985). One reason for the rising interest in such activities may well be the creation of a lead federal agency in the context of budgetary constraints across all governmental levels. Because the federal government is the primary provider of dollars for disaster assistance, an important concern is the reduction of such costs.

Disaster preparedness activities, the second phase of emergency management, are closely related to mitigation. Preparedness activities are undertaken to protect human lives and propery in conjunction with threats that cannot be manipulated by mitigation measures or from which only partial protection can be achieved. Preparedness activities can be divided into two general categories: actions related to providing an alert that an impact is imminent, and actions designed to enhance the effectiveness of emergency operations. Preparedness measures related to providing an alert include the development and improvement of detection and prediction technologies that inform officials about the degree and immediacy of threats. Such technologies are present in riverine flood detection systems, radar detection and tracking of severe storms, and equipment designed to detect functional and coolant irregularities in nuclear power plants. In addition, warning systems that convey information about threats from authorities to the public—regarding, for example, tornadoes, tsunamis, hurricanes, and such—also fall into this category. Preparedness measures aimed at enhancing emergency operations include a variety of activities. These activities include routing plans for evacuations, stockpiling materials for shelters, assembling lists of resources and their location for possible use in responding to a given emergency, and training cadre and conducting drills or rehearsals of emergency plans.

Therefore, like mitigation measures, preparedness activities are conducted or undertaken in advance of any particular disaster event. They represent ways of protecting life and property when disasters do strike. Research has shown that preparedness activities historically also have received comparatively few resources relative to response and recovery. The general cycle is that there is a great deal of interest in preparedness issues immediately following a major disaster that declines significantly as time passes. Because considerable time is often required to translate concern with a hazard into budget allocations and implementable programs, mitigation and preparedness measures have received little emphasis. Using an integrated approach to emergency management, a concerted effort must be made to establish the importance of both mitigation and preparedness activities.

Emergency response activities are conducted during and just after the period of impact, and they focus upon assisting the affected public as well as minimizing damage from secondary or repeated impacts. Some of the more visible response activities include search and rescue, provision of emergency medical care, and the sheltering of evacuees and other victims. Operations also may be mounted to counter secondary threats, such as fighting urban fires in earthquakes, identifying contaminated water supplies and other public health threats in typhoons, identifying contaminated wildlife or fish in connection with a toxic chemical spill, or preparing for floods and mudflows in connection with a volcanic eruption.

Recovery activities begin shortly after disaster impact and may extend for long periods of time. The objective of recovery measures is to restore the physical parts of the community as well as the quality of life to at least the same levels as before the disaster and possibly to introduce improvements. Traditionally, recovery has been thought of in terms of short-range relief and rehabilitation measures and longer-range reconstruction measures. Relief and rehabilitation activities usually include clearing debris and restoring access to the impact area, getting affected business and industry back into operation, restoring government or community services, and developing a temporary system for caring for victims that includes housing, clothing, and food. Reconstruction activites tend to be dominated by the rebuilding of structures— buildings, roads, bridges, dams, and such—and by efforts to restore the area's economic system. Some communities also may treat the reconstruction phase as an opportunity to institute community plans for change that existed before the disaster or may even introduce mitigation measures into the rebuilding that would constitute an improvement upon the predisaster condition (Anderson, 1979).

In most cases, the bulk of the resources used in the recovery phase (particularly reconstruction) is derived from extra-community sources. In the United States, these resources are from private organizations and state governments, but the major contributor is the federal government. As Fritz (1957) has indicated, both in the United States and other countries most of the money and resources devoted to disaster management has been directed to the recovery phase and originates at the federal level.

From this discussion of the phases of emergency management several important points should be clear. First, the discussion has focused on what the desired outcomes of a successful IEMS would be. That is, if operating well, an IEMS would promote mitigation measures, preparedness activities, and capability for response and recovery. Second, and more important, these activities are somewhat time phased. Although the distinction is analytic, mitigation and preparedness measures take place in advance of any specific disaster impact, while response and recovery occur during and following impact activities. Thus, practical problems accompany the development of mitigation and preparedness activities because they usually must be done during so-called normal times, when a threat may not be salient. Historically, it has been difficult to engage in these sorts of activities and the thrust of FEMA toward greater emphasis upon such measures is long overdue. Third, it is clear from the specific examples of activities in each phase discussed above that no single unit or level of government has sufficient scope or resources to successfully manage all phases of disasters. Instead, some form of shared governance must occur. IEMS explicitly recognizes the interdependence of the levels of government in emergency management, yet the specific functions to be carried out by each governmental level are not clear. Certainly, some activities are well suited to federal agency leadership. The importance and cost of gaining technical information and establishing better prediction techniques require primarily a federal initiative. But in the formulation, adoption, implementation, and evaluation of hazards policy there must be a sharing of responsibilities.

The lack of specification of activities within the IEMS system for each level of government is not surprising and may in fact be a strength. The distribution of activities must be worked out over time through a process of bargaining and negotiation. Sensitivity to the political constraints that operate on these different units of government at each level must be considered. There is a myriad of case studies demonstrating what occurs when the federal government attempts to impose programs on state and local actors from above (Drabek, Mushkatel, and Kilijanek, 1983). To better understand the role of the different governmental levels in these activities and the emergency management policy system it is essential to determine what the actors are currently doing in emergency management. By determining their current activities we can see where shifts of responsibility might be worthwhile, where aid in the form of money or technical resources will pay dividends, and where proposals of reallocating responsibilities are likely to meet stiff resistance. It is to these other levels of government that our attention now turns.

State and local governments

States are located at a critical juncture in the federal system: between the federal government and the local governments (municipalities and counties). They are responsible for the health, safety, and welfare of their citizens (police power). Because of this critical location, and more important the police powers, states possess legislation mandates to engage in hazard management activities (May, 1985). Several aspects of state governments' role in emergency management are relevant here. First, states engage directly in hazards management activities, particularly for hazards with a potentially broad scope of impact. For example, threats associated with hurricanes, droughts, and volcanic eruptions affect multiple political jurisidictions (counties and cities); that is, the scope of many disasters is greater than any single local jurisdiction. To be optimally effective, hazard management must be undertaken by both localities and the state. The devices available for emergency management—particularly for mitigation and preparedness—are largely statutes and regulations. State governors also can intervene directly by using special emergency powers, usually applicable during response and recovery periods.

A second aspect of state governments' role in emergency management is coordination. The National Governors' Association recently has emphasized the importance of the state as a coordinator of interactions between the federal government and localities in managing disasters. With respect to all phases of emergency management, the state can be vital in linking localities with the appropriate federal resources. In addition, state governments have the primary responsibility for coordinating efforts within the state. State agencies may link localities for mutual aid agreements and may facilitate these agreements by fostering state laws that encourage their acceptance and formation. State governments may link localities with the private sector, especially during the response phase when there may be a need for special knowledge or equipment to manage disaster threats and consequences. Finally, many states have their own disaster assistance programs that complement federal programs.

Findings from several studies provide insight into the limits of state involvement in emergency management. State emergency services agencies are highly dependent upon federal monies for their staffing and programmatic needs (National Governors' Association, 1979:9). Including federal dollars, in 1979 no state emergency management budget was higher than $3 million and the average was between $400,000 and $600,000. Most important, the federal contribution (on the average) accounted for more than two-thirds of the state budgets for disaster management (National Governors' Association, 1979). This same study of forty-three states found that the median level of non–federally funded positions in state emergency management agencies was five. In addition, one in-depth study of eight states and another study of six states concluded that many states lacked the necessary communications, staffing, funding, and operating procedures to respond effectively to a major disaster. Additionally, state planning, training, and implementation capabilities were all evaluated as being too weak (National Governors' Association, 1979).

In short, the states, despite their occupying an important strategic position, have not had the capacity (or the funds and inclination to increase their capacity) to be a fully responsible partner in emergency management. Yet, there are some signs that this may not be the case under IEMS when federal money is forthcoming. In the central United States seven states have come together to form the Central United States Earthquake Consortium (CUSEC). Financed almost totally by the federal government, CUSEC has begun to formulate earthquake preparedness plans and examine some mitigation activities. In addition, the consortium has better relationships with many of the local governments than the federal agencies and seems to be involving local representatives in the formulation of policy. Similarly, the State of California's Seismic Safety Commission has been actively involved in preparedness and mitigation activities for several years. The California legislature has acted positively by increasing funding for these activities (Olson, 1985). Finally, with the Reagan administration's efforts to decentralize power back to state and local governments, it seems entirely possible that a greater role for the states is on the horizon. Certainly, state capacity building will be necessary if IEMS is to be successful.

Local governments are the crucial element in the formulation and implementation of emergency management policy. While states have the police power to make land use decisions and enact building codes, these powers are usually delegated through enabling legislation to the local governments. In addition, it is the local governments that serve as the primary implementer of local mitigation, preparedness, response, and recovery activities. Hazards policy formulation and implementation may be undertaken by either elected officials (city council members or county commissioners) or by appointed administrative officials (city or county managers or emergency service directors). Policy implementation efforts tend to be carried out by administrative or public safety departments at the local level. Despite the critical roles assigned to local governments in emergency management their performance to date has been spotty (Rossi, Wright, and Weber-Burdin, 1982). The reasons for this lack of a consistent record are structural (capacity) and inherent in some elements of the management process at the local level.

Local government has far more constraints placed upon its revenue production than either the federal or state governments. A study has recently reported that the mean amount of monies allocated by all cities for emergency management was just over $26,000 in 1982 (Hoetmer, 1983). This figure is a mean and obviously distorts the amount of money being spent because of the inclusion of very small cities in the figures. Yet, the mean for the largest cities was under $450,000. Furthermore, cities with populations between 100,000 and 250,000 were found to average expenditures just over $61,000 in 1982. Thus, local governments allocate a strikingly small amount of money for purposes of emergency management. In addition, a recent study by International City Management Association has demonstrated the tremendous diversity that exists at the local level in ways of organizing emergency management departments, functions, and operations (Hoetmer, 1983). Such diversity offers considerable difficulty not only to a federal agency attempting to coordinate local efforts across all disaster events but also to state government.

The lack of capacity and the diversity of local systems alone would be major problems for developing IEMS, but there are three characteristics of the local emergency management process that confound the difficulties. To successfully formulate, adopt, and implement hazard management a local government must (1) be aware a threat exists and consider it important relative to the issues; (2) believe that the threat is susceptible to management; and (3) develop or be presented with a politically and economically feasible policy that can be implemented to manage the hazard.

In practice, most local communities assign very low priority to comprehensive emergency management, although some communities may take an interest in one particular hazard. Rossi et al. (1982) surveyed state and local political influentials and found that problems associated with five natural hazards (flooding, fire, hurricanes, tornadoes, and earthquakes) were near the bottom in importance on a list of eighteen problems confronting state and local governments. While the Wright study has encountered major methodological criticism, it does suggest that in general natural hazards were not defined as serious or pressing problems when compared to other issues (Dra-bek, Mushkatel, and Kilijanek, 1983; Mushkatel and Nigg, 1985). Studies of specific hazards have produced similar findings regarding the lack of salience for hazards. For example, Wyner (1981:24) found that California commu-nities facing significant earthquake threats have engaged in relatively little earthquake hazard reduction planning.

In order to develop a natural hazards management program, both citizens and officials of a community must first be aware that the hazards exist and believe that a risk of significant negative consequences is posed. Numerous studies have reported that hazard or risk perception is a necessary (but not sufficient) step in obtaining risk management action (Burton, Kates, and White, 1978; Hewitt and Burton, 1971; Davenport and Waterstone, 1979). There are differences in how officials and individuals perceive risk, and these differences have implications for the nature of uncertainty, which is a defining characteristic of natural and man-made hazards and also often plays a major role in the definition of these different perceptions. Officials who have respon-sibility for public safety may take seriously a potential threat that could injure many community residents. Individual members of the public, however, might take such a threat much less seriously unless they perceived themselves to be among those people at direct risk (see Hultaker, 1977:14).

Furthermore, one may find situations where community members or sig-nificant interest groups believe that a hazard represents a great danger and they strive to place the issue on the local political agenda. Often, the members of the public who attempt to generate a political response to a hazard are experts in the area (for example, a civil engineer who understands the meaning of the five-hundred–year floodplain or a local professor who understands the impor-tance of building codes that require earthquake-resistant design). Grassroots pressure for community adoption of a given hazard management policy may also come from well-educated lay people who understand the nature of a hazard. Often such situations involve actions in what Louis refers to as con-stituent policy (Louis, 1979).

A second important requisite in hazards management policy formation is that local government officials believe that the hazard that is the object of public policy is susceptible to management. More succinctly, officials must believe that a hazard can be managed. In this context management may refer to any of a variety of activities, including preventing the hazard altogether (by developing strict mechanical standards for vehicles that transport hazardous materials and requiring breach-proof packaging for transported nuclear wastes) or adjusting human use patterns with respect to some hazard (by keeping homes and businesses out of floodplains or demanding strict building codes against earthquakes). It is essential, however, that there be some identifiable human or governmental action that can be undertaken to minimize the negative consequences associated with the hazard. Interestingly, when there is significant disagreement among technical experts regarding the extent of a threat, or its manageability or survivability, political bodies often hesitate to adopt positive hazard management postures. When technical experts provide no consistent guidance, the management of a hazard moves into a conflictual political arena and may be subject to the same kinds of forces as other political and social value questions (Drabek, Mushkatel, and Kilijanek, 1983). In the United States, the question of civil defense measures has taken on a political dimension in part due to disagreement among experts regarding the threat (Perry, 1982; Drabek, Mushkatel, and Kilijanek, 1983).

Finally, for a local government to act, an effective politically feasible program must be available. That is, one of the policy alternatives being considered must appear to be effective in managing the hazard. Such a policy must not run counter to established community or elite values, and it must be economically feasible. The importance of having an acceptable proposal upon which to act should not be underestimated. As Davies points out, "legislatures work almost exclusively as boards of review . . . what actually happens is that new ideas in the form of bill drafts come to legislators . . . [A bill is] accompanied by supporting advocacy which convinces legislators that the bill is sound and that they will not incur serious political vulnerabilities if they support it" (1975:2). This perspective is consistent with that of Atkisson and Petak, who argue that in spite of claims to the contrary, most governmental policy makers are not characterized as "pioneers in public problem identification and problem-solving activities, designers of legislation, or creators of a legislative political environment . . . [where] it becomes possible to enact or successfully oppose . . . any specific policy proposal" (1981:4). An important point, then, is that for a hazard policy to be politically feasible it must be presented to the legislature (local government) in a form that permits officials to act. Additionally, the policy must be in a form that minimizes political vulnerability and especially political and economic costs. Local officials can and do fine tune largely acceptable proposals into a fully acceptable form in light of the prevailing political climate.

In summary, there appear to be two primary avenues through which hazard management policies come before local government. First, local officials can, because of their broad public safety responsibilities, incorporate some elements of hazards management into their political agenda. Second, interest or constituent (professional) groups can lobby to have public officials address issues of hazard management. In practice, a combination of local officials, professional or client groups, and citizen interests interact to create or sustain a community hazards management policy. As Atkisson and Petak suggest in their discussion of impediments to community seismic safety if a particular issue is to be perceived as important by policy makers "some substantial segment of the community must become convinced that the problem exists" (1981:96).

With respect to community hazard management, administrative and public safety departments are primarily involved in policy implementation and only secondarily in policy formulation. Such departments may serve as identifiers of new threats or gaps in existing hazard management policy. These departments may also call on technical experts to advise them on some specific policy option. In the final analysis, however, administrative and public safety departments have responsibility for *interpreting* and *implementing* public policy relative to hazards management and these functions overshadow their role vis-à-vis policy formulation.

The administrative and public safety mission of these departments focuses upon action: mitigating against, preparing for, responding to, and recovering from acute environmental threats. The recognition of a potential danger is one motivating factor for each of these activities, since if no problem or potential risk is perceived, no action is likely to be taken. Administrators of other departments (such as public works) in a community, when involved in the hazards field, tend to be most concerned with planning and coordination in connection with disasters rather than immediate response, search and rescue, or other operational aspects of emergency management. This description of activities, of course, excludes those administrators such as police chiefs, fire chiefs, or emergency services officials who have public safety and emergency response as their primary responsibility. City managers and county administrators may have general oversight responsibilities for the functioning of their jurisdiction or for a particular area such as transportation, housing, or public works. It must be remembered, however, that the responsibilities of such officials are broad and numerous political priorities intervene to reduce the time that can be devoted to such concerns.

Administrators whose duties include land use planning, building regulation, public works, and utilities are likely to be concerned with mitigation and recovery matters. This role seems to be broadening, however, to include disaster preparedness. During a recent conference on earthquakes and related hazards, it was pointed out that "effective hazard reduction measures are critical for emergency preparedness . . . city planning directors, attorneys, and others will make as many of these decisions, likely more, than disaster directors" (Council of State Governments, 1979:45). Thus, through an emphasis on mitigation and post-disaster recovery, local administrators can have an indirect responsibility for emergency preparedness. When identifying recovery responsibilities of administrative officers, it is important that a linkage be made between recovery planning and comprehensive community planning. Rubin (1979:7) identifies several steps that are important to achieving successful recovery: (1) coordinating public and private participation in the planning process; (2) facilitating complex intergovernmental relations; and (3) capitalizing on existing federal programs to replace or improve capital stock and to provide programs and services for local residents. Hinojosa and Gelman (1977:34) have described the major planning and administrative tools (geologic studies and seismic risk matrix zoning) used in the recovery process.

In addition to mitigation and long-term recovery responsibilities, most public administrators also will play some role in the immediate response phase of a community emergency. Hence, although most administrators may prefer to leave the implementation of preparedness and response plans procedures to their public safety offices, in times of disaster they will play a major role in coordinating government efforts. As Kartez and Kelley point out, individual emergency plans "prepared by separate offices . . . are most likely to stem from some overall policy or emergency response philosophy encouraged by the jurisdiction's elected officials or chief executive officer" (1980:30). Certainly there are jurisdictions where, because of the strong personalities of individuals in some positions, independent planning efforts will take place. However, in most cases the administrative officer in a jurisdiction will have responsibility not only for overall preparedness and response, but also for mitigation and long-term recovery.

In the hazards management process, both administrators and staff of public safety departments have more direct responsibilities for preparedness and response than do other administrative departments. These public safety departments include fire departments, police departments, emergency medical services, and disaster preparedness offices. Depending on the type of disaster, organizational duties can range from immediate preparedness (warning, setting up roadblocks, sandbagging, evacuation) to immediate response (search and rescue, rubble clearing) and long-term recovery. Officials in disaster preparedness offices also may be required to develop parts of a community's mitigation program. Public safety–related departments also may have the task of developing preparedness plans prior to any disaster, but the overall direction of such efforts is usually determined by the jurisdiction's elected officials or chief executive officer.

The Coastal Area Planning and Development Commission in Brunswick, Georgia (1980:5) surveyed twenty-five coastal and Great Lakes states to determine where legal responsibility rested for disaster preparedness planning, response (evacuation order), and recovery. The study revealed that in most states (60 percent) the primary responsibility for planning resided with the highest locally elected official. Only 36 percent of the states assigned sole responsibility for this activity to the state emergency services agency. Furthermore, in 64 percent of the states, local governments were found to be primarily responsible for disaster planning (either solely or shared with other agencies). With regard to emergency response, 76 percent of the states assigned the authority to order evacuations to local governments. These findings emphasize that regardless of where the primary responsibility lies for developing the plans, "actual implementation will take place at the local level" (Coastal Area, 1980:6). Furthermore, if a governor or a local elected official orders an evacuation, neither of those officials would actually implement the evacuation.

Each agency responsible for public safety usually develops its own preparedness plan and set of procedures (Hildebrand, 1980). Such plans and procedures may reflect an overall community philosophy, but often these plans or procedures will be poorly referenced to each other, resulting in minimal coordination and great dependence on initiative taking in emergencies (see Wenger, Faupel, and James, 1980:154). In one community the following separate plans and procedures existed: the county disaster plan; a separate emergency plan for each school prepared by the principal; an overall school emergency procedure planning guide; a storm response manual for both gas and electricity prepared by the utility; planning procedures for the fire department; a police department emergency plan; a citywide post-disaster cleanup plan; a countywide post-disaster plan; an emergency medical services response plan; and an emergency plan for each of the military facilities in the area. Few of these plans are referenced or coordinated with each other (see Greene and Gori, 1982:10).

Our review of the local role in emergency management has been necessarily lengthy. As can be seen from the preceding discussion, the activities of local governments in emergency management policy are both diverse and rich. Yet, this description of local activities also should be placed in the context described earlier regarding the limited capacity of local governments and the low level of importance state and local influentials place on hazards policy. Within this context, the activities of local governments become even more impressive. How, then, will IEMS impact or be affected by the activities of state and local governments?

Clearly, the current system is characterized by a sharing of responsibilities and governance. The state role must be enhanced for purposes of coordination between the federal agencies and local governments. In addition, state governments must become more active in the formulation of policy rather than merely passing this function on to local units as in the case of land use planning mitigation activities. FEMA can assist state governments provided its own capacity is increased in the area of technical knowledge (May, 1985).

Local grovernments also need to have federal resources allocated for purposes of expanding their capacity to engage in hazard management. This assistance can take the form of more federal and state monies for mitigation and preparedness and planning. In addition, states can aid by providing expertise, facilitating and providing incentives for mutual aid agreements, and a variety of other activities. Local government must also be more responsible in its actions to its own constituents. This responsibility means bringing the issues associated with hazard management to public attention as well as the attention of key actors in the government. Too often citizens have not been viewed as a political resource by emergency managers. Citizen involvement can not only result in greater political support for emergency management, but also can be essential in the formulation and implementation of disaster policies.

Citizen participation in emergency planning

In connection with evacuation planning in particular, it has been argued that operational success is greatly enhanced by citizen participation (Perry and Nigg, 1985). In the context of our research in Denver, Mount Vernon, and Abilene, this assertion applies to both minority and majority citizens. To a certain extent, attempts at citizen involvement will reach both ethnic minority and majority groups without any special effort on the part of organizations seeking citizen participation. This participation will be most visible when minority and majority groups are of similar socioeconomic standing and share a common language.

In the United States, the more established minority groups such as blacks and Mexican-Americans are likely to be reached via the same kinds of citizen participation measures as are effective with majority citizens. The problem of citizen participation in the hazard management process, however, is relevant for all ethnic groups and for both natural and man-made hazards. For this reason, the discussion of citizen participation is bifurcated. The first section overviews the problem of citizen participation and describes general strategies and techniques for involving citizens in hazard management. This topic is important because nearly all hazard management efforts fail to adequately take account of the role of the public. The second section focuses on the problem of obtaining citizen involvement in hard to reach populations; these include recent ethnic minority immigrants, ethnic minority citizens whose language is not English, and special groups such as the physically handicapped.

Citizen involvement in hazard management

This section reviews general strategies to obtain citizen input in the evacuation planning process. Once again it is written from the perspective of a county of municipal director of emergency services. One premise underlying this work is that an evacuation plan must have a built-in capacity to respond to and incorporate feedback. Most planning guides stress the need for periodic review and updating of plans to accommodate changes in the emergency response system. An evacuation plan should be flexible enough to incorporate comments and suggestions that come from other officials or departments within the community as well as outside emergency management agencies. Yet, evacuation plans also need to be designed to encourage comments and feedback from the citizenry that can be accommodated and incorporated into the plan. Citizen participation may help to insure that a warning message effectively communicates with the population at risk. Citizens must understand what is expected of them under the plan and believe they have a shared interest with authorities to make the provisions of the plan work. Citizen participation in planning is a way of achieving this understanding and shared interest.

These benefits may be realized only if inputs from citizens can be obtained and integrated into the planning process. From a social psychological standpoint, asking citizens to participate in the planning process commits them to being part of the response process and encourages compliance with the evacuation effort. Yet, in virtually every case, the most effective way to obtain citizen participation is to actively seek it. Fostering citizen involvement requires emergency managers to assume a proactive posture vis-à-vis the community. Of course budget and staff limitations prescribe definite parameters on the extent to which a proactive role can be assumed. However, within this context there are a number of techniques for increasing citizen involvement. Some of these devices can be used with a minimum resource expenditure and others are substantially more costly.

There are three major objectives to citizen involvement in evacuation planning. The first is *information exchange,* where officials seek citizen feedback regarding specific procedures and policies while providing information to citizens regarding the rationale underlying official actions. *Educational contacts* encompass official efforts to familiarize citizens with the basic provisions of the evacuation plan. Finally, *support-building exchanges* emphasize enhancement of the credibility of the plan (and of the planners and response personnel) in the eyes of the public. There are several options that may be used to exchange information about local evacuation planning.

One of the first obstacles that must be overcome in informing the community about emergency evacuation plans is to effectively communicate to citizens that community officials are engaged in planning for emergencies. Sometimes this communication involves informing the public that a local department of emergency services exists. Unfortunately, most citizens rarely think about emergency services until a disaster strikes, and when it is over they rapidly forget (Wolensky and Miller, 1981). Hence, there is a need for periodic educational contacts with the community. Two techniques are well suited to this purpose: mailed brochures and mass media interviews. For a relatively low cost community officials can develop brochures (for example, on the need for hazards management in general or specifically describing an evacuation plan) that can be bulk mailed to the community. Such brochures have the advantage of being written information that citizens can retain for future use as well as reminders that the emergency services department is active.

In Valley, Nebraska the volunteer fire department developed a brightly colored brochure on five-by-seven-inch cardboard with space for emergency telephone numbers on top and the meaning of different warning messages on the bottom. The brochure was designed to be kept near a telephone, where it could easily be referenced in the event of a disaster (Perry, Lindell, and Greene, 1981:18–24). Brochures can be printed relatively inexpensively in large quantities and, after one mailed wave, they also can be distributed by hand in response to inquiries made by citizens. In San Bernardino County, California short brochures that cover general survial, desert survival, winter survivial, earthquakes, and floods are developed in conjunction with recurrent seasonal threats for direct distribution to citizens (Bethell, 1981). Furthermore, several federal agencies—the National Weather Service, Forest Service, U.S. Geological Survey, and the Federal Emergency Management Agency—routinely produce brochures on a variety of emergency topics. These brochures can be obtained by local officials (usually at low cost) and distributed to citizens by mail or by hand. Such mailings can be made on a periodic basis, perhaps quarterly, and can be designed to provide current information on emergency services activities and seasonal hazards.

In cases where limited budgets either preclude such activities or limit the number of mailings, emergency managers might obtain permission from state authorities to send relevant pamphlets with hunting and fishing licenses and boat and recreational vehicle registration renewals (Bethell, 1981). Also, arrangements can be made to have material printed in documents that are routinely available to the public. For example, the Skagit County (Washington) Department of Emergency Services has arranged with the local phone company to have a set of blue pages inserted in phone books (Sheahan, 1982). Although the precise content of these blue pages is yet to be determined, present plans include listing emergency phone numbers, brief instructions for reporting and responding to recurrent local threats, and perhaps locations of potential evacuation reception centers. This very innovative strategy achieves wide distribution at low cost. Furthermore, since the instructions are printed in a commonly used and retained public document, the likelihood of loss or misplacement is substantially reduced.

Another method of bringing information to a large segment of the public at low cost is through interviews of emergency services personnel in the local mass media or informational spots on public service programming. One means of insuring that such interviews occur in a timely fashion is to periodically contact local newspapers or weekly magazine feature editors with a seasonally appropriate suggestion for a story as well as some information on a given hazard: winter storms, summer/fall tornadoes, or spring floods (Sheahan, 1982). A similar approach can be used with local radio and television talk shows and news programs (Bethell, 1981). By approaching different radio stations and using different time slots, a creative emergency services official can reach many different segments of the community in a short period of time.

Both of these techniques have the advantage of reaching large audiences at moderate cost but the disadvantage of using essentially one-way communication. The emergency services official gets his or her message out, but except in rare circumstances the audience cannot respond. The following techniques involve the opportunity for two-way communication and rely principally upon existing personnel and equipment. The first technique is for emergency services staff to serve as listening posts and information disseminators in their own neighborhoods. This type of communication involves picking up and distributing (largely verbal) information at the grassroots level. The value of such exchanges, particularly over the long run, should not be underestimated.

A second technique for interacting with the public involves setting up a hazard information telephone number. This need not be any more elaborate than advertising an office phone number and training existing staff to handle inquiries. Citizens could be informed of the information line—perhaps via a mailed brochure—and staff could develop a procedure for promptly responding to questions. This type of phone-in arrangement is quite useful in that it serves to gather and disseminate information on a routine basis and has the potential to be expanded into a rumor control and/or warning confirmation line during times of disaster (Perry, 1979b:75).

There are potential limitations in using telephones to disseminate hazard relevant information or as a mechanism for rumor control during a time of emergency. In general, over the course of a year, one would not anticipate large volumes of calls involving citizen inquiries. Such non-emergency calls probably would not tax either the ability of staff to respond or the capability of telephone equipment to handle calls. However, if a telephone number is to be used during emergencies to disseminate information, officials even in small communities should anticipate the possibility of very large volumes of calls that could potentially overload telephone exchanges. Two strategies might be used to prevent or minimize difficulties associated with the high volume of calls. First, several phone numbers (in addition to an emergency services office, perhaps a fire department, police department, city manager's office, public works office, and/or social services office) could be used in an effort to distribute calls across numerous exchanges. This option demands that coordination between offices be maintained so that all citizens receive the same information from each office. Second, at some cost arrangements could be made for special telephone equipment to handle large numbers of calls with appropriate personnel to answer inquiries. In any case, if telephones are to be used either to disseminate information in general or during emergencies, adequate measures must be taken to insure that the system can be responsive to the needs or demands of the community. A system that quickly overloads or results in the simultaneous dissemination of conflicting messages in an emergency produces greater negative consequences than would likely be the case if no system existed.

A third technique for communicating with the public is to establish direct contact with citizens in the community. This communication is traditionally accomplished by speaking at neighborhood meetings, community organization meetings, and schools. Neighborhood meetings can deal with very specific and timely topics, they can reach otherwise difficult to contact groups, and they provide both face-to-face contact and the opportunity for dialogue. For example, a community or neighborhood organization might welcome a dialogue on how to prepare for a hurricane timed to coincide with the start of hurricane season. Detailed information could be provided residents on what to expect in their specific neighborhood, and evacuation routes and procedures could be discussed. A discussion of this specificity is not as feasible on a communitywide basis, although meetings at community organizations and schools are still very important in disseminating hazards information and emergency procedures. An important issue is to remember that neighborhood groups and community organizations tend to have fairly homogeneous memberships. In order to communicate with a significant portion of the community one must make contacts with a number of different types of groups.

Finally, a more direct type of citizen involvement can be achieved by creating citizen advisory committees and citizen cadre opportunities. Advisory committees are usually small in size and attached to departments, but they may be used for specific topics as well, including the problem of evacuation planning. The creation of an advisory committee represents a considerable commitment. At a minimum, regular meetings should be scheduled and officials must devise an acceptable mechanism for soliciting and evaluating information. This information must be either used or an explanation offered to explain why it was not utilized. The citizen advisory committee, if administered appropriately, can provide valuable, timely suggestions on specific points of planning interest and also serve a strong support-building function in the community.

While citizen advisory committees tend to involve people in the administrative aspects of evacuation planning, citizen cadre opportunities tend to involve volunteers in selected operational duties. Citizen cadres require some degree of training and usually function as auxiliary personnel who act in support of regular emergency personnel. Citizen cadres have functioned as sandbagging personnel in floods, as traffic direction officers, in search and rescue operations, to provide security in evacuated areas, and to help administer family locator services and other shelter services. The central idea in using citizen cadres is to incorporate people into the evacuation response process in a constructive way. Such auxiliary personnel can ease the tremendous demands placed on regular manpower during the operational phase of an evacuation. Furthermore, an appropriately trained volunteer represents a community member with a working knowledge of emergency procedures and the logic behind them. Such persons can serve as support builders vis-à-vis the larger community, explaining and justifying emergency procedures to others.

In summary, the general purpose of all these techniques is the same: to allow emergency authorities to better know their community and to familiarize citizens with emergency response planning and operations. Not all these techniques are appropriate in the same community. They have been elaborated to demonstrate the range of possible programs that can be selected relative to existing budgetary and other constraints. These alternatives may be adapted to the specific needs of a community.

Hard-to-reach population groups

In any community undertaking the dissemination of hazard information there is the problem that certain segments of the population are harder to reach than others. In the hazards management process these groups include the elderly, some ethnic minority groups (including the non–English speaking), the poor, and the handicapped (Andrews, 1982:108). The following discussion briefly summarizes why such groups, particularly ethnic minorities, are difficult to reach and makes several suggestions to overcome problems associated with both language and cultural differences.

The first step in designing an information program aimed at a particular subgroup is the identification of group members and their particular needs. In the case of ethnicity (as well as other identifiable subgroups) it is crucial to know the community. An emergency manager can obtain information about the ethnic makeup of the community in a variety of ways. Indeed, usually anyone who has lived in an area for a period of time is likely to be familiar with local ethnic groups and the location of any ethnic enclaves. Since people's perceptions and their contacts are influenced by their particular dwelling place and associations, however, it is advisable to supplement personal knowledge with systematically obtained data. This information can be gained by visiting places in the community such as churches, sporting events, and grocery stores that are frequented by different ethnic groups and by talking to community leaders. These interactions should provide information on particular problems of the community group that might be relevant to emergency planning, including language issues. Such information can also be supplemented with census data on ethnic makeup. Additional information can be obtained through conversations with local officials—for example, elected officials who represent minority interests and bankers and business people who might have particular knowledge of the minority communities. Such information might identify problems or issues that would be relevant to emergency management.

To the extent that non-English speakers tend to be either poor or members of recent immigrant groups, some knowledge of their presence in a community can be obtained by inquiring at departments that manage social services. In addition, many state governments issue city and county data books that report basic demographic information (age, sex, race/ethnicity, etc.) for large and moderate-size cities. Of course, these sources afford information on the makeup of the population but not the porportions of non-English speakers. Yet, data on the presence or concentration of large numbers of non-native English speakers can be gained that can serve as an alert to the possibility of language difficulties. The presence of non–English speaking people may be most quickly detected by seeking out informants in the community.

By enhancing his or her knowledge of a community's demographic structure in this fashion, an emergency manager can also become sensitive to the living patterns of relevant ethnic minority groups. For emergency planning it is important to know whether ethnic minority groups (and potential non-English speakers) are dispersed through the community or if they are concentrated in specific areas. Often it is likely that if there are sufficient non-English speakers to constitute a factor in emergency planning, they will be clustered in some type of ethnic enclave. For a large number of non-English speakers, to function unobtrusively in a community the presence of same-ethnicity bilinguals is necessary to serve as insulation from the majority population. In most cases, when ethnic groups are dispersed throughout a population, we can safely assume that they possess sufficient language skills (or access to bilinguals) to enable some interaction with other community members. For example, particularly among Mexican-Americans in the Southwest, we often find some members of an extended family household who are Spanish speaking only; the presence of other bilinguals in the extended family affords ample translators. Hence, in most circumstances, the presence of some dispersed non-English speakers in the community does not pose significant language difficulties for emergency response and planning activities. Indeed, the presence of dispersed non-English speakers would probably be difficult to detect using most conventional means of assessing the demographic structure of the community. Ready access to translators tends to allow such persons to remain relatively "invisible" as far as social and demographic records are concerned.

If a community structure reveals neighborhood clusters of ethnic minorities, there is a reasonable chance that if non-English speakers are present in significant numbers, they will reside in these clusters. The most efficient approach to assessing the approximate proportion of non-English speakers in any given ethnic/racial neighborhood grouping is to make initial contact with merchants in the area, particularly grocery stores and small shops. Such merchants often deal on a regular basis with nearby residents and can usually provide accurate information on language patterns, neighborhood leaders, and voluntary associations. This process of contact is important because the simple presence of ethnic enclaves is not always a signal of the presence of non-English speakers. The two general problems of language barriers and cultural differences are examined here because these factors are likely to affect dissemination strategies aimed at hard-to-reach groups. These problems are less likely to arise among older or more acculturated groups (except perhaps Native Americans) or among groups where socioeconomic status is at least similar to the majority population. Thus, the issues addressed below are important for recent immigrants and other minority groups who have either resisted acculturation or who have experienced sufficient prejudice and discrimination to preclude acculturation.

For non-English speakers, language constitutes an obvious limitation to involvement in the emergency planning process and tends to limit community participation, except within like-cultural groups. A language barrier also can present potentially serious problems during the response phase if individuals are unable or slow to understand emergency instructions. This situation may be further complicated if messages need to be translated, because problems can arise as a result of dialect variations within the same language group. In addition there may be numerous different language groups in the same community, necessitating several different translations and thereby slowing the process of dissemination and raising the question of consistency of messages. Furthermore, the logistics of timely multiple translations of a message are sufficiently complex to strain the administrative process in even the best organized department of emergency services.

If a community can support non-English newspapers, radio stations, or shops that carry non-English magazines and books, it is likely that at least some foreign language speakers in the area are not bilingual. Thus, once an area of non-English speakers has been identified, the problem becomes how to communicate emergency-relevant information. In some cases where a single language group is represented (for example, Spanish), a reasonably straightforward way of translating relevant materials can be developed. Both warning messages and planning information can be handled in this manner. When written translation is not feasible—because of multiple languages, or because the native language is not a written language, or because the target group might not be literate—some strategy of contact with the minority group must be used to impart information. In the process of contacting neighborhood leaders or organizations to assess the presence of non-English speakers, emergency managers should first establish contact with bilinguals. Through further contact and cooperation with these bilinguals, he or she can determine the most effective strategies for disseminating information to non-English speakers. In the case of emergency planning information, available alternatives may include joint participation of emergency services personnel with bilinguals in organizing a neighborhood meeting or an appearance at a neighborhood voluntary association meeting. Visual materials also can be very important in the process of communicating with people who are learning English.

Person-to-person communication or a network of such contacts can be used for developing the capacity for issuing a warning. Since warnings demand timely dissemination during an emergency period, emergency managers might arrange for a neighborhood warning relay system to effectively communicate a message among non-English speakers. Such an approach is similar in principle to telephone ring-down systems, which have been used in small communities for flood warnings (cf. Perry, Lindell, and Greene, 1981). The basis for this system is for authorities to communicate a warning message directly to selected citizens (in this case, bilinguals) who then each relay the message to the other citizens. Of course, the warning mode may vary—telephone or face-to-face contacts have been shown to work about equally well. By utilizing such a system, local authorities can promptly issue a warning largely without concern about language problems. To effectively maintain such systems requires periodic contacts with citizens' groups to be sure that roles are understood and that any citizens who drop out of the system are promptly replaced. In communities where such systems are used in connection with floods, for example, authorities routinely schedule one such contact just prior to the beginning of the flood season.

Another matter, related to the issue of language, is that some population groups may view natural hazards—and the emergency planning process—in fundamentally different ways from (majority group) community authorities, depending upon their cultural perspective (Wright and Phillips, 1980). A recent study of perceptions of earthquake threat in California found that ethnic minority group identification influenced the way people understood and responded to the threat (Turner et al., 1980). Specifically, Nigg (1982:82–83) reports that Anglos, blacks, and Mexican-Americans differed substantially with regard to (1) levels of fear and concern about future earthquakes, (2) fatalistic attitudes regarding the importance of preparedness, (3) knowledge about the accuracy of earthquake predictions, (4) faith in the efficacy of science and the government, (5) information seeking regarding earthquake threat, (6) levels of personal preparedness, and (7) awareness of specific endangering conditions. One would expect that these cultural differences might also be pronounced among recent immigrant groups, such as refugees from Southeast Asia.

Another aspect of cultural differences is that some minority group members perceive authority figures—particularly uniformed government representatives—differently from majority group members. Among members of some urban ethnic/racial minority groups in the United States, public safety personnel, particularly police, are not necessarily viewed in positive terms or as sources from whom to expect help and protection.

With regard to these kinds of cultural differences emergency managers are faced with the problem that these citizens doubt the efficacy of emergency preparedness activities. In addition, they may disagree with the nature of the actions that should afford protection from the threat, and might be reticent to deal with authorities. Such difficulties may be approached in part as communications problems with people unaccustomed to the English language. Thus, emergency managers are faced with the task of educating people about the role of authorities in emergency response and enhancing basic knowledge of environmental hazards. While the process of changing this situation is inevitably slow due to the nature of the embeddedness of culturally founded beliefs, it can be approached by using essentially the same strategies utilized in information campaigns described in connection with language difficulties.

6 Retrospect: ethnic differentials in disaster behavior

The purpose of this chapter is to summarize the general findings from our analyses of ethnic differentials in warning response and disaster preparedness behavior. The structure of the chapter reflects the topical structure of the book and consequently focuses upon three issue areas. The first section deals with disaster warning processes, examining the sources of first warning, how such warnings are interpreted, and citizens' behavior following initial warning receipt. The second part of the chapter focuses on social processes that occur after warning receipt: warning confirmation, warning compliance, and post-warning evacuation responses. The last section reviews the problem of citizen involvement in emergency preparedness planning and reiterates findings pertaining to evacuation compliance, reasons for undertaking protective actions, sources of information about environmental hazards, and desired modes of participation in the emergency management process.

Disaster warning processes

We have argued that disaster warning message dissemination is itself a social process that triggers other social processes. Much of our initial work focused upon the first warning message received: the sources from which it came, citizens' perceptions of the reliability of these sources, the content of the message, and citizens' first responses after hearing the initial warning message.

Warning source

In connection with the Abilene flood, the three ethnic groups were initially warned by different sources. More than half of the blacks were first warned by an authority; slightly more than one-fourth were initially warned via mass media, and only two respondents were warned by relatives or friends. On the other hand, more than 60 percent of whites first heard of the flood threat through the mass media; relatives or friends were the second most frequently cited source and these were first warned by authorities. Mexican-American respondents were split almost equally between mass media and relatives and friends; about 10 percent reported being first warned by authorities.

Because of the progressive nature of the warning process in Abilene (the areas with highest proportions of minority citizens were threatened first and thus warned first by the authorities), minority citizens had a slightly greater opportunity to be warned by authorities than did whites. The authorities used door-to-door contacts in issuing warnings and progressed through the danger areas, thereby creating sequential lag wherein heavily minority areas were warned early in the process and heavily white areas were warned later. However, at the same time authorities began issuing warnings, mass media began broadcasting warning bulletins, so all citizens tuned to the mass media had an equal chance of hearing an initial warning message via this source. Dependence upon the media for first warning was highest among whites and Mexican-Americans, where approximately half of the respondents in each ethnic group were first warned by radio or television.

To receive a first message from relatives or friends requires a two-step process. First, the relative or friend must receive a warning or some information about the environmental threat. Then, that warning recipient must contact another person and relay the message. Consequently, in our samples the proportion of persons warned by relatives or friends serves as an index of the level of social network activity among warning recipients. In Abilene, this social networking behavior was highest among Mexican-Americans, suggesting that kinship and friendship contacts serve as important channels for information exchange. Considerably fewer whites—who had an equal opportunity for such networking—and blacks—with a somewhat reduced opportunity—used those channels to disseminate threat information.

In Mount Vernon, the two ethnic groups were residentally interspersed and consequently each group had an approximately equal chance to receive first warning from any of the three sources. White warning recipients were about equally split between an authority as first source and relatives or friends. A relatively smaller proportion of whites cited the mass media as initial warning source. The most frequent source of first warning among Mexican-Americans was relatives or friends, followed by the mass media and authorities. It is interesting to note that in Mount Vernon the majority of each ethnic group reported relatives or friends as first warning source. This relatively high level of networking among both ethnic groups is probably related to the characteristics of the community and the type of environmental threat involved. The Abilene flood represented a familiar, slow-developing threat in a small town setting with a history of similar threats. Under those circumstances we found that Mexican-Americans relied to a greater extent on social networks than either whites or blacks. This finding is consistent with the results of other flood-threatened communities with similar characteristics (cf. Perry, Lindell, and Greene, 1981; Perry and Mushkatel, 1984). Mount Vernon is also a semi-rural community facing a technological threat that had been recently faced by neighboring communities. Two factors distinguished the Mount Vernon case from Abilene: (1) the precise nature of the threat—a derailed tank car carrying liquid propane—was unfamiliar to warning recipients, and (2) the onset of the threat was rapid and unexpected by the public and the time available for citizens to comply with the warning was short. One would expect Mexican-Americans in Mount Vernon to engage in a relatively high level of networking contacts because kin and friendship networks are commonly used channels of information exchange during non-emergency times (Moore, 1976:102–113; Alvirez and Bean, 1976). Under the circumstances described above, however, the level of social network contacts among whites also increases (in Mount Vernon) to levels approximating those of minority citizens.

The patterns of first warning source among Denver respondents approximate those seen in the Mount Vernon data. Among blacks about half of the respondents were first warned by relatives or friends, another one-third by an authority, and about 20 percent via the mass media. A rank ordering of first warning sources for whites duplicates the order for blacks: relatives or friends, authorities, and mass media. The majority of Mexican-Americans—nearly three-fourths—were warned by relatives or friends, with much smaller but equal proportions citing an authority and the mass media. It is interesting to note that the proportions of blacks and whites first warned via mass media are virtually identical, with an only slightly smaller proportion of Mexican-Americans citing radio or television as first warning source. Consequently, in Denver the mass media were cited as initial warning source less often than authorities and relatives or friends by all three ethnic groups and by similar proportions of respondents within each ethnic group. Blacks received an initial warning message from authorities more often than whites, who in turn cited this source more often than Mexican-Americans. Finally, the greatest proportion of Denver respondents in each ethnic group cited relatives or friends as their first warning source. Furthermore, a considerably larger proportion of Mexican-Americans than whites or blacks were initially warned by relatives or friends.

An examination of the data on citizens of different ethnicity warned first by relatives or friends shows several general patterns across the three communities. First, a greater proportion of Mexican-Americans were first warned via social networks in Denver than in either Mount Vernon or Abilene. Second, the proportion of whites first warned by relatives or friends increases substantially as we move from Abilene to Mount Vernon and increases moderately when we move from Mount Vernon to Denver. Third, the proportion of blacks first warned via social networks increases substantially from Abilene to Denver. Fourth, the proportion of whites warned by relatives and friends in Denver is similar to the proportion of blacks first warned by the same source in Denver.

From these empirical patterns, by taking into account characteristics of the disaster threat, we can draw three general inferences about the use of social networks to relay warning information by different ethnic groups. First, Mexican-Americans tend to rely upon social networks to relay warning information to a greater extent than blacks or whites. This assertion is consistent with our data on the Abilene flood and seems to hold true generally when the threat agent is familiar to the public and characterized by gradual onset and when the community involved is semi-rural or a small town (cf. Perry, Lindell, and Greene, 1981; Perry, 1983; Perry and Greene, 1982a). Second, when response time is relatively short and the public is unfamiliar with the nature of the threat agent, the proportion of whites who relay warning information via social networks increases, while the proportion of Mexican-Americans (who normally have a higher base rate for such exchanges) stays about the same. This interpretation is supported in our data when the proportions of citizens first warned by friends or relatives are compared between Abilene and Mount Vernon, where the principal structural differences between events relate to response time and threat agent. Finally, communication of warning information via social networks is highest among all three ethnic groups when the threat agent is unfamiliar, response time is short, environmental cues of pending danger are present, and the endangered area is urban. Furthermore, the increase in levels of warning information exchange among Mexican-Americans is likely to be greater than that observed among blacks and whites.

In all cases, the frequency of social network contacts was higher among Mexican-Americans than among either blacks or whites. Also, the increase in proportion of network contacts among Mexican-Americans is higher than among blacks and whites as we compare the Abilene threat with those in Mount Vernon and Denver. Other warning response data also support the thesis that when the public is unfamiliar with the threat (Perry and Mushkatel, 1984) and when environmental cues representing danger are present (Perry, 1985; Perry, Lindell, and Greene, 1981; Gruntfest, Downing, and White, 1978), warning recipients tend to accelerate the extent to which they seek information regarding the threat and also tend to comply more readily with officially recommended protective measures. Our data suggest that urban-dwelling citizens, particularly Mexican-Americans, engage in higher levels of warning information exchange than do those who live in semi-rural or small town settings. This finding must be interpreted cautiously, however, because of the paucity of rural-urban warning response comparisons available in the empirical literature (Drabek, 1983).

Warning source credibility

Respondent assessments of the relative credibility or reliability of first warning sources varied both by ethnicity and the type of environmental threat. Most citizens first warned by an authority rated the source as highly reliable. With one exception, this claim holds true across all three ethnic groups and all three disaster events. All Mexican-Americans warned by authorities of the

Abilene flood and the Denver nitric acid spill and nearly 90 percent of those in the Mount Vernon propane gas threat rated this source as highly reliable. Among whites, nearly all of the respondents in Abilene, Mount Vernon, and Denver rated authorities as highly reliable. In Denver, almost all of black warning recipients also rated authorities as a highly reliable source. The only exception is to be found among black flood warning recipients, where only slightly more than half rated authorities as a highly reliable source. In Abilene, blacks warned by an authority were highly polarized; the respondents rated this source as either highly reliable or sometimes not reliable. No compelling explanation readily suggests itself to account for the lower confidence ratings by blacks in Abilene. Mexican-Americans and whites show similar proportions across all three sites and blacks in Denver were similar to whites and Mexican-Americans. It appears likely that situational factors specific to blacks warned in Abilene (perhaps a neighborhood antipathy regarding police) account for the lower ratings of authorities among this ethnic group.

When the mass media were the initial warning source, consistently smaller proportions of blacks and whites rated them as highly reliable than was the case when an authority was the first source. Approximately one-half of the whites first warned by the mass media in all three sites rated the source as highly reliable. Approximately half of the black warning recipients in Abilene and in Denver rated mass media as highly reliable. Compared with the other two ethnic groups, significantly higher proportions of Mexican-Americans in all three threat settings rated mass media as highly reliable. Thus, while blacks and whites were less confident of the mass media, Mexican-Americans rated this source as highly reliable across types of disaster threat and across community settings. Records of interviewer debriefings show that Mexican-American respondents tended to listen to Spanish language radio broadcasts and expressed the belief that both English and Spanish radio and television broadcasts content was governed by standards that would forbid airing false statements about a pending disaster. Moore (1976:96–100) has commented on the role of communication within the Mexican-American community, indicating the importance of institutions such as Spanish radio broadcasts as representing ethnic community solidarity, to be distinguished from communication links dependent upon the Anglo community. Given this ethos, the higher proportions of Mexican-Americans describing the mass media as a highly reliable first warning source are readily interpretable.

Therefore, in terms of issuing disaster warnings to Mexican-Americans, the mass media—particularly Spanish language broadcasts—are apt to be treated as reliable sources. This is not the case with blacks and whites; both ethnic groups tended to be skeptical of mass media warnings. A predominant objection raised by whites regarding media warnings was that "they are always looking for a story—they make everything sound bad so you never know what's really happening." Black respondents expressed reservations about media consistent with a variety of research on the behavior of black Americans: mass media tend to be controlled by the white majority and rarely deal with issues relevant to blacks or to the preservation of a black community (Altshuler, 1970:66–69; Staples, 1976:38–39).

The reliability ratings given relatives and friends as a first warning source show some differences by ethnicity and disaster events. In Abilene, a small town confronted by a familiar flood threat, all of the minority citizens first warned by relatives or friends rated this source as highly reliable. Comparatively, only about half the whites rated relatives and friends as highly reliable. This pattern is compatible with what one would expect based upon the race relations literature (cf. Jackson, 1973:437; Staples, 1976; Grebler, Moore, and Guzman, 1970:350–378). That is, minority citizens are more likely to attribute higher levels of credibility to same ethnicity contacts from kin and friendship networks than white citizens. An important qualifier here is that we are dealing with a familiar threat in a small town setting.

The data from Mount Vernon allow us to examine credibility attributions of whites and Mexican-Americans also in a small town but in response to an unfamiliar environmental threat. In this setting, the proportions of whites and Mexican-Americans ranking relatives or friends as highly reliable are very low. In Mount Vernon the danger about which citizens were warned was a *potential* propane gas containment breach—an unfamiliar threat, accompanied by no visible environmental cues, thereby making it difficult for citizens to evaluate it. In similar situations, citizens have tended to place less confidence in social network contacts, who have the same faculties for threat evaluation as the warning recipients, and greater confidence in warnings from authorities, who are presumed to have access to specialized threat information (cf. Perry, 1985; Perry and Mushkatel, 1984). The Mount Vernon data show this same pattern and demonstrate that the argument applies to at least two ethnic groups: whites and Mexican-Americans.

The Denver data add still another dimension to understanding the credibility of relatives or friends as warning sources. Two features distinguish the Denver disaster from those in Abilene and Mount Vernon: the nitric acid produced numerous visible cues that something was amiss and warning recipients lived in a large urban area. In this setting, almost all blacks, whites, and Mexican-Americans first warned by a relative or friend described that source as highly reliable. It can be argued that the attribution of credibility to relatives or friends is a function of two primary factors. First, even though citizens were unfamiliar and inexperienced with nitric acid threats, visible cues (fire, odor, vapor cloud, and presence of police, fire, and emergency services personnel and vehicles) definitely established the existence of danger. Second, because the urban setting was characterized by multiple opportunities for citizens to obtain threat-relevant information, warning recipients could reasonably assume that relatives or friends delivering a warning message possessed some special information, perhaps as a function of being warned themselves by authorities at an earlier time, simply collecting information from other sources, or by having observed the threat itself. Under these specific conditions, it became plausible for citizens, regardless of ethnicity, to view a relative or friend from whom first warning was just received as a highly reliable source.

In summary, six general conclusions may be drawn regarding attributions of credibility to authorities, mass media, and relatives or friends as first warning sources. First, warning recipients tend to regard authorities (police, fire fighters, uniformed emergency personnel) as highly reliable warning sources; this conclusion holds across all three types of disaster events for blacks, whites, and Mexican-Americans. Second, blacks and whites viewed the mass media as less reliable warning sources in all three disaster events. Third, Mexican-Americans rated the mass media as highly reliable warning sources across all three sites. Fourth, when the threat involved is familiar to the public and the setting is semi-rural or a small town, minority citizens are more likely than whites to regard relatives or friends as reliable first warning sources. Fifth, when the setting is a small town but the threat is unfamiliar, both minority and white warning recipients tend to define relatives or friends as less reliable warning sources. Finally, when the threat is unfamiliar but accompanied by visible environmental cues and the setting is urban, blacks, whites, and Mexican-Americans regard relatives or friends as credible warning sources.

Message content

Our analyses of the specificity of initial warning message content relative to the source yielded three general conclusions. First, across all three disaster events and all three ethnic groups, citizens first warned by an authority were most likely to hear the most specific warning message. Second, in small town or semi-rural settings where forewarning is short, citizens of all ethnic groups warned via mass media were more likely to hear specific messages than those warned by relatives or friends. Third, when forewarning is short but the population warned is urbanized, the proportion of all ethnic groups warned via mass media is smaller, and those warned through relatives or friends are more likely to hear specific warning messages.

It was also found that as warning content becomes more specific, citizens' initial warning belief and perception of personal risk increase. Thus, warning content is an important tool through which emergency managers may influence warning belief and personal risk assessments. This task is important because it is known that ultimately warning belief and risk assessment are correlated with the extent to which citizens comply with the suggested protective measures in disaster warnings. Because of the small numbers of cases involved, however, caution was urged in generalizing the results of the analyses of warning content.

Past experience

We also examined the impact of past disaster experience upon citizens' first assessments of warning belief and personal risk. Three conclusions were drawn regarding the relationship between disaster experience and warning belief. When confronted with a familiar threat, whites with prior disaster experience exhibit higher levels of warning belief, while experience has no effect on warning belief among minority group warning recipients. Second, when whites are faced with an unfamiliar threat accompanied by visual cues allowing them to link the otherwise unfamiliar threat to other disaster experiences, prior experience is strongly correlated with high levels of warning belief. Third, when faced with an unfamiliar threat that is *not* accompanied by visual cues, prior disaster experience is not related to warning belief among either whites or Mexican-Americans. Finally, based on comparisons across three different warning settings, prior experience is uncorrelated with level of warning belief among Mexican-Americans.

Our analyses of the correlation of past experience with personal risk indicate that across all three ethnic groups prior disaster experiences have no impact on initial risk assessment when the threat involved is familiar to warning recipients. The correlation between prior experience and perceived risk is more equivocal when dealing with less familiar threats. When the threat is unfamiliar and no visual cues are present, whites with prior experience do assess risk higher than those without experience. Under these same conditions, Mexican-Americans with experience also perceive risk as slightly higher than those lacking experience.

Similarly, when visual cues accompany an unfamiliar threat, whites and Mexican-Americans reporting prior experience again define personal risk to be slightly higher than their counterparts without experience. Unfortunately, except for the Mount Vernon whites, the magnitude of the relationship between disaster experience and perceived risk is relatively low. Thus, the most appropriate interpretation of these data is to note the differences between the Abilene data and the other two disaster settings and suggest that further studies of experience and risk assessment in response to unfamiliar threats is necessary to clarify the question of how the two variables are interrelated (if at all) in these settings.

Initial warning response

Our last series of analyses explore the extent to which citizens' first actions after hearing a warning are determined by their initial assessments of warning belief and personal risk. This first action or first warning response is of particular interest because it marks a decision point that profoundly affects the speed with which an individual evaluates warning messages and consequently arrives at a final decision regarding warning compliance. The relationship between initial warning belief and first response can be summarized by elaborating seven general conclusions. First, across all three disaster settings, Mexican-Americans were more likely to engage in family-oriented actions (at both levels of warning belief) than blacks or whites. Second, across all disaster settings, there is a strong positive relationship between increasing levels of warning belief and the probability of undertaking a protective action among whites and blacks; this relationship does not hold for Mexican-Americans. Third, both whites and Mexican-Americans are less likely to do nothing as an initial warning response when the threat agent is unfamiliar and no visible cues are present than is the case when the threat is familiar or unfamiliar but accompanied by visible cues. Fourth, in settings where the threat is familiar or unfamiliar with visible cues, whites are less likely to engage in family-oriented actions than when confronted by an unfamiliar threat with no visible cues. Mexican-Americans undertake relatively more warning confirmation actions when responding to first warning of an unfamiliar threat not accompanied by visual cues than is the case with either a familiar threat or an unfamiliar one with visual cues. Sixth, blacks are more likely to engage in family-oriented activities when the threat is unfamiliar (even when accompanied by visible cues) than when the threat is familiar. Finally, Mexican-Americans engage in warning confirmation behaviors less frequently in response to familiar or unfamiliar threats with cues than when facing unfamiliar threats lacking visible cues.

In general, among all ethnic groups and in all three research sites, there is a positive relationship between increased levels of perceived personal risk and the probability of undertaking a protective action as a first warning response. This correlation is weakest, however, among Mexican-Americans; across all three warning settings there is a strong tendency for these citizens to initially engage in family-oriented activities.

Social processes following warning receipt

When a warning message is delivered to a threatened population, citizens begin a process of information gathering. That is, they attempt to confirm the elements of the warning message with some collection of sources thought to be knowledgeable. In this way, citizens arrive at a personal definition of the situation as either threatening or nonthreatening. Our analyses of the types of confirmation sources first contacted by warning recipients can be summarized in the form of three general conclusions. First, in all three settings, most whites trying to confirm a warning message first contacted the mass media. Furthermore, whites used relatives or friends as a first confirmation source more often in familiar threats than in unfamiliar threats whether visible disaster cues were present or not. These patterns do not change as we move across the rural-urban continuum. Second, the greatest proportions of Mexican-Americans use mass media as a first confirmation source in familiar threats or unfamiliar threats accompanied by visible environmental cues. A rural-urban differential also exists among Mexican-Americans in that those living in less urban areas (whether the threat is familiar or unfamiliar) use relatives or friends as a first confirmation source less frequently than those living in ur-banized areas. Finally, blacks are more likely to first contact a relative or friend to confirm a warning in rural settings than in an urban area, where mass media are more likely to be used as a first confirmation source.

One important index of citizens' perceived reliability of the first source contacted for confirmation is the number of additional sources subsequently contacted for further information. In this case, the concept of source reliability is also bound up with the idea of consistency of message content. That is, the more reliable the first source is believed to be and the more consistent subse-quent messages are with the first, the lower the number of additional sources contacted. Our data showed that although comparatively few citizens chose authorities as a first confirmation source, those who did—across all three sites and among blacks, whites, and Mexican-Americans—tended to contact a minimum number of additional sources. This suggests that when a message warning of an environmental danger is confirmed by an authority, citizens feel confident enough about the reliability of the message to abbreviate the infor-mation-seeking process regarding the threat. This finding has important im-plications for the design of warning systems. The less time citizens spend in the confirmation or information-seeking process, the shorter the elapsed time between initial warning receipt and the time individuals make a decision to comply with (or reject) the warning message. Furthermore, the shorter this elapsed time, the faster the process of warning response will be, and conse-quently the period of time citizens are exposed to danger is reduced. Since first confirmation of a warning message with authorities is correlated with a reduction in the number of additional sources contacted, thereby reducing total warning response time, measures aimed at enhancing the likelihood of official confirmation can produce shorter warning response times.

Among citizens who contacted mass media as a first confirmation source there are differentials in the number of additional sources contacted both by ethnicity and between disaster events. Minority citizens seek more additional warning confirmation sources than whites where the disaster agent is familiar and the setting is a small town. In response to the Abilene flood, the largest proportions of blacks and Mexican-Americans who first confirmed the warning via mass media sought three or more additional sources. The majority of Abilene whites whose first confirmation source was the mass media followed up by contacting only one or two additional sources.

In general, citizens who first confirmed a warning about an unfamiliar threat (with or without visible cues) via mass media were less likely to seek additional confirmation sources than when the warning setting involved a familiar threat. In Mount Vernon, most whites and Mexican-Americans using mass media as a source for initial confirmation sought further information from only one or two additional sources. In Denver, only one or two additional sources were contacted by almost all of the blacks and about half of the whites and Mexican-Americans. Thus, in a rural setting where the threat is unfamiliar and not accompanied by environmental cues, both whites and Mexican-Americans who first confirmed a warning message with mass media tended to contact relatively fewer additional sources. However, when confronted by an unfamiliar threat accompanied by cues in an urban setting, minority citizens tended to accept first confirmation by mass media and seek fewer additional confirmation sources than their white counterparts.

These findings emphasize the importance of the mass media as a warning confirmation source in dealing with disaster threats that are largely unfamiliar to the public at risk. Emergency managers can potentially reduce citizen warning response time in unfamiliar threat situations by insuring that, as part of the warning dissemination process, local mass media also receive detailed warning information. This increases the chance that citizens who do use mass media as first confirmation sources will hear a warning compatible with the official message.

Familiarity with threat

Our data also showed that, in general, warning recipients in all three ethnic groups seeking first confirmation from relatives or friends tend to contact more additional sources when the threat is familiar than when it is unfamiliar. In fact, relatives or friends are rarely used as a first confirmation source by any ethnic group when the threat is unfamiliar. When relatives and friends are used as first confirmation sources in familiar threats, minority citizens are more likely to seek larger numbers of additional sources than whites.

Finally, in examining the warning confirmation process, we reviewed the range of confirmation sources contacted by warning recipients. The results of these analyses may be summarized as four propositional statements. In response to familiar threats, blacks, whites, and Mexican-Americans engaged in warning confirmation with multiple sources contact the mass media most frequently, followed by relatives and friends. When dealing with an unfamiliar threat (in either an urban or rural setting), Mexican-Americans also use mass media and relatives or friends most frequently when contacting sources for warning confirmation. In connection with an unfamiliar threat in an urban area, blacks and whites most frequently contact authorities and mass media as warning confirmation sources. Finally, faced with an unfamiliar threat in a rural or small town setting, whites also confirm warnings most often with authorities, but relatives or friends displace the mass media in this setting as the second most frequently contacted confirmation source.

Warning belief and personal risk

We have argued that citizens make final decisions regarding warning compliance on the basis of information obtained during the warning confirmation process. It is during this process that warning recipients revise their initial assessments of warning belief and personal risk and, based upon these latter two variables, make the decision of whether to comply with (or ignore) an evacuation warning. Our data on the Abilene flood showed that across all three ethnic groups, as level of warning belief increases, so does the probability of evacuation (that is, warning compliance). The positive correlation between level of warning belief and probability of evacuation also held for blacks, whites, and Mexican-Americans in Mount Vernon and Denver. Three qualifications were offered, however, regarding warning belief in connection with the two relatively unfamiliar threat agents and the more familiar flood threat in Abilene. First, proportionately fewer citizens in all three ethnic groups developed a low warning belief in the two unfamiliar threats than was the case in Abilene. Second, among those citizens with low warning belief, greater proportions *evacuated anyway* when the threat was unfamiliar than when the threat was familiar. Finally, even greater proportions of citizens with high warning belief evacuated in unfamiliar threats than in the flood threat. Thus, in general—and across all three ethnic groups—fewer citizens developed a low warning belief and more complied with the target warning response at both levels of warning belief when faced with an unfamiliar threat than when the threat was familiar.

There are distinct differences in risk perception and warning response behaviors between the familiar flood threat and the less familiar hazardous materials threats in Mount Vernon and Denver. The important common pattern in the two types of warning settings is that among blacks, whites, and Mexican-Americans, as perceived risk increases from low to high, the proportion of citizens who evacuate increases. However, the magnitude of the correlation between risk and warning compliance is much greater in the unfamiliar threat settings (Mount Vernon and Denver) than when a more familiar threat was involved. In fact, with the exception of two high-risk Mexican-Americans in Mount Vernon (representing 1.6 percent of the total), all respondents in the two unfamiliar threats who perceived risk as high complied with the evacuation warnings. Furthermore, even among citizens who believed personal risk was low, those responding to a warning that involved an unfamiliar threat were more likely to evacuate than those faced with a comparatively familiar flood threat.

Part of the over-representation of evacuees among citizens defining risk as low in Mount Vernon and Denver may be an empirical artifact. It is known that citizens faced with an unfamiliar threat are less able to identify a range of different protective measures than those facing more familiar threats, particularly floods (Perry and Mushkatel, 1984:231). Consequently, citizens facing unfamiliar threats may have relatively fewer protective options to choose among than people confronted with a more familiar environmental danger. Under these conditions we would expect citizens to undertake officially recommended warning responses (in these data, evacuation) in greater proportions as a default means of reducing the likely negative consequences of disaster impact. Our data on citizens who perceive personal risk to be low supported this interpretation.

In summarizing our analyses of the relationships of warning belief and perceived risk with warning compliance, the most striking finding is the absence of differentials by ethnic group membership. Thus, among blacks, whites, and Mexican-Americans, as the levels of warning belief and perceived risk increase, so does the probability of warning compliance. Although these fundamental relationships hold across warning settings, three differentials were detected according to the relative familiarity of the public with the threat agent. First, the correlation between warning belief and warning compliance is stronger in unfamiliar threats. Second, citizens who perceive risk as low are more likely to undertake protective measures different from the target warning response in familiar as opposed to unfamiliar threats. Finally, citizens who believe personal risk is high almost always comply with the target warning response when the threat agent is unfamiliar.

Shelter behavior

In examining post-evacuation responses, our interest focused upon the questions of where evacuees went when they complied with the warning message, how they knew this shelter was available, and what mode of transportation was selected to leave the danger area. Our data lead us to make four inferences about shelter choice patterns. In general, without regard to ethnicity, evacuees tend to seek shelter in the homes of friends or relatives. Three qualifications of this conclusion are necessary. When the period of evacuation is known in advance to be short, minority and majority group evacuees will avoid public shelters in preference to staying with friends or relatives. In less urban settings, Mexican-Americans are less likely to use public shelters than blacks or whites. In highly urbanized areas, blacks utilize public shelters more often than whites or Mexican-Americans.

It is often argued that the warning message is the appropriate place to communicate information about shelter availability. In practice, however, different officials usually have responsibility for warning dissemination and shelter provision. In some cases it is probable that personnel disseminating warnings may have only a general understanding of shelter arrangements. Our data reinforced this impression of differing responsibilities, showing that comparatively small proportions of evacuees cited the warning message as the place they learned about a shelter. The only exception is in the Denver data, where about half of black evacuees reported hearing about shelter in the warning message. The proportions of whites and Mexican-Americans who learned of shelter from the warning in Denver were similar to the proportions in the other sites. The high figure for Denver blacks is no doubt related to the higher levels of public shelter use among these citizens.

The majority of evacuees, however, in all three sites and including majority and minority citizens discover the shelter facilities they eventually use by making the first contact themselves. Thus, locating shelter, particularly with friends or relatives, tends to be a process in which the evacuees themselves take the initiative and make first contact, usually through use of the telephone. There are two interesting departures from this pattern that account for relatively smaller but nonetheless noticeable proportions of shelter seekers. First, in Mount Vernon, characterized by a projected short period of absence for evacuees, larger and approximately equal proportions of whites and Mexican-Americans located shelter by simply stopping at the first safe location they came upon. This tactic for determining shelter availability was less frequently used by all three ethnic groups in the Abilene and Denver evacuations, where the term of absence was not known in advance and presumed to be longer.

The second variation on finding shelter relates to a process that has been designated "evacuation by invitation." More than a decade ago, Drabek (1969:345) found that warning recipients in a flood disaster were contacted by relatives or friends who invited them to come to their homes. Our data indicate that invitations to evacuate were issued in all three warning settings to members of all three ethnic groups; in Denver such invitations accounted for 26.5 percent of blacks, 20.6 percent of whites, and 22.2 percent of Mexican-Americans. These findings support Drabek's results but add the qualification that the effect exists in urban areas even when the period of forewarning is relatively short.

The coordination and use of evacuation plans also involve logistics issues resulting from the movement of people. When a warning message calls for evacuation, local authorities are requesting that citizens undertake a specific adaptive action where timing is often critically important and effective adaptation of the community as a whole depends upon a coordinated exodus. Under such circumstances, the question of how citizens exit the area to be evacuated arises. Our analyses showed that in general, among blacks, whites, and Mexican-Americans across all three sites, the majority of evacuees departed the danger area in a family-owned vehicle. In the less urbanized sites—Abilene and Mount Vernon—a slight ethnic differential exists: minority citizens were less likely to evacuate in a family car and more likely to use some form of officially provided transportation. In Denver, almost all whites and Mexican-Americans evacuated in a family car. On the other hand, only about half of the Denver blacks used a family vehicle and one-third used some official transportation. These data highlight two important issues. First, most evacuees leave in a family car and consequently the number of exiting vehicles in almost any evacuation is large enough to merit careful attention from emergency managers. Second, official transportation is needed, and used, by evacuees, particularly ethnic minorities.

Citizen involvement in emergency preparedness

In examining the extent of citizen participation in emergency management, our interest focused upon three issue areas: reasons for warning compliance and undertaking protective measures, hazard information sources, and citizen involvement in community emergency management.

Much of our research has dealt with the problem of citizen adoption of adaptive (protective) behaviors in the face of environmental threats. We reviewed reasons given by citizens for engaging in particular adaptive behaviors. In so doing we were able to catalog citizen perceptions of their own motivations for obeying or ignoring the instructions of emergency management authorities.

In connection with the hazardous materials emergency in Mount Vernon, the reason for evacuating most frequently endorsed by whites was that local officials told them to do so. This reason was followed, in descending order of citation frequency, by watching neighbors evacuate and seeing the accident site. Mass media warnings were infrequently cited as the most important reason for evacuating, and none of the white respondents mentioned past disaster experience as a reason for evacuation compliance. Mexican-Americans most often cited officials' warnings and seeing the accident site as reasons for evacuating. These respondents also cited, although less frequently, warnings from friends and neighbors and the departure of neighbors as reasons for evacuation compliance. None of the Mexican-Americans mentioned either media warnings or past experience.

Therefore, in responding to a relatively unfamiliar threat, the majority of whites cited warning information from officials as the most important reason for deciding to evacuate; warnings from friends and relatives trailed at some distance as the second most frequently given reason. Among Mexican- Americans, officials' warnings and seeing the impact site were most frequently given as the primary reason for evacuation compliance. These findings suggest that, when faced with a technological and unfamiliar threat, citizens will seek out sources perceived to have relevant expertise upon which to base a warning compliance decision; in most cases such expertise will be attributed to emergency authorities. Our citizen perception data suggest that for minority respondents, witnessing the impact site (that is, assembling personal evidence of danger) is equally important or at least perceptually equivalent to officials' warnings.

The flood data revealed a different pattern of reasons given for evacuation compliance. It was argued that these differences are attributable to different characteristics of the flood threat. Most blacks identified officials' warnings as the most important reason for evacuating. Other reasons given by substantially smaller proportions of blacks included past flood experience, warnings from friends and relatives, and departure of neighbors. Mexican-Americans cited past flood experience most often, followed by officials' warnings and warnings from friends and neighbors. The majority of whites, like Mexican-Americans, cited past flood experience as the most important reason for evacuating. Among whites, the departure of neighbors also weighed heavily as a reason for evacuation compliance, followed at some distance by warnings from friends and relatives, officials' warnings, and mass media warnings.

With respect to flood evacuation warning compliance, the two groups of minority citizens identified the same three reasons for evacuating—officials' warnings, past experience, and warnings from friends and relatives—although the relative order of importance differs. It remains, however, that taken together past experience and officials' warnings accounted for nearly two-thirds of the blacks and more than three-fourths of the Mexican-Americans. Past experience with flooding was also an important motivation for whites to comply with the evacuation warning, but these citizens endorsed a wider range of reasons for evacuating than the two minority groups. Among whites, the evacuation of neighbors and mass media warnings assumed positions of greater relative importance than among blacks or Mexican-Americans. Even acknowledging these differences, however, the same combination of factors that accounted for most minority citizens—past experience, officials' warnings, and warnings from friends and neighbors—also accounts for more than two-thirds of the whites. These findings support the contention that, across the three ethnic groups, when dealing with a familiar (or recurrent) threat, past experience is an important factor in evacuation compliance. One may add to this the idea that warning information supplied by officials and friends and relatives also has a positive impact on compliance.

The Denver data are similar to Mount Vernon in that the threat involved was unfamiliar to the public but distinguished by the urban environment. Interestingly, although the relative orderings differ, the same three reasons given for evacuating predominate the choices expressed by blacks, whites, and Mexican-Americans: warnings from officials, warnings from relatives and friends, and the departure of neighbors and friends. As we found in Mount Vernon, officials' warnings were important in the evacuation decision-making process in Denver. In fact, warnings from officials were cited as the most important reason for evacuating by the largest proportions of blacks and whites and the third largest proportion of Mexican-Americans. These data support our previous argument that in unfamiliar threat settings citizens from all ethnic backgrounds tend to look to authorities as a leading source of threat-relevant information. In contrast to the more familiar flood threat in Abilene, past experience was not often cited as a reason for warning compliance by blacks, whites, or Mexican-Americans in Denver. But unlike their more rural counterparts in Mount Vernon, Denver urban dwellers emphasized the role of social networks in their decisions to evacuate. Among blacks, warnings from friends and relatives were the second most frequently mentioned compliance reason, followed by the departure of neighbors and friends. Whites cited neighbors and friends evacuating as the most important reason for leaving with the second greatest frequency and warnings from friends and relatives next most often. The largest proportion of Mexican-Americans gave warnings from friends and relatives as the most important reason for evacuating, followed by the departure of neighbors and friends.

Finally, an important observation can be made regarding officials' warnings and evacuation compliance. In all three threat settings none of the citizens (regardless of ethnicity) completely or even largely disregarded officials' warnings in making evacuation compliance decisions. This finding emphasizes the idea that information from emergency management officials is a significant motivating factor for citizens in coping with both familiar and unfamiliar types of environmental threat. Furthermore, while emergency managers can have no influence over a citizen's past disaster experience and little influence over such things as warnings from friends and relatives, they exercise considerable control over officials' warning information. Aside from underscoring the significance of careful warning message construction and dissemination, these data demonstrate that officials' warnings also contribute to warning compliance indirectly to the extent that they motivate the neighbors of potential evacuees to leave the threatened area.

Protective measures

Our data on citizen propensities to undertake protective measures (in addition to or instead of evacuating) yielded several important findings. It was found that citizens faced with a relatively familiar threat such as a flood engaged in a wider range of protective actions with greater frequency than citizens who attempted to cope with an unfamiliar threat. An important implication of this finding is that if citizens know about specific protective measures, they will use them. Also, in some cases, particularly blacks and whites faced with flooding, people who undertook any protective action at all tended to use multiple measures rather than just one. Finally, especially with an unfamiliar threat, citizens did cite authorities as one important source of advice in choosing whether to adopt some protective action. These findings all point to the idea that citizens *do* engage in protective actions and that emergency management authorities *can* influence citizen behavior.

With respect to the question of whether citizens would engage in a different protective action—if they know of several—from what authorities desire, the answer is yes. Two qualifications follow, however, First, it is probably better for citizens to engage in some protective action than none if they ultimately choose not to engage in the protective target authorities have in mind. Second, and more important, is the idea that one of the tasks of effective emergency management is to induce people to engage in the most appropriate protective action. Citizens are likely to always consider alternatives to officially advised actions. It is directly through the structure of the warning message—and indirectly through their demeanor and reputation—that emergency managers must convince threatened citizens that the recommended protective action is most appropriate. Furthermore, one should not rule out the idea of multiple protective measures in connection with any given disaster event.

Established communication channels

In order to effectively plan for disseminating information regarding environmental threats from natural and man-made hazards, it is important to understand which communication channels or information sources have been traditionally used by citizens. Findings are reported separately for each community because differing community characteristics and emergency management policies are likely to affect observed patterns of utilization of hazard information sources.

With regard to the use of traditional channels for communicating information about environmental hazards to citizens, we can derive four conclusions from the Mount Vernon data. First, newspapers and radio are two channels that are very likely to reach both ethnic groups. Each of these media were among those most frequently cited by whites as well as Mexican-Americans as sources of hazard information in the past.

Second, television, local magazine articles, and social networks are channels that whites cited with moderate frequency as hazard information sources. Television and magazines are tools for information dissemination that are less susceptible to use by emergency managers. Aside from news releases, public service announcements, and coverage of response to specific community disasters, uses of television to disseminate emergency response and planning are highly limited and require substantial resources and in some cases technical skills. Like television, regional and local magazines are comparatively complicated channels for disseminating hazard information, even though this source has some appeal to whites. Preparation of short hazard awareness of response articles or participation in a focused interview constitute the primary modes of access to magazines available to emergency managers.

Among Mexican-Americans television and social networks were frequently used sources of hazard information. Although less so than for Mexican-Americans, whites too reported that social networks were important channels for receiving hazard information. In this case, referring to social networks is another way of describing the process of obtaining information about hazards on a word-of-mouth basis from important people in the individual's social sphere. While it is true that there is little emergency managers can do to affect or use this channel, it is important that they be aware of its existence and its special significance for Mexican-Americans. Social networks should not be seen as a primary channel through which to disseminate specific hazard information; the difficult and complex aspects of gaining access and the high likelihood that information will become garbled in transmission mediate against such uses. Information that passes through social networks is probably most usefully conceived of in terms of the support-building function of citizen participation.

The Mount Vernon data showed that local political authorities, emergency authorities, and speakers at local civic and voluntary organizations are the established channels used least frequently by both ethnic groups. Of course this does not mean that these channels are undesirable, only that in the past they have enjoyed little utilization by citizens. In any use of speakers or some other direct dissemination strategy, emergency managers should keep the technique's primary weak point in mind: the coverage obtained by any single effort will be limited. While speakers can disseminate very specific hazard information, to convey the message to any significant portion of the population requires many separate contacts with different organizations or groups.

The Abilene data showed patterns of source utilization similar to those observed in Mount Vernon. Interestingly, blacks and whites showed similar use patterns for the five most frequently used sources, and the distribution for these two ethnic groups mirrors that of Mount Vernon whites. The use pattern for Abilene Mexican-Americans is different from blacks and whites in that community but similar to Mount Vernon Mexican-Americans.

Abilene blacks most frequently cited television, newspapers, and radio as sources of information about environmental hazards. Whites also cited these sources as those used most often, but in a different order: newspapers, television, and radio. Both blacks and whites cited magazines and social networks as sources used with moderate frequency, although a greater relative proportion of whites relied on magazines. Finally, political officials, emergency authorities, and speakers at organizations were the sources mentioned least often by both of these ethnic groups.

The sources of hazard information most frequently mentioned by Abilene Mexican-Americans were television, social networks, and newspapers, and radio was cited with moderate frequency. It should be noted that this hierarchy of source utilization is the same as that given by Mount Vernon Mexican-Americans, except that the order of importance of radio and television is reversed. Abilene Mexican-Americans reported infrequent use of political officials, emergency authorities, magazines, and speakers as sources of hazard information.

Before presenting conclusions from the Denver data, several observations can be made regarding urban-rural differences in the source utilization data. These differentials generally hold across ethnic groups. Although they are still used relatively infrequently when compared to other sources, Denver urbanites were more likely to have obtained information from speakers at organizational meetings than citizens in less urban settings. Urban dwellers also reported higher levels of past contacts with local emergency authorities than observed in Mount Vernon or Abilene. Furthermore, slightly greater proportions of Denver respondents claimed to have obtained emergency response information from newspapers, magazines, and social networks. Like their less urban counterparts, Denver respondents reported that they rarely had obtained information regarding environmental hazards from local political officials.

The most frequently cited sources of past information among all three ethnic groups in Denver were social networks, radio, television, newspapers, and magazines. There are ethnic differentials regarding the relative frequency with which these sources were named. Minority citizens tended to emphasize social networks as sources of past hazards information to a greater extent than whites. Both blacks and Mexican-Americans identified the broadcasting media (radio and television) as the second most frequently used sources of past information as well as designating newspapers as the third most frequently used source. Most whites reported newspapers were a source of hazard information in the past. Radio was named by the next largest proportion of whites, followed by magazine articles and television.

Preferred communication channels

Our analyses of citizen perceptions of the best ways to communicate hazard information have several important implications for emergency managers who are planning dissemination programs. Radio was the one channel that was rated as a desirable dissemination mode among all three ethnic groups at all three research sites. This finding is significant because local radio is a high coverage, low cost communication channel that is readily available to emergency managers. Furthermore, radio is a versatile channel in that an emergency manager (perhaps in the form of a structured interview or a public service spot) can disseminate specific hazard relevant information and/or simply raise a particular hazard issue and advise interested listeners where additional information can be acquired (for example, by picking up a brochure at a police or fire station or the local emergency services office). To a limited extent, emergency managers can also participate in dialogues with citizens via this medium, perhaps by arranging to participate in a call in program designed to solicit questions from listeners. Amid these virtues, one must keep in mind the principal vices of radio: different stations will have different audiences and broadcasts at different times of day will have different audiences. Fortunately, for purposes of selling advertising, most radio stations are aware of what audience they serve and who is likely to be listening at different hours. Hence, an emergency manager planning an effective dissemination campaign must be aware of these limitations and probably will be forced to include several radio stations in the plan as well as broadcasts at different times.

With regard to ethnic variations, whites and blacks showed a preference for information received via the mail and through newspapers. These communication channels have the advantage of providing citizens with hazard information in written form that can be kept and referenced by those sufficiently motivated to do so. Mailed brochures have the advantage that emergency managers retain complete control of the content and style of information presentation. To attain maximum effectiveness, though, mailed brochures have a disadvantage in that the amount of information in any single message must be kept to a minimum and concisely presented. On the other hand, newspapers share with radio the problem of audience variation and require more of an emergency manager's time and resources for effective utilization.

Minority respondents rated neighborhood meetings higher as a preferred communication channel than whites. While conducting neighborhood meetings may be an effective way of reaching some segments of the community, this communication mode is by far the most taxing relative to emergency management time and resources. Neighborhood meetings have the advantages of allowing two-way communication and face-to-face contact, and the information to be disseminated can be tailored to the specific audience. Such meetings carry the disadvantages of requiring much advance preparation of material, finding a location, advertising a suitable meeting time and place, and demanding that at least one emergency manager work outside normally prescribed hours. Also, it should be remembered that while the opportunity to build positive rapport with citizens is great, if the neighborhood meeting is not carefully planned in advance, problems could arise.

Citizen involvement

We argued that community emergency management should be seen as an activity guided by drawing upon the technical expertise of emergency managers but accomplished jointly with the citizens to be protected. The rationale here is that citizens are more likely to comply with emergency measures they believe they have had a hand in devising. Also, and perhaps more important, having citizens involved in emergency planning affords emergency managers the chance to obtain immediate feedback on citizen perceptions of the acceptability or workability of different management strategies.

Interestingly, in both Abilene and Mount Vernon, so few Mexican-Americans volunteered for any of the activities that very little interpretation of the data is possible. The two most appropriate conclusions are that, in general, these choices for involvement were not appealing to the Mexican-Americans in these communities, but among those who did indicate a choice, work as auxiliary police or fire personnel seemed to be preferred. Larger proportions of blacks and whites indicated a willingness to work in some volunteer capacity, but in most cases only about one-fourth of the members of each ethnic group volunteered for a given activity. As expected, then, most citizens would not choose to do volunteer work in an emergency management capacity.

Among whites in Mount Vernon and Abilene, the most popular choices were participation on a task force or advisory committee. Whites reported less interest in serving as auxiliary fire or police personnel and least interest in working in an emergency services office. Respondent comments indicated the perceived commitment and time involved in working as auxiliary police or fire fighters was too great. Some respondents also mentioned that volunteering for office work was inappropriate because they believed they lacked necessary skills (those most often mentioned included the ability to type and operate radio equipment). The attractiveness of serving on committees from the whites' point of view was that the task appeared to have definite parameters; particularly, a defined work commitment and completion time.

The largest proportion of blacks volunteered for service on a task force dealing with a specific emergency management problem. The next most endorsed volunteer activity among blacks was the option to work as auxiliary personnel in a police or fire department. Work on a general advisory committee was less often endorsed by blacks and very few agreed to volunteer as office help in an emergency services department.

The Denver data were noteworthy because there are no differences by ethnicity in the rank ordering of the four types of volunteer activity by frequency of citizen endorsements. The volunteer activity preferred by the largest proportions of blacks, whites, and Mexican-Americans was membership on a task force charged with addressing a specific problem. Work as an auxiliary police officer or fire fighter was the second most popular choice. It should be noted that greater relative proportions of minority citizens than whites in Denver endorsed these two options for participating in emergency management. Participation on an advisory committee was the third most frequently chosen mode of involvement among all three ethnic groups in Denver.

Three variations among the study communities should also be mentioned. The urban Mexican-Americans in Denver were far more willing to be involved in volunteer capacities than Mexican-Americans in the less urbanized sites at Mount Vernon and Abilene. The proportions of blacks opting for volunteer involvement in Abilene and Denver are similar; for these citizens the urban/less urban dimension has little impact on participation levels. Whites resemble blacks in that their desired participation levels are similar across all three communities. Finally, serving as volunteer office help was the least frequently endorsed participation mode among all three ethnic groups at all three sites.

While the differences among the ethnic groups were not large enough to argue that any ethnic differentials exist, two points do deserve comment. First, in the less urban settings, Mexican-Americans show little inclination to be involved in any of the four capacities mentioned; in Denver the desired participation levels were much higher. Second, blacks seem slightly more open to participation as auxiliary police or fire personnel than whites. With regard to these data in general we should also keep two qualifications in mind. It is known that low income citizens tend to volunteer less often than higher income citizens. Because the Mexican-Americans in our samples represent the lower income categories, their apparent reticence to participate may be due to an income difference rather than to ethnic group membership. Furthermore, we have asked citizens about participating in only four fairly constrained kinds of activity. It would not be appropriate to assume that because the proportions of volunteers were fairly low when asked about these activities, volunteers would be equally slow to participate in other capacities. The mode and success of any citizen involvement effort depends upon the imagination and resourcefulness of the emergency manger who implements the program.

Bibliography

Ackerman, C. 1980. *Flood Hazard Mitigation*. Washington, D.C.: National Science Foundation, Engineering and Applied Science Division.

Altshuler, Alan. 1970. *Community Control: The Black Demand for Participation*. New York: Pegasus.

Alvirez, David, and Bean, Frank. 1976. "The Mexican American Family." In C. H. Mindel and R. W. Habenstein (eds.), *Ethnic Families in America*. New York: Elsevier.

American National Red Cross. 1975. *Disaster Relief Program*. Washington, D.C.: American Red Cross National Headquarters.

Anderson, James. 1979. *Public Policy-Making*. New York: Holt, Rinehart and Winston.

Anderson, Jon. 1968. "Cultural Adaptation to Threatened Disaster." *Human Organization* 27 (Winter):298–307.

Anderson, William A. 1965. *Some Observations on a Disaster Subculture*. Columbus: Ohio State University Disaster Research Center.

——. 1969a. *Local Civil Defense in Natural Disaster*. Columbus: Ohio State University Disaster Research Center.

——. 1969b. "Disaster Warning and Communication in Two Communities." *Journal of Communication* 19 (June):92–104.

Andrews, Richard. 1982. "Lessons from Seismic Safety Planning in California." In W. W. Hays (ed.), *Preparing for and Responding to a Damaging Earthquake in the Eastern United States: Proceedings of Conference XIV*. September 16–18,

Knoxville, Tenn. U. S. Geological Survey Open File Report 82-220, pp. 106–123.

Atkisson, Arthur, and Petak, William. 1981. *Seismic Safety Policies and Practices in U.S. Metropolitan Areas.* Washington, D.C.: Federal Emergency Management Agency.

Bandura, Albert. 1977. *Social Learning Theory.* Englewood Cliffs, N.J.: Prentice Hall.

Barnes, Kent, Brosius, James, Cutter, Susan, and Mitchell, J. K. 1979. *Response of Impacted Populations to the Three Mile Island Nuclear Reactor Accident.* New Brunswick, N.J.: Department of Geography, Rutgers University.

Barton, Allen. 1970. *Communities in Disaster.* New York: Anchor Books.

Bates, Fred, Fogelman, C., Parenton, V., Pittman, R., and Tracy, G. 1963. *The Social and Psychological Consequences of Natural Disaster.* Washington, D.C.: National Academy of Sciences–National Research Council.

Bauman, Duane, and Sims, John. 1978. "Flood Insurance." *Economic Geography* 54 (July):189–196.

Beach, Horace, and Lucas, Rex. 1960. *Individual and Group Behavior in a Coal Mine Disaster.* Washington, D.C.: National Academy of Sciences–National Research Council.

Bennet, Glin. 1970. "Bristol Floods 1968." *British Medical Journal* 3 (August):454–458.

Bernert, E. H., and Ikle, Fred. 1952. "Evacuation and Cohesion of Urban Groups." *American Journal of Sociology* 58 (September):133–138.

Bethell, William. 1981. Personal communication to Ronald W. Perry. San Bernardino, Calif.: San Bernardino County Department of Emergency Services.

Bianchi, Suzanne, and Farley, Reynolds. 1979. "Racial Differences in Family Living Arrangements and Economic Well-Being: An Analysis of Recent Trends." *Journal of Marriage and the Family* 41 (August):537–551.

Blackwell, James. 1975. *The Black Community.* New York: Dodd, Mead.

Boardman, David. 1981. "Derailment Forces Massive Evacuation." *Skagit Valley Herald*, volume 97, number 44 (April 24):1.

Boardman, David, and Burkart, Steve. 1981. "Derailment Forces 1000 to Evacuate." *Skagit Valley Herald*, volume 97, number 43 (April 23):1.

Bolin, Robert. 1976. "Family Recovery from Natural Disaster." *Mass Emergencies* 1:267–277.

Bucher, Rue. 1957. "Blame and Hostility in Disaster." *American Journal of Sociology* 62:467–475.

Burkhart, Steve. 1981. "Derailment Reporting Delay Draws City's Anger." *Skagit Valley Herald*, volume 97, number 44 (April 24):1.

Burton, Ian. 1972. "Cultural and Personality Variables in the Perception of Natural

Hazards." In J. Wohlwill and D. Carson (eds.), *Environment and the Social Sciences*. Washington, D.C.: American Psychological Association.

Burton, Ian, and Kates, Robert. 1964. "The Perception of Natural Hazards in Resource Management." *Natural Resources Journal* 3 (January):412–441.

Burton, Ian, Kates, Robert, and White, Gilbert. 1978. *The Environment as Hazard*. London: Oxford University Press.

Cantwell, Brian. 1981. "Railroad Calls Mishap 100% Safe." *Argus,* volume 90, number 18 (April 30):1.

Carter, Michael, Clark, John, Leck, Robert, and Fine, Gary. 1977. "Social Factors Affecting the Dissemination of and Response to Warnings." Paper read at the Eleventh Technical Conference on Hurricanes and Tropical Meteorology, Miami Beach, Fla.

Clarke, James. 1973. "Race and Political Behavior." In Kent Miller and Ralph Dreger (eds.), *Comparative Studies of Blacks and Whites in the United States*. New York: Seminar Press.

Clifford, Roy. 1956. *The Rio Grande Flood*. Washington, D.C.: National Academy of Sciences–National Research Council.

Coastal Area Planning and Development Commission. 1980. *Summary of a Coordination, Education and Mitigation Model for Disaster Preparedness in Coastal Areas*. Brunswick, Ga.: Coastal Area Planning and Development Commission Bulletin.

Cohen, Steven, and Kapsis, Robert. 1978. "Participation of Blacks, Puerto Ricans, and Whites in Voluntary Associations." *Social Forces* 56 (June):1053–1071.

Committee on Government Operations. 1978. *Hazardous Materials Accident Reporting*. Government Activities and Transportation Subcommittee of the Committee on Government Operations, U.S. House of Representatives, Ninety-fifth Congress, second session: Washington, D.C.: U.S. Government Printing Office.

Corbett, Jack, and Svenson, Arthur. 1981. "Perspectives on Local Natural Hazard Management." Paper read at the Western Political Science Association, Denver, Colo.

Council of State Governments. 1979. *The States and Natural Hazards*. Lexington, Ky.: Council of State Governments.

Crawshaw, Ralph. 1963. "Reactions to a Disaster." *Archives of General Psychiatry* 9 (August):157–162.

Dacy, D., and Kunreuther, H. 1969. *The Economics of Natural Disaster*. New York: Free Press.

Danzig, Elliott, Thayer, Paul, and Galanter, Lila. 1958. *The Effects of a Threatening Rumor on a Disaster Stricken Community*. Washington, D.C.: National Academy of Sciences Publication number 517.

Davenport, Sally, and Waterstone, Penny. 1979. *Hazard Awareness Guidebook: Planning for What Comes Naturally.* Austin, Tex.: Texas Coastal and Marine Council.

Davies, J. W. 1975. *An Introduction to Public Administration.* New York: The Free Press.

Davis, Lee. 1979. *Frozen Fire.* San Francisco, Calif.: Friends of the Earth.

Defense Civil Preparedness Agency. 1978. *Emergency Broadcast System: The Life Saving Public Service Program.* Washington, D.C.: Department of Defense.

Diggory, James. 1956. "Some Consequences of Proximity to a Disease Threat." *Sociometry* 19 (March):47–53.

Drabek, Thomas. 1968. *Disaster in Isle 13.* Columbus: Ohio State University Disaster Research Center.

―――. 1969. "Social Processes in Disaster." *Social Problems* 16 (Winter):336–347.

―――. 1980. *Search and Rescue Missions in Natural Disasters and Remote Settings.* Washington, D.C.: National Science Foundation, Problem Focused Research Division.

―――. 1983. Personal communication to Ronald W. Perry. Denver, Colo.: Department of Sociology, University of Denver.

―――. 1985. "Managing the Emergency Response." *Public Administration Review* 45 (January):85–92.

Drabek, Thomas, and Boggs, Keith. 1968. "Families in Disaster." *Journal of Marriage and the Family* 30 (August):443–451.

Drabek, Thomas, and Key, William. 1976. "The Impact of Disaster on Primary Group Linkages." *Mass Emergencies* 1 (2):89–106.

Drabek, Thomas, Key, William, Erickson, Pat, and Crowe, Juanita. 1975. "The Impact of Disaster on Kin Relationships." *Journal of Marriage and the Family* 37 (August):481–494.

Drabek, Thomas, Mushkatel, Alvin, and Kilijanek, Thomas. 1983. *Earthquake Mitigation Policy.* Boulder, Colo.: Institute of Behavioral Science, University of Colorado.

Drabek, Thomas, and Stephenson, John. 1971. "When Disaster Strikes." *Journal of Applied Social Psychology* 1:187–203.

Drayer, Calvin. 1957. "Psychological Factors and Problems, Emergency and Long-Term." *The Annals* 309 (January):151–159.

Dynes, Russell. 1970. *Organized Behavior in Disaster.* Lexington, Mass.: Heath-Lexington Books.

Dynes, Russell, and Quarantelli, Enrico L. 1976. "The Family and Community Context of Individual Reactions to Disaster." In Howard Parad, H. L. L. Resnik, and Libbie Parad (eds.), *Emergency and Disaster Management.* Bowie, Md.: The Charles Press Publishers.

———. 1979. "Group Behavior under Stress." *Sociology and Social Research* 52 (July):416–429.

Dynes, Russell, Quarantelli, Enrico, and Kreps, Gary. 1972. *A Perspective on Disaster Planning*. Columbus: Ohio State University Disaster Research Center.

Erickson, Pat, Drabek, Thomas, Key, William, and Crowe, Juanita. 1976. "Families in Disaster." *Mass Emergencies* 1:206–213.

Erikson, Kai. 1976. *Everything in Its Path*. New York: Simon and Schuster.

Fawcett, Howard. 1981. "The Changing Nature of Acute Chemical Hazards." *Journal of Hazardous Materials* 4 (March):313–320.

Field, Donald, Barron, James, and Long, Burl. 1974. *Water and Community Development*. Ann Arbor, Mich.: Ann Arbor Science Publishers.

Fogelman, Charles. 1958. "Family and Community in Disaster." Ph.D. dissertation, Louisiana State University, Baton Rouge.

Form, William, and Loomis, Charles. 1956. "The Persistence and Emergence of Social and Cultural Systems in Disasters." *American Sociological Review* 21 (April):180–185.

Form, William, and Nosow, Sigmund. 1958. *Community in Disaster*. New York: Harper Brothers.

Foster, Harold. 1980. *Disaster Planning*. New York: Springer-Verlag.

Foster, Harold, and Wuorinen, Vilko. 1976. "British Columbia's Tsunami Warning System." *Syesis* 9 (1):113–122.

Friedsam, Hiram. 1962. "Older Persons in Disaster." In George Baker and Dwight Chapman (eds.), *Man and Society in Disaster*. New York: Basic Books.

Fritz, Charles E. 1957. "Disasters Compared in Six American Communities." *Human Organization* 16 (Summer):6–9.

———. 1961a. "Disasters." In R. Merton and R. Nisbet (eds.), *Contemporary Social Problems*. New York: Harcourt, Brace and World.

———. 1961b. *Disaster and Community Therapy*. Washington, D.C.: National Academy of Sciences–National Research Council.

———. 1968. "Disasters." In *International Encyclopedia of the Social Sciences*. New York: Macmillan and The Free Press.

Fritz, Charles E., and Marks, Eli. 1954. "The NORC Studies of Human Behavior in Disaster." *Journal of Social Issues* 10 (3):26–41.

Fritz, Charles E., and Mathewson, J. H. 1957. *Convergence Behavior in Disasters: A Problem in Social Control*. Washington, D.C.: National Academy of Sciences–National Research Council.

Fritz, Charles E., and Williams, Harry. 1957. "The Human Being in Disasters: A Research Perspective." *The Annals* 309:42–51.

Garb, Solomon, and Eng, Evelyn. 1969. *Disaster Handbook*. New York: Springer.

Giuffrida, Louis. 1983. "The Integrated Emergency Management System." *Emergency Management Review* 1 (Fall):9–11.

Glass, Albert. 1970. "The Psychological Aspects of Emergency Situations." In Charles Abram (ed.), *Psychological Aspects of Stress*. Springfield, Ill.: Charles C. Thomas.

Goering, John. 1982. "Race, Housing and Public Policies." *Urban Affairs Quarterly* 17 (June):463–490.

Gortner, Harold. 1977. *Administration in the Public Sector*. New York: John Wiley and Sons.

Grebler, Leo, Moore, Joan, and Guzman, Ralph. 1970. *The Mexican-American People*. New York: Free Press.

Greene, Marjorie, and Gori, Paula. 1982. *Earthquake Hazards Information Dissemination: A Study of Charleston, South Carolina*. Open File Report 82-233. Reston, Va.: U.S. Geological Survey.

Greene, Marjorie, Perry, Ronald W., and Lindell, Michael. 1981. "The March, 1980 Eruptions of Mt. St. Helens: Citizen Perceptions of Volcano Hazard." *Disasters* 5 (1):49–66.

Grodzins, Morton. 1966. *The American System*. Chicago: Rand McNally.

Gruntfest, Eve. 1977. *What People Did during the Big Thompson Flood*. Boulder: Department of Geography, University of Colorado.

Gruntfest, Eva, Downing, T. E., and White, Gilbert. 1978. "Big Thompson Flood Exposes Need for Better Flood Reaction System to Save Lives." *Civil Engineering* 78 (February):72–73.

Hamilton, R., Taylor, R. M., and Rice, G. 1955. *The Social Psychological Interpretation of the Udall, Kansas Tornado*. Wichita, Kans.: University of Wichita Press.

Hank, Marilyn, Pollack, Andy, and McMullen, Mary. 1981. "Elm Creek Is Cause of Concern." *Abilene Reporter News*, volume 101, number 120 (October 14):1.

Hannigan, John, and Kueneman, Rodney. 1978. "Anticipating Flood Emergencies: A Case Study of a Canadian Disaster Subculture." In Enrico L. Quarantelli (ed.), *Disasters*. Beverly Hills, Calif.: Sage Publications.

Hanson, John. 1981. *Getting the Disaster Facts*. Washington, D.C.: National Governors' Association.

Healy, Richard J. 1969. *Emergency and Disaster Planning*. New York: John Wiley and Sons.

Helms, John. 1981. "Threat Perception in Acute Chemical Disasters." *Journal of Hazardous Materials* 4 (March):321–329.

Hershiser, Marvin, and Quarantelli, Enrico L. 1976. "The Handling of Dead in a Disaster." *Omega* 7 (3):195–208.

Hewitt, Kenneth, and Burton, Ian. 1971. *The Hazardousness of a Place*. Toronto: University of Toronto Press.

Hildebrand, Michael. 1980. *Disaster Planning Guidelines for Fire Chiefs.* Washington, D.C.: Federal Emergency Management Agency.

Hill, Rueben, and Hansen, Donald. 1962. "Families in Disaster." In G. Baker and D. Chapman (eds), *Man and Society in Disaster.* New York: Basic Books.

Hinojosa, Jesus, and Gelman, William. 1977. "After the Earthquake." *Practicing Planner* 231 (March):35–40.

Hirose, Hirotada. 1979. "Volcanic Eruption and Local Politics in Japan." *Mass Emergencies* 4 (1):53–62.

Hoetmer, Gerald. 1983. *Emergency Management: Individual and County Data.* Washington, D.C.: International City Management Association, Baseline Data Reports, volume 15.

Holland, Paul, and Leinhart, Samuel. 1979. *Perspectives on Social Network Research.* New York: Academic Press.

Hultaker, Orjan. 1977. *Evakuera.* Uppsala: Uppsala University.

Ives, Sallie, and Furuseth, Owen. 1980. "Immediate Response to Headwater Flooding in Neighborhoods in Charlotte, North Carolina." Report to the National Science Foundation. Charlotte: Department of Geography, University of North Carolina.

Jackman, M. R., and Jackman, R. W. 1980. "Racial Inequalities in Home Ownership." *Social Forces* 58 (6):1221–1234.

Jackson, Jacquelyne. 1973. "Family Organization and Technology." In K. S. Miller and R. M. Dreger (eds.), *Comparative Studies of Blacks and Whites in the United States.* New York: Seminar Press.

Janis, Irving. 1962. "Psychological Effects of Warnings." In G. Baker and D. Chapman (eds.), *Man and Society in Disaster.* New York: Basic Books.

Janis, Irving, and Mann, Leon. 1977. "Emergency Decision Making." *Journal of Human Stress* 3 (June):35–45.

Johnson, Susan, and Burdge, Rabel. 1973. "Personal and Social Adjustment to Reservoir Development." Seattle: Conference on Water and the Community, University of Washington.

Jones, James. 1972. *Prejudice and Racism.* Reading, Mass.: Addison-Wesley.

Jones, Roy, and Reed, Jerry. 1981. "Residents Stand Vigil over Creek." *Abilene Reporter News,* volume 101, number 120 (October 14):2.

Kain, J. F., and Quigley, J. M. 1975. "Housing Markets and Racial Discrimination." New York: National Bureau of Economic Research.

Kartez, Jack, and Kelly, William. 1980. *Emergency Planning and the Adaptive Local Response to Mt. St. Helens Eruption.* Pullman, Wash.: Washington State University.

Kates, Robert. 1971. "Natural Hazard in Human Ecological Perspective." *Economic Geography* 47 (July):438–451.

———. 1976. "Risk Assessment of Environmental Hazard." SCOPE Report number

8, International Council of Scientific Unions. Paris, France: Scientific Committee on Problems of the Environment.

Keeling, Terry. 1980. "The National Flood Insurance Program: A Local Perspective." In E. J. Baker (ed.), *Hurricanes and Coastal Storms.* Gainesville: Florida Sea Grant College.

Key, William. 1967. *When People Are Forced to Move: Final Report of Forced Relocation.* Topeka, Kans.: The Menninger Clinic.

Killian, Lewis. 1952. "The Significance of Multiple-Group Membership in Disaster." *American Journal of Sociology* (January):309–314.

———. 1954. "Some Accomplishments and Some Needs in Disaster Study." *Journal of Social Issues* 10 (3):68–79.

———. 1956. *An Introduction to Methodological Problems of Field Studies in Disasters.* Washington, D.C.: National Academy of Sciences–National Research Council.

Kirby, Anne. 1974. "Individual and Community Responses to Rainfall Variation in Oaxaca, Mexico." In Gilbert White (ed.), *Natural Hazards.* London: Oxford University Press.

Kreps, Gary. 1973. *Decision Making under Conditions of Uncertainty.* Columbus: Ohio State University Disaster Research Center.

———. 1979. "A Framework for Comparing Nuclear and Nonnuclear Disasters in Terms of Key Defining Properties of Disaster Events and Generic Functions of Disaster Response." Williamsburg, Va.: Department of Sociology, College of William and Mary.

———. 1981. "The Worth of the NAS-NRC (1952–1963) and DRC (1963–Present) Studies of Individual and Social Response to Disaster." In James Wright and Peter Rossi (eds.), *Social Science and Natural Hazards.* Cambridge, Mass.: Abt Books.

Kunreuther, Howard. 1974. "Economic Analysis of Natural Hazards: An Ordered Choice Approach." In G. White (ed.), *Natural Hazards.* New York: Oxford University Press.

Kusler, John. 1982. *Innovation in Local Floodplain Managements.* Boulder: Institute of Behavioral Science, University of Colorado.

Kutchins, Kay. 1978. "Plan for an Emergency before It Happens." *Journal of American Waterworks Association* 70 (6):308–310.

Lachman, Roy, Tatsuoka, Maurice, and Bonk, William. 1961. "Human Behavior during the Tsunami of May, 1960." *Science* 133 (May):1405–1409.

Lampham, V. 1971. "Do Blacks Pay More for Housing?" *Journal of Political Economy* 79:1244–1257.

Lerner, Preston. 1981. "West Texas: A History of Floods." *Abilene Reporter News,* volume 101, number 119 (October 13):1.

Lessa, William. 1964. "Social Effects of Typhoon Ophelia (1960) on Ulithi." *Micronesia* 1:1–47.

Lewis, James, O'Keefe, Phillip, and Westgate, Kenneth. 1977. "A Philosophy of Precautionary Planning." *Mass Emergencies* 2:95–104.

Lucas, Rex. 1966. "The Influence of Kinship upon Perception of an Ambiguous Stimulus." *American Sociological Review* 31 (April):227–236.

Mack, Raymond, and Baker, George. 1962. *The Occasion Instant*. Washington, D.C.: National Academy of Sciences–National Research Council.

Madsen, William. 1964. *Mexican Americans of South Texas*. New York: Holt, Rinehart and Winston.

Makosky, Frank. 1977. "The Forecast Officer's Severe Weather Role." Paper read at the Tenth Annual Conference on Severe Local Storms, Omaha, Nebr.

May, Peter. 1985. *Recovering from Catastrophes: Federal Disaster Relief Policy and Politics*. Westport, Conn.: Greenwood Press.

May, Peter, and Williams, Walter. 1985. *Disaster Policy Implementation*. New York: Plenum Press.

McAdoo, Harriette. 1981. *Black Families*. Beverly Hills, Calif.: Sage Publications.

McCubbin, Hamilton. 1979. "Integrating Coping Behavior in Family Stress Theory." *Journal of Marriage and the Family* 41 (May):237–244.

McGrath, Joseph. 1970. "A Conceptual Formulation for Research on Stress." In J. McGrath (ed.), *Social and Psychological Factors in Stress*. New York: Holt, Rinehart and Winston.

McLoughlin, David. 1983. "Integrated Emergency Management." *Hazard Monthly* 3 (March):1–4.

McLuckie, Benjamin. 1970. *Warning Systems in Disaster*. Columbus: Ohio State University Disaster Research Center.

McLuckie, Benjamin, and Whitman, Robert. 1971. *A Study of Warning and Response in Ten Colorado Communities during the Floods of June 1965*. Columbus: Ohio State University Disaster Research Center.

McMullen, Mary. 1981a. "Ex-Goodlow Residents Glad They Are Out." *Abilene Reporter News*, volume 101, number 119 (October 13):1.

———. 1981b. "City Quickly Looking for Disaster Assistance." *Abilene Reporter News*, volume 101, number 123 (October 17):1.

McPherson, H. J., and Saarinen, Thomas. 1977. "Flood Plan Dwellers' Perception of the Flood Hazard in Tucson, Arizona." *Annals of Regional Science* 12 (July):25–40.

Mendoza, Patricia. 1981. "Responding to Stress: Ethnic and Sex Differences in Coping Behavior." In Augustine Baron (ed.), *Explorations in Chicano Psychology*. New York: Praeger.

Menninger, W. C. 1952. "Psychological Reactions in an Emergency." *American Journal of Psychiatry* 109 (August):128–130.

Midlarsky, Elizabeth. 1968. "Aiding Responses: An Analysis and Review." *Merril Palmer Quarterly* 14:229–260.

Mileti, Dennis. 1974. "A Normative Causal Model Analysis of Disaster Warning Response." Ph.D. dissertation, University of Colorado, Boulder.

————. 1975. *Natural Hazards Warning Systems in the United States.* Boulder: Institute of Behavioral Sciences, University of Colorado.

Mileti, Dennis, and Beck, Woody. 1975. "Communication in Crisis." *Communication Research* 2 (January):24–49.

Mileti, Dennis, Drabek, Thomas, and Haas, Gene. 1975. *Human Behavior in Extreme Environments.* Boulder: Institute of Behavioral Sciences, University of Colorado.

Mileti, Dennis, and Harvey, Patricia. 1977. "Correcting for the Human Factor in Tornado Warnings." Paper read at the Tenth Conference on Severe Local Storms, Omaha, Nebr.

Miller, Kent, and Dreger, Ralph. 1973. *Comparative Studies of Blacks and Whites in the United States.* New York: Seminar Press.

Mindel, Charles, and Habenstein, Robert. 1976. *Ethnic Families in America.* New York: Elsevier.

Mogil, Michael, and Groper, Herbert. 1977. "NWS's Severe Local Storm Warning and Disater Preparedness Programs." *Bulletin of the American Meteorological Society* 58:318–329.

Mogil, Michael, Monro, John, and Groper, Herbert. 1977. "The National Weather Service Flash Flood Warning and Disaster Preparedness Programs." Paper read at the Second Annual Conference on Hydro-Meteorology, Toronto, Ontario.

Moore, Harry E. 1958a. *Tornadoes over Texas.* Austin: University of Texas Press.

————. 1958b. "Some Emotional Concomitants of Disaster." *Mental Hygiene* 42 (January):45–50.

Moore, Harry E., Bates, F., Lyman, M., and Parenton, V. 1963. *Before the Wind: A Study of Response to Hurricane Carla.* Washington, D.C.: National Academy of Sciences–National Research Council.

Moore, Harry E., and Friedsam, Hiram. 1959. "Reported Emotional Stress Following a Disaster." *Social Forces* 38 (December):135–139.

Moore, Joan. 1976. *Mexican Americans.* Englewood Cliffs, N.J.: Prentice Hall.

Mueller, John, Schuessler, Karl, and Costner, Herbert. 1977. *Statistical Reasoning in Sociology.* Boston: Houghton Mifflin.

Murphy, Leonard. 1973. *San Fernando, California Earthquake of February 9, 1971, Volume II.* Washington, D.C.: U.S. Government Printing Office.

Murton, Brian, and Shimabukuro, Shimzo. 1974. "Human Adjustment to Volcanic Hazard in Puna District, Hawaii." In Gilbert White (ed.), *Natural Hazards.* New York: Oxford University Press.

Mushkatel, Alvin, and Nigg, Joanne. 1985. *Opinion Congruence and the Formulation of Seismic Safety Policies.* Tempe, Ariz.: Office of Hazard Studies, Arizona State University.

Mushkatel, Alvin, and Weschler, Louis. 1985a. "Emergency Management and the Intergovernmental System." *Public Administration Review* 45 (January):49–56.

———. 1985b. "Intergovernmental Implementation of Building Codes with Seismic Provisions." *Policy Studies Review,* in press.

National Academy of Sciences. 1975. *Earthquake Prediction and Public Policy.* Report of the Panel on Public Policy Implications of Earthquake Prediction of the Advisory Committee on Emergency Planning. Washington, D.C.: National Academy of Sciences–National Research Council.

National Governors' Association. 1979. *Comprehensive Emergency Management: A Governor's Guide.* Washington, D.C.: National Governors' Association, Center for Policy Research.

———. 1982. "Comprehensive Emergency Management Bulletin." Washington, D.C.: Office of State Services, National Governors' Association.

National Science Foundation. 1980. *Flood Hazard Mitigation.* Washington, D.C.: Problem-Focused Research, National Science Foundation.

Nigg, Joanne, M. 1982. "Societal Response to the Earthquake Threat in the Eastern United States: Issues, Problems and Suggestions." In W. W. Hays (ed.), *Preparing for and Responding to a Damaging Earthquake in the Eastern United States: Proceedings of Conference XIV.* September 16–18, Knoxville, Tenn. U.S. Geological Survey Open File Report 82-220, pp. 77–91.

Norton, Frank, and Haas, Eugene. 1970. "The Cities and Towns." In Committee on the Alaska Earthquake, *The Great Alaska Earthquake of 1964.* Washington, D.C.: National Research Council.

O'Brien, David. 1975. *Neighborhood Organization and Interest-Group Processes.* Princeton, N.J.: Princeton University Press.

Office of Emergency Preparedness. 1972. *Report to the Congress: Disaster Preparedness.* Washington, D.C.: U.S. Government Printing Office.

Office of Technology Assessment. 1979. *Issues and Options in Flood Hazards Management.* Washington, D.C.: U.S. Government Printing Office.

Oliver, John. 1978. *Natural Hazards Response and Planning in Tropical Queensland.* Boulder, Colo.: Natural Hazards Research and Applications Information Center.

Olsen, Marvin. 1970. "Social and Political Participation of Blacks." *American Sociological Review* 35 (August):682–697.

Olson, Richard, and Nielson, Douglas. 1982. "Public Policy Analysis and Hazards Research." *Social Science Journal* 19 (January):89–105.

Olson, Robert A. 1973. "Individual and Organizational Dimensions of the San Fernando Earthquake." In L. Murphy (ed.), *San Fernando Earthquake of February 9, 1971.* Washington, D.C.: U.S. Government Printing Office.

————. 1985. *Final Strategies for California Earthquake Programs: A Report to the State Legislature.* Sacramento, Calif.: House of Representatives Joint Rules Committee (contract number LCB20661).

Ornstein, Allan. 1974. *Race and Politics in Community Organizations.* Pacific Palisades, Calif.: Goodyear Publishing Company.

Otway, Harry. 1973. "Risk Estimation and Evaluation." In *Proceedings of the IIASA Planning Conference on Energy Systems, IIASA-PC-3.* Laxenburg, Austria: International Institute for Applied Systems Analysis.

Owen, H. James. 1977. "Guide for Flood and Flash Flood Preparedness Planning." Washington, D.C.: National Weather Service, Disaster Preparedness Staff.

Parker, Gordon. 1977. "Cyclone Tracy and Darwin Evacuees: On the Restoration of the Species." *British Journal of Psychiatry* 130 (6):548–555.

Parr, Arnold. 1969. "A Brief on Disaster Plans." *EMO National Digest* 9:13–15.

Pearlin, Leonard, and Schooler, Carmi. 1978. "The Structure of Coping." *Journal of Health and Social Behavior* 19 (March):2–21.

Perry, H. S., and Perry, Stewart. 1959. *The Schoolhouse Disasters: Family and Community as Determinants of the Child's Response to Disaster.* Washington, D.C.: National Academy of Sciences–National Research Council.

Perry, Ronald W. 1979a. "Evacuation Decision-Making in National Disasters." *Mass Emergencies* 4 (1):25–38.

————. 1979b. "Incentives for Evacuation in Natural Disaster." *Journal of the American Planning Association* 45 (October):440–447.

————. 1982. *The Social Psychology of Civil Defense.* Lexington, Mass.: Heath-Lexington Books.

————. 1983. "Environmental Hazards and Psychopathology." *Environmental Management,* in press.

————. 1985. *Comprehensive Emergency Management: Evacuating Threatened Populations.* Greenwich, Conn.: JAI Press.

Perry, Ronald W., and Greene, Marjorie. 1982a. *Citizen Response to Volcanic Eruptions.* New York: Irvington Publishers.

————. 1982b. "The Role of Ethnicity in the Emergency Decision-Making Process." *Sociological Inquiry* 52 (Fall):306–334.

Perry, Ronald, Greene, Marjorie, and Mushkatel, Alvin. 1983. *American Minority Citizens in Disaster.* Seattle, Wash.: Battelle Human Affairs Research Center.

Perry, Ronald W., Lindell, Michael, and Greene, Marjorie. 1981. *Evacuation Planning in Emergency Management.* Lexington, Mass.: Heath-Lexington Books.

Perry, Ronald W., and Mushkatel, Alvin. 1984. *Disaster Management.* Westport, Conn.: Greenwood Press.

Perry, Ronald W., and Nigg, Joanne. 1985. "Emergency Management Strategies for Communicating Hazard Information." *Public Administration Review* 45 (January):72–77.

Petak, William, and Atkisson, Arthur. 1982. *Natural Hazard Risk Assessment and Public Policy.* New York: Springer-Verlag.

Pettigrew, Thomas. 1971. *Racially Separate or Together?* New York: McGraw-Hill.

Phillips, Leslie. 1968. *Human Adaptation and Its Failures.* New York: Academic Press.

Pinkney, Alphonso. 1975. Black Americans. Englewood Cliffs, N.J.: Prentice-Hall.

Platt, Ruitherford. 1976. "The National Flood Insurance Program: Some Midstream Perspectives." *Journal of the American Institute of Planners* 42 (July):303–313.

Pollack, Andy. 1981a. "Lyle Lake Overflows Spillway." *Abilene Reporter News*, volume 101, number 119 (October 13):1.

———. 1981b. "Flooding Leaves Its Muddy Mark on Local Homes." *Abilene Reporter News*, volume 101, number 121 (October 15):2.

———. 1981c. "Rough Estimate of Flood Damage Is $2.7 Million." *Abilene Reporter News*, volume 101, number 122 (October 16):1.

Prince, S. H. 1920. *Catastrophe and Social Change.* New York: Columbia University Press.

Quarantelli, Enrico L. 1960. "A Note on the Protective Function of the Family in Disasters." *Marriage and Family Living* 22 (August):263–264.

———. 1977. "Social Aspects of Disasters and Their Relevance to Pre-Disaster Planning." *Disasters* 1 (1):98–107.

———. 1980a. *Evacuation Behavior and Problems.* Columbus: Ohio State University Disaster Research Center.

———. 1980b. *The Consequences of Disasters for Mental Health: Conflicting Views.* Columbus: Ohio State University Disaster Research Center.

Quarantelli, Enrico L., with Baisden, Barbara, and Bourdess, Timothy. 1980. *Evacuation Behavior and Problems: Findings and Implications from the Research Literature.* Columbus: Ohio State University Disaster Research Center, Miscellaneous Report 27.

Quarantelli, Enrico L., and Dynes, Russell. 1970. "Property Norms and Looting: Their Patterns in Community Crisis." *Phylon* 31 (Summer):168–182.

———. 1972. "When Disaster Strikes." *Psychology Today* 5 (February):67–70.

———. 1977. "Response to Social Crisis and Disaster." *Annual Review of Sociology* 2:23–49.

Quarantelli, Enrico L., Lawrence, Charles, Tierney, Kathleen, and Johnson, Thomas. 1979. "Initial Findings from a Study of Sociobehavioral Preparations and Planning for Acute Chemical Hazards." *Journal of Hazardous Materials* 3 (February):77–90.

Quarantelli, Enrico L., and Taylor, Verta. 1977. "Some Views on the Warning Problem in Disasters as Suggested by Sociological Research." Paper read at the American Meteorological Society Conference on Severe Local Storms, Omaha, Nebr.

Raiffa, Howard. 1968. *Decision Analysis.* Reading, Mass.: Addison-Wesley.

Ramirez, Oscar, and Arc, Carlos. 1981. "The Contemporary Chicago Family." In Augustine Baron (ed.), *Explorations in Chicano Psychology.* New York: Praeger Publishers.

Rapkin, C. 1966. "Price Discrimination against Negroes in the Rental Housing Market." In C. Rapkin (ed.), *Essays in Urban Land Economics.* Los Angeles: University of California Press.

Reed, Jerry. 1981. "Red Cross Finds 26 Homes Ruined." *Abilene Reporter-News,* volume 101, number 122 (October 16):16.

Regulska, Joanna. 1979. "Public Awareness Programs for Natural Hazards." Paper prepared for Hazard Awareness Workshop, Corpus Christi, Tex.

Robinson, Donald. 1959. *The Face of Disaster.* New York: McGraw-Hill.

Rose, Peter I. 1973. "Race and Ethnicity." In Rodney Stark (ed.), *Society Today,* 2nd edition. Del Mar, Calif. CRM Books.

Rossi, Peter, Wright, James, and Weber-Burdin, Eleanor. 1982. *Natural Hazards and Public Choice.* New York: Academic Press.

Rowe, William. 1977. *An Anatomy of Risk.* New York: John Wiley and Sons.

Rubin, Claire B. 1979. *Natural Disaster Recovery Planning for Local Public Officials.* Washington, D.C.: Academy for Contemporary Problems.

Scanlon, Joseph. 1980. *The Peel Regional Police Force and the Mississauga Evacuation.* Toronto, Canada: Emergency Communications Research Unit, Carleton University.

Schiff, Myra. 1977. "Hazard Adjustment." *Environment and Behavior* 9 (June):233–254.

Sheahan, Thomas. 1982. Personal communication to Ronald W. Perry. Mount Vernon, Wash.: Skagit County Department of Emergency Services.

Shibutani, Tamotsu, and Kwan, Kian. 1965. *Ethnic Stratification: A Comparative Approach.* New York: Macmillan.

Sillar, William. 1975. "Planning for Disasters." *Long Range Planning* 8 (October):2–7.

Sims, John, and Bauman, Duane. 1972. "The Tornado Threat." *Science* 176:1386–1392.

Slovic, Paul, Kunreuther, Howard, and White, Gilbert. 1974. "Decision Processes, Rationality and Adjustments to Natural Hazards." In Gilbert White (ed.), *Natural Hazards.* New York: Oxford University Press.

Slovic, Paul, Lichtenstein, Sarah, and Fischhoff, Baruch. 1980. *Images of Disaster: Perception and Acceptance of Risks from Nuclear Power.* Eugene, Oreg.: Decision Research, Inc.

Sorkin, Alan. 1982. *Economic Aspects of Natural Hazards.* Lexington, Mass.: Lexington Books.

Sotomayor, Marta. 1971. "Mexican-American Interaction with Social Systems." *Social Casework* 52 (May):316–322.

Srole, Leo, Langner, Thomas, Michael, Stanley, Opler, Marvin, and Rennie, Thomas. 1962. *Mental Health in the Metropolis: The Midtown Manhattan Study.* New York: McGraw-Hill.

Stallings, Robert. 1967. *A Description and Analysis of the Warning Systems in the Topeka, Kansas Tornado of June 8, 1966.* Columbus: Ohio State University Disaster Research Center.

———. 1971. *Communications in Natural Disaster.* Columbus: Ohio State University Disaster Research Center.

Staples, Robert. 1976. *Introduction to Black Sociology.* New York: McGraw-Hill.

Staples, Robert, and Mirande, Alfredo. 1980. "Racial and Cultural Variations among American Families: A Decennial Review of the Literature on Minority Families." *Journal of Marriage and the Family* 42 (November):887–903.

Stark, Rodney. 1972. *Police Riots.* Belmont, Calif.: Wadsworth.

Sterling, Joyce, Drabek, Thomas, and Key, William. 1977. "The Long-Term Impact of Disaster on the Health Self-Perceptions of Victims." Paper read at meetings of the American Sociological Association, Chicago, Ill.

Stiles, William. 1957. "How a Community Met Disaster: The Yuba City, California Flood." *The Annals* 309 (January):163–174.

Terrell, H. S. 1971. "Wealth Accumulation of Black and White Families." *Journal of Finance* 26:363–379.

Tierney, Kathleen. 1978. *Emergent Norm Theory as Theory.* Columbus: Ohio State University Disaster Research Center.

———. 1980. *A Primer for Preparedness for Acute Chemical Emergencies.* Columbus: Ohio State University Disaster Research Center.

Tierney, Kathleen, and Baisden, Barbara. 1979. *Crisis Intervention Programs for Disaster Victims.* Rockville, Md.: National Institute of Mental Health.

Titmuss, Richard. 1950. *Problems of Social Policy.* London: HM Stationery Office.

Tolsdorf, Christopher. 1976. "Social Networks, Supports and Coping." *Family Process* 15 (4):407–417.

Tomeh, Aida. 1973. "Formal Voluntary Organizations: Participation, Correlates and Interrelationships." *Sociological Inquiry* 43:89–122.

Trainer, Matricia, and Hutton, Janice. 1972. "An Approach to the Differential Distribution of Deaths from Disaster." Paper read at the meetings of the Midwest Council on Social Research in Aging, Kansas City, Kans.

Travis, Richard, and Riebsam, William. 1979. "Communicating Environmental Uncertainty." *Journal of Geography* 78 (5):168–172.

Turner, Barry. 1978. *Man Made Disasters.* London: Wykeham Publications Limited.

Turner, Ralph. 1964. "Collective Behavior." In Robert Faris (ed.), *Handbook of Modern Sociology.* Chicago: Rand-McNally.

Turner, Ralph, and Killian, Lewis. 1972. *Collective Behavior.* Englewood Cliffs, N.J.: Prentice-Hall.

Turner, Ralph, Nigg, Joanne, Paz, Denise, and Young, Barbara. 1981. *Community Response to Earthquake Threat in Southern California. Part Ten: Summary and Recommendation.* Los Angeles: Institute for Social Science Research, University of California.

Tyhurst, J. S. 1957. "Psychological and Social Aspects of Civilian Disaster." *Canadian Medical Association Journal* 76:385–393.

Vallance, Theodore, and D'Augelli, Anthony. 1982. "The Helpers Community: Characteristics of Natural Helpers." *American Journal of Community Psychology* 10 (2):197–205.

Van den Berghe, Pierre. 1967. *Race and Racism.* New York: John Wiley.

Vander Zanden, James. 1966. *American Minority Relations.* New York: The Ronald Press.

Von Furstenberg, G. M., Harrison, B., and Horowitz, A. R. 1974. *Patterns of Racial Discrimination.* Lexington, Mass.: Heath-Lexington.

Walker, David. 1981. *Toward a Functioning Federalism.* Cambridge, Mass.: Winthrop Publishers.

Wallace, Anthony. 1956a. *Tornado in Worcester.* Washington, D.C.: National Academy of Sciences.

———. 1956b. *Human Behavior in Extreme Situations.* Washington, D.C.: National Academy of Sciences–National Research Council.

———. 1957. "Mazeway Disintegration." *Human Organization* 16 (Summer):23–27.

Waterstone, Marvin. 1978. *Hazard Mitigation Behavior of Urban Flood Plan Residents.* Boulder, Colo.: Natural Hazards Research and Applications Information Center.

Watson, Eunice, and Collins, Alice. 1982. "Natural Helping Networks in Alleviating Family Stress." *The Annals* 461 (May):102–112.

Webber, D. L. 1976. "Darwin Cyclone: An Exploration of Disaster Behaviour." *Australian Journal of Social Issues* 11 (1):54–63.

Weller, Jack, and Quarantelli, Enrico L. 1973. "Neglected Characteristics of Collective Behavior." *American Journal of Sociology* 79:665–685.

Wenger, Dennis E. Faupel, Charles E., and James, Thomas F. 1980. *Disaster Beliefs and Emergency Planning.* Final Report to the National Science Foundation. Newark: University of Delaware.

White, Gilbert. 1974. *Natural Hazards: Local, National and Global.* New York: Oxford University Press.

———. 1975. *Flood Hazard in the United States.* Boulder: University of Colorado.

White, Gilbert, Calef, Wesley, Hudson, James. 1958. *Changes in Urban Occupance of Flood Plains in the United States.* Chicago, Ill.: Department of Geography, University of Chicago.

White, Gilbert, and Haas, Gene. 1975. *Assessment of Research on Natural Hazards.* Cambridge, Mass.: MIT Press.

Whyte, Anne. 1980. *Survey of Households Evacuated during the Mississauga Chlorine Gas Emergency.* Toronto, Canada: Institute for Environmental Studies, University of Toronto.

Whyte, Anne, and Burton, Ian. 1980. *Environmental Risk Assessment.* New York: John Wiley and Sons.

Williams, Allen. 1969. "The Effects of Urban Renewal upon a Black Community: Evaluations and Recommendations." *Social Science Quarterly* 50 (June):701–710.

Williams, Harry. 1957. "Some Functions of Communications in Crisis Behavior." *Human Organization* 16 (Summer):15–19.

————. 1964. "Human Factors in Warning and Response Systems." In George Grosser, Henry Wechsler, and Milton Greenblatt (eds.), *The Threat of Impending Disaster.* Cambridge, Mass.: MIT Press.

Williams, Harry, and Fritz, Charles. 1957. "The Human Being in Disaster: A Research Perspective." *The Annals* 309 (January):42–51.

Williams, Walter. 1980a. *Government by Agency.* New York: Academic Press.

————. 1980b. *The Implementation Perspective.* Los Angeles: University of California Press.

Willie, Charles. 1970. *The Family Life of Black People.* Columbus, Ohio: Charles Merrill.

Wilmer, Harry. 1958. "Toward a Definition of the Therapeutic Community." *American Journal of Psychiatry* 114:824–834.

Windham, George, Posey, E., Ross, P., and Spencer, B. 1977. *Reactions to Storm Threat during Hurricane Eloise.* State College: Mississippi State University.

Withey, Stephen. 1962. "Reaction to Uncertain Threat." In G. Baker and D. Chapman (eds.), *Man and Society in Disaster.* New York: Basic Books.

————. 1964. "Sequential Accommodations to Threat." In G. H. Grosser (ed.), *The Threat of Impending Disaster.* Cambridge, Mass.: MIT Press.

Wolensky, Robert, and Miller, Edward. 1981. "The Everyday versus the Disaster Role of Local Officials." *Urban Affairs Quarterly* 16 (June):483–504.

Wright, Charles, and Hyman, Herbert. 1966. "Who Belongs to Voluntary Associations?" In W. Glaser and D. Sills (eds.), *The Government of Associations.* Totowa, N.J.: Bedminster Press.

Wright, George, and Phillips, Lawrence. 1980. "Cultural Variation in Probabilistic Thinking: Alternative Ways of Dealing with Uncertainty." *International Journal of Psychology* 15 (4):239–257.

Wright, James, Rossi, Peter, Wright, Sonia, and Weber-Burdin, Eleanor. 1979. *After the Clean-up.* Beverly Hills, Calif.: Sage Publications.

Wyner, Alan. 1981. "Seismic Safety Planning in California." Paper read at the annual meeting of the Western Political Science Association, San Diego, Calif.

Young, Carl, Giles, Dwight, and Plantz, Margaret. 1982. "Natural Networks: Help-Giving and Help-Seeking in Two Rural Communities." *American Journal of Community Psychology* 10 (4):457–469.

Young, Michael. 1954. "The Role of the Extended Family in a Disaster." *Human Relations* 7:383–391.

Zaltman, Gerald, and Duncan, Robert. 1977. *Strategies for Planned Change.* New York: Wiley Interscience.

Zeigler, Don, Brunn, Stan, and Johnson, J. H. 1981. "Evacuation from a Nuclear Technological Disaster." *The Geographical Review* 71 (January):1–16.

Zurcher, Louis. 1968. "Social Psychological Functions of Ephemeral Roles: A Disaster Work Crew." *Human Organization* 27 (Winter):281–297.

Index

Abilene, Texas, 10–12; warnings in, 26; shelter patterns in, 80; refusals to evacuate in, 95
Acculturation, 152
Adaptive behaviors, 89–104
American ethnic groups, 1
American Indians, 15
Authority, 26–31; and warning compliance, 93; and protective measures, 102; as warning source, 156–59
Auxiliary police, 123

Barton, Allen, 8
Behavioral response options, 51; among minority groups, 95
Bilingualism, 124; in emergency management, 150–54
Blacks: warning sources, 27–28; and credibility attributions, 34; and disaster experience, 47; and warning confirmation, 63–64; and shelter utilization, 80; and warning compliance, 94–95; hazard information sources, 104–9; social networks among, 158–59
Brunswick, Georgia, 142
Building codes, 128

California Seismic Safety Commission, 136
Cambodian immigrants, 16
Citizen participation, 115–24; in evacuations, 144–50
Citizen task forces, 121–24
Citizen volunteers, 121–24
City manager roles, 140
Civic organizations, 148–49
Coastal Area Planning and Development Commission, 142
Communication channels, 25–26; and

Communication channels (*cont'd*)
  warning message noise, 36; radio as,
  119; in routine hazard information,
  175–78
Comprehensive Emergency
  Management, 4; and minority
  citizens, 4–7; in Texas, 10–11; in
  Washington, 15; and warning process,
  23; and warning messages, 36; and
  warning confirmation centers, 64–65;
  shelter checkpoints in, 82–83; and
  traffic management, 86; disseminating
  information in, 102–4; and
  hazard awareness, 119–21;
  intergovernmental relations in, 126;
  and state government, 135–36
Constituent policy, 138
Convergence, 84
Council of State Governments, 141
Credibility: in warning, 31–35; of mass
  media, 32; conclusions regarding, 35
Crisis Relocation Planning, 86
Cultural perspectives, 153–54

Damage sustained, 48–50
Data analysis, 20
Death rates, 2
Defense Civil Preparedness Agency, 84
Denver, Colorado, 15–17; warnings in,
  26; shelter utilization in, 80; refusals
  to evacuate in, 94–98
Denver Office of Emergency
  Preparedness, 16
Denver and Rio Grande Railroad, 16
Department of Commerce, 129
Disaster alert, 4
Disaster brochures, 146–47
Disaster planning cycle, 145–46
Disasters: defined, 8; characteristics of,
  9–10

Drabek, Thomas, 26; on rural-urban
  differences, 62; on evacuation
  warning, 82; on emergency
  management, 130–31
Dynes, Russell, 9

Earthquake proofing, 3
Earthquakes, 153–54
Emergency Broadcast System, 25;
  expansion of, 84
Emergency planning: and warning
  confirmation, 64–66; and shelter
  management, 78–80; transportation
  incentives in, 85–88; auxiliary police
  in, 123; citizen task forces in, 124;
  and drills, 132; citizen involvement
  for, 144–50
Environmental cues, 34; and disaster
  experience, 44–46; and warning
  confirmation, 64; in warning
  dissemination, 162
Ethnic community solidarity, 160–61
Ethnic enclaves, 151–52
Evacuation, 70; in riverine floods, 83;
  transportation in, 85–87;
  clearinghouse for, 86–87; reasons
  given for, 89–93; citizen involvement
  in, 144–50; by invitation, 171
External validity, 19–21

Family-oriented actions, 164–65
Fatalism, 153
Federal Emergency Management
  Agency, 11; and intergovernmental
  system, 129–30
Federal Highway Administration, 129
Federal Insurance Administration, 129
Federalism, 126
Fritz, Charles, 8

Great Northern Railway, 12

Handicapped citizens, 150
Hazard awareness, 104–14; ways to
improve, 145–54
Hazard information: sources of, 104–9;
preferences for communication of,
115–21; techniques for disseminating,
145–54
Hazardous materials: in Washington,
13–14
Hazard-resistant dwellings, 2
Hurricanes, 5

Immigrant groups, 150–52
Implementation, 127–39
Integrated Emergency Management,
130. See also Comprehensive
Emergency Management
Intergovernmental relations, 126–35

Kartez, Jack, 141
Kreps, Gary, 9

Land use planning, 141
Liquified petroleum, 14
Literacy, 152–53
Local emergency services: and public
information, 105–9; use of radio,
119; and bilingualism, 124; and state
government, 135–36; federal
resources for, 143; and special
populations, 150–54
Local government, 135–44

Majority groups. See Whites
Mass media: issuing warnings, 25;
evaluations of, 33; in warning
confirmation, 63–64; as emergency

information sources, 111–15; as first
warning source, 160–61
Message content, 35–36; specificity of,
39–41; and warning belief, 42; and
shelter availability, 80
Mexican-Americans: warning sources,
27–29; and credibility attribution, 34;
and disaster experience, 47; and
warning confirmation, 63–64; and
shelter utilization, 80; and warning
compliance, 94–95; hazard
information sources, 104–9; social
networks among, 158–59
Minority groups, 3–8. See also Blacks,
Mexican-Americans
Mitigation measures, 131–32; in
hazardous materials, 138–39
Moore, Joan, 160–61
Mt. Baker volcano, 13
Mt. Vernon, Washington, 12–15;
warnings in, 26; shelter utilization in,
80; refusals to evacuate in, 95–96
Multiple protective measures, 103–4
Murton, Brian, 102

National Oceanic and Atmospheric
Administration, 16
National Opinion Research Corporation,
3
National Governor's Association, 135
National Science Foundation, 3
National Weather Service, 11
Neighborhood meetings, 148–49
Nitric acid, 16–17
Non-English speaking citizens, 150–53
Nuclear power, 23

Past disaster experience, 44–50; and
warning belief, 163

Perceived risk: and warning compliance, 73–76; and warning belief, 168–70
Policy systems, 126–27
Political climate, 139–40
Political efficacy, 1
Polk's City Directory, 18
Post-compliance processes, 76–87. *See also* Evacuation
Preparedness measures, 4–5; in Texas, 12; in natural threats, 70; among minority groups, 97–99. *See also* Response measures
Private sector, 135
Propane gas, 78
Public information, 104–15
Public service announcements, 111–12
Public works departments, 140–41
Puna District, Hawaii, 103

Quarantelli, Enrico L., 84

Radar detection methods, 132
Recovery operations, 133; in long-term, 141
Red Cross, 2; in Texas, 11–12
Relief, 133
Replication, 20–21
Response measures, 5; citizen involvement in, 144–50
Return rates, 18
Risk assessment, 48; in initial response, 57–58
Roadside checkpoints, 83
Rumor control, 83
Rural settings: and warning issuance, 29–30; and credibility, 34–35; and warning confirmation, 63–64; and unfamiliar threats, 69; and shelter seeking, 80

Sample procedure, 17–19
San Bernardino, California, 146
Sandbagging, 70
Scope of impact, 9; in hazardous materials incidents, 15. *See also* Disasters
Seasonal hazard bulletins, 111–12
Sheltering, 78–80; citizen preferences for, 82. *See also* Evacuation
Shimabukura, Shimzo, 102
Silicon Valley, 15
Situational definitions, 44
Skagit County, Washington, 106–7
Small Business Administration, 129
Social contacts: as warning source, 33–34; and evacuation decisions, 174
Social networks: and warning, 28; and warning credibility, 159–60; as sources of warning information, 165
Social structural issues, 2–4
Southeast Asians, 154
Spanish language: in media, 33; and public information, 115–24. *See also* Bilingualism
Speed of onset, 9; and protective action, 103–4; and community structure, 158; and mass media, 167
Stark, Rodney, 21
State government, 135–36
Survivability, 139. *See also* Death rates

Target warning response, 102–3
Telephone systems, 84
Texas and Pacific Railway, 10
Threat agents: in warning response, 55; unfamiliar to public, 68–69; and public shelter use, 80
Threat assessment, 23; specialized equipment for, 63; and local government, 136–39

Three Mile Island, Pennsylvania, 73
Toxic chemicals, 5; and abatement policy, 129
Transportation, 85–87
Tsunami, 5
Turner, Ralph, 153–54

Unfamiliar threats, 68–69; and warning belief, 72; responses to, 167–68
Urban fires, 5
U.S. Geological Survey, 146

Valley, Nebraska, 146
Volcanic eruptions, 82

Waco, Texas, 2
Warning: process, 23; modes of, 25; source of, 25–35; credibility in, 30–35; content of, 35–44; and hazard experience, 45–50; and warning compliance, 69–76; use of telephones in, 84

Warning belief: and disaster experience, 47; and initial warning response, 54–55; and personal risk, 57–58; confirmation of, 59–60; and warning compliance, 73
Warning compliance, 69–76
Warning confirmation, 59–69; sources for, 165–67
Warning denial, 59–60
Warning response process, 50–51; information seeking in, 64; and warning belief, 73; and perceived risk, 75–76; and evacuation compliance, 93; protections in, 102–3
Whites: warning sources, 27–29; and risk perception, 48; and family-oriented actions, 54; and warning confirmation, 63–64; and shelter utilization, 80; and warning compliance, 94–95; hazard information sources, 104–9; social networks among, 158–59
Wildlife management, 5

www.ingramcontent.com/pod-product-compliance
Lightning Source LLC
Chambersburg PA
CBHW020703270326
41928CB00005B/241